D0009848

THE BONE WOMAN

Random House Trade Paperbacks

New York

THE BONE WOMAN

—

A Forensic Anthropologist's Search
for Truth in the Mass Graves of
Rwanda, Bosnia, Croatia, and Kosovo

—

CLEA KOFF

For the seekers of the silvery threads

. . .

Published in the United States by Random House Trade
Paperbacks, an imprint of The Random Publishing Group,
a division of Random House, Inc., New York.

RANDOM HOUSE TRADE PAPERBACKS and colophon are
trademarks of Random House, Inc.

This work was originally published in hardcover by
Random House, an imprint of The Random House
Publishing Group, a division of Random House, Inc., in 2004.

Library of Congress Cataloging-in-Publication Data

Koff, Clea.
The bone woman: a forensic anthropologist's search
for truth in the mass graves of Rwanda, Bosnia,
Croatia, and Kosovo / Clea Koff.
p.   cm.
ISBN 0-8129-6885-9
1. Forensic anthropology—Rwanda.   2. Forensic
anthropology—Former Yugoslav republics.   3. Body, Human—
Identification.   4. Genocide—Rwanda.
5. Genocide—Former Yugoslav republics.
6. Koff, Clea.   I. Title.

GN69.8.K64   2004
599.9—dc22   2004041213

Printed in the United States of America

Random House website address: www.atrandom.com

2 4 6 8 9 7 5 3 1

Book design by Barbara M. Bachman

Acknowledgments

IT IS DIFFICULT to put into words my gratitude toward the following people, but I do know that I was able to write this book because they have been a part of my life: Suttirat Anne Larlarb, Sam Brown, David Koff, Msindo Mwinyipembe Koff, Kimera Koff, Geri Koff, Paul and Gwera Mwinyipembe, Bob Koff, the late Carole Ferry, Amy Uyematsu, Dr. LuAnn Wandsnider, and my grandfather Harry N. Koff, who gave me a book about Pompeii when I was seven and for years after that gave me books on the importance of words and of storytelling, but wasn't here to see what those books inspired me to do.

I thank Isobel Dixon of Blake Friedmann Literary Agency, Patty Moosbrugger of Stuart Krichevsky Literary Agency, and Lee Boudreaux of Random House for making sure that my friends and family were not the only ones to read these stories.

Contents

—

THE BONE WOMAN

BEFORE

AT 10:30 IN THE MORNING ON TUESDAY, JANUARY 9, 1996, I WAS on a hillside in Rwanda, suddenly doing what I had always wanted to do. I took stock of my surroundings as though taking a photograph. I looked up: banana leaves. Down: a human skull. To my left: more banana leaves. To my right: a forest of small trees. Directly in front of me: air. I was sitting on a steep slope, in the midst of a banana grove. My knees were pulled up tight to stop me from slipping down; the skull hadn't been so fortunate. It had rolled down to this point from higher up the slope, leaving behind its body. This particular indignity had not been inflicted on this skull alone; indeed, I was surrounded by skulls, surrounded by people who had been killed on this very slope one and a half years earlier. Most of their heads had rolled away since then. I was there to find the heads and get them back to their bodies. After that reunion, we would have a chance at determining age, sex, stature, and cause of death, and maybe even who these people were. I crouched quietly, "listening" to the skull. It was facedown; so far, I had been able to focus only on the wound to the occipital: a strong blow to the back of the head with something sharp and big. I looked at the wound, the way the bone bent inward, and the V shape of the cut in cross section. A mosquito buzzed by my ear and landed on the rim of the cut on the skull. "You won't get much joy there, mate: the blood's long gone from him," I thought, and brushed it away.

The way the skull was resting, I could see the maxillary (upper) teeth. One of the third molars had been erupting when this person was killed. I had just had my own wisdom teeth extracted before leaving for Rwanda and I ran my tongue thoughtfully over the fleshy sockets in my gums. It's interesting how you can immediately look for points of comparison between your own body and the body in front of you. Is it empathy with their plight, or relief that you're still alive? I didn't have time to contemplate this point further, as my body recovery partner, Roxana, came crashing through the leaves to my right, bringing with her Ralph, the photographer who would record the exact location and position of the skull. Next to the skull we rested a photo board—this provided an identification number as well as the date—and an arrow pointing north. In the silence, we listened to the Nikon shutter open and close, twice.

This done, we could move the skull. I picked it up and turned it to see the face. And there it was in front of me: a tight, deep, diagonal cut across the eyes and bridge of the nose. The cut had broken all the delicate bones that form that identifiable feature on all of us. It was painful to look at, so I put the skull down, exchanging it for a clipboard onto which Roxana and I recorded the condition of the bone, the number of teeth recovered, and the location of the skull on the hillside. When we had gathered all the information, we stabilized the skull where we had found it and ascended the slope, ducking under low-lying banana fronds and sidestepping sunbleached vertebrae, into a grassy area replete with fragments of clothing. We were looking for our skull's body. After clearing away the grass with our trowels, we found that some of the clothing held bones, partially buried in soil that had eroded from higher up the slope. Was this our man? The search was on.

This search and dozens like it continued for two weeks with varying success. There were four anthropologists scattered about the hillside, all of us engaged in the same task. Meanwhile, two archaeologists were on the crest of the hill, delineating the edges of the feature we would spend two months investigating: the mass grave behind the Kibuye church.

I WAS TWENTY-THREE YEARS old then and part of a team of sixteen archaeologists, anthropologists, pathologists, and autopsy assistants sent to Kibuye by the United Nations International Criminal Tribunal for Rwanda (ICTR) after the 1994 genocide. ICTR is the sister tribunal to ICTY, the International Criminal Tribunal for the former Yugoslavia, which is prosecuting those responsible for war crimes and "ethnic cleansing" in Bosnia-Herzegovina, Croatia, and, now, Kosovo. ICTR and ICTY have the distinction of being the first international criminal tribunals since the Nuremberg trials following World War II. In 1995, ICTR's then chief prosecutor, Richard Goldstone, made an unprecedented request. He asked Physicians for Human Rights, a Boston-based nongovernmental organization, to bring together a team of forensic experts who could investigate mass graves for which ICTR had already indicted alleged perpetrators.

Judge Goldstone had turned to the right place. PHR had a network of health professionals at its fingertips and had previously retained forensic pathologists to conduct autopsies in cases of state-sponsored human rights abuses in Israel. For the tribunal job, they also had the services of Dr. William Haglund, the UN's senior scientific expert, who would personally select the team.

When I got the call from Bill, I was a graduate student in forensic anthropology, but I had known for years that my goal was to help end human rights abuses by proving to would-be killers that bones can talk. Fortunately, I'd made no secret of this as I went through university; when Bill asked the forensic anthropologist Dr. Alison Galloway to recommend students for the Rwanda mission, she apparently told him I was the only one she knew who was trained in forensic anthropology *and* was interested in human rights investigations.

My inspiration was a man named Clyde Snow. I first read about him in *Witnesses from the Grave: The Stories Bones Tell,* which chronicles his creation of the Argentine Forensic Anthropology Team (EAAF). EAAF is now a world-renowned organization of experts, but in 1984 they were a quiet group of graduate students brave enough to unearth and try to identify the remains of Argentines "disappeared" during the military junta of the 1970s and 1980s. When I read *Witnesses from the Grave,* I was determined to help their efforts—but first I had to gain the skills. Not only would I have to go to graduate school to train in forensic anthropology, I also had to finish the remaining three years of my anthropology degree at Stanford University.

I had gone to university already knowing that I wanted to work with human remains. This was actually a narrowing of a broad (and slightly odd) childhood interest in bones and things past. When I was seven, I was collecting the dead birds I found outside our Los Angeles house and burying them in a little graveyard. A few years later, in Kenya with my family, I collected bleached animal bones in Amboseli National Park while monkeys yelled in the trees above me. I put all the bones back the next day, after I had cleaned them gently. By the time I was thirteen, we were living in Washington, D.C., and I was burying dead birds in plastic bags so I could dig them up later—I was curious how long it took them to "turn into" skeletons. I took the stinking bags to my (somewhat horrified) science teacher for extracurricular and wholly self-motivated death investigations. But when I was seventeen, in my last year of high school, I was firmly put on the track of *human* osteology. I chanced upon a National Geographic television documentary about how the ash from Italy's Mount Vesuvius had preserved the remains of people killed in the volcano's eruption nearly two thousand years ago. I was amazed when the anthropologist on the program said that she could tell from a set of bones that they were of a young female servant who had had to carry heavy loads. I watched, enthralled, and took copious notes, including a "note to self": study archaeology at Stanford.

But about halfway through the Stanford-in-Greece archaeological dig the following year, I realized I didn't want to exhume ancient graveyards for research purposes. Those people had been buried "properly." I wanted to investigate clandestine graves and the surface remains of crime victims, or of people whose deaths were accidental. My real interest was people who'd been recently killed and whose identities were unknown. *Witnesses from the Grave* taught me that forensic anthropologists deal with those bodies—and, more than that, that forensics could also be used to bring killers to justice.

Forensic anthropology is all about Before and After. Forensic anthropologists take what is left *after* a person has died and examine it to deduce what happened *before* death—both long before (antemortem) and just before or at the same time (perimortem). In addition to helping authorities determine the identity of deceased people, forensic anthropology has a role in human rights investigations, because a dead body can incriminate perpetrators who believe they have silenced their victims forever. This is the part of forensic anthropology that drives me, this "kicking of bad-guy ass" when it's least expected.

I think I appreciate this use of forensics because I grew up well aware of the concepts and conditions of suppression and discrimination. My parents, David and Msindo, made documentary films about subjects like colonialism and resistance in Africa, the Israeli-Palestinian conflict, and the intersection of race and class in Britain. And they weren't the type of parents to pack their kids off to bed while they had political discussions with their friends. My brother, Kimera, and I were always at the dinner table or the film screenings, learning terms like "lumpenproletariat" before we had even heard of *Sesame Street*.

Our parents took us with them even when they traveled for filming, and we were participants at our destinations, not tourists. Traveling like this while young, combined with not being allowed much television, helped us grow up with little sense of national identity. Of course, our parents couldn't have encouraged such a thing even if they'd wanted to: David has spent years abroad, although he's a second-generation American of a Polish and Russian family, while Msindo was raised in England although she's Tanzanian with half-Ugandan family. Instead of a national identity we had a strong family identity.

The only time our parents didn't keep us with them was when they went to Boston to protest against the censorship of their film *Blacks Britannica*. Suddenly, the focus of their work became tangible in our lives: they were away for half a year while Kimera and I stayed in Norfolk, England, on a friend's pig farm. On my sixth birthday, separated from our parents, I knew that a serious injustice had been done to our parents' film, and therefore to our parents, and therefore to our family. A few years later, I feared that some authority figure could again arbitrarily split up my family. We were at the Nairobi airport when the passport control officer said he was going to detain my mother because he disagreed with the politics of the president of Tanzania, my mother's country of birth. He directed the rest of my family to get on the plane without her. We almost missed the flight that day, and I nearly fainted from crying so hard. I was nine years old and I still remember the smirk on the officer's face as he abused his power and enjoyed it.

So when I read about the Argentine Forensic Team in *Witnesses from the Grave* eight years later, I recognized their work as precisely the kind I wanted to do. For me, one photograph said it all: Clyde Snow standing up during the trial of officials responsible for the abduction and murders of thousands of people, showing a slide of the skull of one of those victims, Liliana Pererya. Through Clyde, this young woman was telling the court that she had been shot in the back of the head not long after giving birth to the baby she was carrying when she disappeared. Her remains were the physical evidence that would corroborate the living witnesses' testimony. The state-sanctioned murderers doubtless thought they'd heard the last of her, but Clyde's work was making them think again.

When I entered the master's program in forensic anthropology at the University of Arizona, I took the biggest step toward my dream. The U of A program applied human osteology to forensic cases through an arrangement with the Pima County medical examiner's (ME's) office to handle all unidentified bodies. The first time I visited the U of A Human Identification Laboratory I saw walls of narrow cardboard boxes containing the skeletons of as-yet unclaimed people, an adjoining wet lab for removing flesh from bone under a fume hood, a darkroom for developing dental X rays, and, in a distant corner, a coffeepot simmering quietly on a countertop. When I left the lab that day, I was so happy that I cried; the lab felt like a place where I belonged. There were only eight other students in the program, most of whom had been there for several years already. I would be surrounded by mentors and, best of all, the director of the program, Dr. Walt Birkby, was one of America's greatest forensic anthropologists. But that wasn't the only reason I wanted to fit in: the lab was his shop, and he was an ex-Marine with an iron-gray buzz cut and a staccato delivery. I didn't want to find out what he would do if a student wasn't up to his standards.

Fortunately, Walt took a liking to me, I think in part because of my enthusiasm and in part because of the training I already had in human osteology from Stanford, so I moved quickly from observing cases at the ME's office to processing them. The first time I saw a body—as distinguished from a skeleton—at the ME's, I wasn't shocked: I had seen bodies before, though just the odd few, when my Stanford osteology classmates and I had visited the medical students dissecting corpses for their anatomy class next door. At that time, I didn't think much of "fresh," fleshed bodies, because it seemed all that tissue just got in the way of seeing the bones. But those do-nated cadavers couldn't have been more different from the first body I saw at the ME's. She had been lying in the desert for some time and was well on her way to full mummification. Her skin was so tanned and hard she re-minded me of a big handbag—except high up on her inner thigh, where the skin had been protected from the sun. On initial observation, there was no visible trauma to suggest cause of death. "Looks like JP FROG," Walt said and then added, for my benefit, "Just Plain F—in' Ran Outta Gas."

Walt was climbing a ladder to take photographs before working on the body, so I turned to look at our second case, which was waiting on the next table. This body, too, was a woman's, but she had died in her house and hadn't been discovered for several days. As I glanced at her, I thought I saw her cheeks move. I thought, "Couldn't be," and went for a closer look: not only were her cheeks moving, but her tongue was actually turning in her partly open mouth because there were so many maggots in there, eating and jostling for position. I don't know what bothered me more, seeing that many live maggots or seeing a dead body move. Since everyone in the au-topsy suite was wearing full protective gear, including a mask over nose and mouth, you couldn't tell what people were thinking unless they spoke, but my eyes must have widened when I looked at the maggots because Todd Fenton, one of Walt's longtime students, quietly said to me, "You'll get used to them." By this time, Walt was descending the ladder behind us and delegating tasks to start processing the first case.

Regardless of a corpse's state of decomposition, the forensic anthropol-ogist's goal when processing a case is to analyze the specific bones that ex-hibit sex differences and age-related changes, as well as the bony elements that indicate ancestry and enable an estimate of height. In general, we de-termine age by examining the face of the pubic symphysis (the very front of the two hip bones); the state of fusion of the epiphyses (end caps) of the long bones (arms and legs) and the medial clavicle (middle of the collar bone); and the morphology (shape) of the tips of the third and fourth ribs where they curve to meet the sternum. Of course, dentition is a great help with age as well, as teeth develop in rough accordance with chronological age. To determine the sex of an adult body without external genitalia (or with genitalia made unrecognizable by decomposition), several bones come into play: the entire set of bones that make up the pelvic girdle exhibit distinctions between males and females, as do the skull and several aspects of the long bones. "Race," or ancestry, is an estimation that, again, relies upon the anthropologist's interpretation of the morphology of bones throughout the body, with teeth and hair potentially contributing information. We estimate the stature of a body by measuring the length of particular long bones and entering those measurements into a formula that takes into account the sex and race of the body.

Now, when I say "regardless of a corpse's state of decomposition," I mean that even if the body is fresh—the person died that very day—you must use a scalpel to cut away tissue from the areas of interest until you expose bone. Then you use a Stryker saw (an instrument with a round blade that vibrates back and forth quickly, unable to cut tissue but able to saw through bone) to free up the section of bone you need to examine. You do not just cut or saw anywhere you feel like: there are ways to remove tissue with minimal disturbance of surrounding flesh or bone. For example, you must follow proper procedure for sawing out the maxillae and mandible (essentially, the mouth) in order to take dental X rays; otherwise you risk cutting through the tips of tooth roots that sit in the maxillary sinus cavities.

I'm not going to pretend that a Stryker saw didn't intimidate me the first time I had to use one. The saw is quite heavy; it can slide around in your hand if your surgical gloves are wet, and if it touches liquid (say, blood in the intestinal region) it can spray that liquid everywhere. Plus, it's difficult to believe a saw can't cut you. But Angie Huxley, another of Walt's senior students, said the magic words when I picked up the saw: "You can do it, Clea." It helped, too, that the environment of the Pima County ME's office was efficient. Efficiency is good when you're doing something for the first time—it means that everyone's concentrating on his or her own job and not watching you hold a Stryker saw with two hands as if you're corralling a cat for a bath.

The lab protocol dictated that once we removed the bony elements of interest, we signed them out from the ME's office (to maintain the chain of custody), and took them to the wet lab at the university, where we cleaned them in several stages to remove tissue and fats. Then we anthropologically analyzed them, took a full set of dental X rays, and processed the films right there in the lab darkroom. We would then submit to the ME's office a report of our findings. Once the ME's office could send dental X rays of missing persons whose characteristics matched our anthropological report, Walt could compare the sets to determine if the root formation, dental characteristics, and restorations (fillings, bridges, dentures, and so on) could be from our case.

My perspective on the evaluation of a skeleton for identification purposes is that, as anthropologists, we must take into account as much information as is available to us. Nothing is gained from using only one measurement, even a measurement considered reliable. I think of us as interpreters of the skeleton's language. Experience is the key to interpreting that language as accurately as possible, and experience comes from working on and observing as many cases as possible alongside a practiced professional.

While I was gaining that experience at the Human ID Lab, I still thought that only international human rights investigations would have a humanitarian quality. A single case in Arizona dispelled that notion, and when I was invited to Rwanda, I remembered how fulfilling that case had been. We had brought an unidentified person's dentition and other bones back to the lab from the ME's. Several of us decided to finish processing the case that afternoon, since we already had the dental X rays of a missing person whose body the police suspected this might be. We established the age, sex, ancestry, and stature of the body, and we assessed its physical anomalies. We shot the postmortem dental X rays and processed them in the darkroom. Once the films were ready, Walt compared them with the missing person's X rays. It was a match. The decedent was a young man who had gone missing more than a year earlier.

After I packed my bag to leave that day, I went to say good night to Walt. As I reached the tall bookcase that separated his office from the main room, I realized he was on the phone to the medical investigator who was handling the young man's case and would communicate with his family. "You can tell his folks he'll be home for Thanksgiving," Walt said, leaning back in his chair. There was pride in his voice—a voice that was usually either stern or joking—and my heart swelled because I had been a part of this: our work meant the return of someone to his family, someone they might not have been able to identify on their own, someone they'd been *missing*. I have often read that surviving relatives feel that having a body, or even just a piece of one, is the key to closure and the gateway to grieving.

As I had imagined before graduate school, working with Walt in the ME's office was wonderful; but working on real cases had unexpected consequences. I began to draw inward, preferring to be home alone, where I read cozy British mysteries in an attempt to block out what I was seeing every week: the bodies of people who'd overdosed on drugs while with friends (friends so strung out that they hadn't known what to do with the body except to dump it in the middle of nowhere), murdered ex-wives (shot *and* beaten, and in that order), foreign nationals who had died of exposure after paying a coyote to help them cross the U.S.-Mexico border only to be abandoned in a relentless desert. Murders, suicides, car accidents, boating accidents, hiking falls; and on and on.

Eventually, I got spooked. I lived alone in a complex of hundreds of apartments spread across several acres at the edge of the desert. I was constantly checking my balcony doors to make sure they were locked. I even replaced the shower curtain with a transparent one so that if someone broke in, at least I'd see him coming. I had a neighbor I rarely saw—I think he was a salesman—and sometimes I convinced myself I could smell "decomp" emanating from under his front door.

Then, one evening, I was eating supper and watching the television news. The newscast played the 911 emergency tape of a woman telephoning for help as she was being attacked. I had just been at the ME's office with Walt, examining that very woman. Walt had been asked to determine the sequence of physical trauma. I remember the beginning of stubble on her shaved legs, her painted nails, the ragged bullet holes visible in her scalp when it was reflected down over her face, postcraniotomy. But when I heard the 911 tape, these memories weren't ordered and discrete, like I just recounted them. It was more like hearing the voice of someone I knew, but someone I knew was dead. It scared the hell out of me.

In the midst of all this, the genocide in Rwanda took place, from April to June 1994. When I watched the TV reports describing the carnage as tribal conflict, I knew enough to know better. Simplistic reporting didn't obscure the images, however, and I wondered to myself, "Who's going to go over there and identify all those bodies?" Less than two years later, I was on a plane to Rwanda.

I JOINED THE MISSION with great excitement because I was finally going to be applying my forensic skills to the human rights abuse investigations that had motivated me for years. Accordingly, I wasn't particularly worried that I would get spooked as I had in Arizona. I also didn't expect to be demoralized by whatever we unearthed—after all, I was a trained scientist by then. I didn't take stock of the fact that I was well prepared for the bodies but perhaps for nothing else.

Sure enough, when the mission was over and I returned home, my internal compass had been oriented to a different north. I see now that this was due in part to specific traumatic events during the mission and in part to identifying with Rwandans because I have family in three of the surrounding countries. In the end, however, my feelings of fulfillment intertwined with the unexpected and painful challenges of the work in such a way that I only wanted to do one thing: work on more missions.

At first I just needed to see if the work would be the same at another site, so I worked in Rwanda a second time, also in 1996. When I accepted a mission to Bosnia later that year with the UN International Criminal Tribunal for the former Yugoslavia, I wanted to know how the work was different in another country. The next thing I knew, I was a core member of the UN forensic team, going on to investigate graves in Croatia and Kosovo. I did it often enough that being on a mission became more "my life" than my life was, and I did it long enough to see the evolution of forensic investigation in the international setting, and for the setting to change around us.

As for the work itself—the graves and the bodies—that became familiar, too. In Rwanda, there might be hundreds of bodies in a single grave, predominately women and children, killed by blunt or sharp force trauma. In Bosnia, there might be two hundred bodies per grave, predominately men, their hands tied behind their backs, killed by high-velocity gunshot wounds (GSW). In Kosovo we found several people in each grave, family groups, killed by both GSW and burning.

By the time I worked in Kosovo, I was an old hand at most of the protocols and quirks of Tribunal forensic missions; yet when I was in the morgue and saw the bodies—so many young, so many very old—I was reminded of Rwanda almost daily. The morgue itself couldn't have been more different from the inflatable autopsy tent we had in Rwanda; this morgue was a built structure with running water, electricity, and even fume hoods. But the bodies coming through that building could have been the same as those in Rwanda: a middle-aged woman carrying a child's (her child's?) pacifier, an old man wearing three layers of trousers, another woman carrying a stash of jewelry in an inner pocket. So many people shot in the back and buttocks, just as those in Rwanda had had the backs of their heads cut. In both places it was a story of people running away, or already incapacitated, a story of people who didn't, couldn't, get away.

The bodies we recovered in Kosovo were those that hadn't been removed by the police and Yugoslav National Army before our arrival. Some showed signs of the perpetrators' attempts to hide the evidence (not so easy, really). That behavior was the first effect of forensic science's entrance into the international consciousness. But it wasn't the only such effect. I have come to understand that the global role of forensic science is not only to deter killing but also to contribute, in a postconflict setting, to improved and real communication between "opposing" parties. This is done by helping to establish the truth about the past—what happened and to whom— which in turn strengthens ties between people in their own communities. Despite the facts—whether religious, ethnic, or historical—that are supposed to differentiate places like Rwanda and Kosovo, their dead reveal their common humanity, one that we all share.

If someone had asked me about my career goal on my first mission to Rwanda, I would have said that I aspired to give a voice to people silenced by their own governments or militaries, people suppressed in the most final way: murdered and put into clandestine graves. Looked at from this perspective, working for the two United Nations international criminal tribunals as a forensic expert really was a dream come true for me. I felt this most keenly my first day on the job in Rwanda: I was crouched on a forty-five-degree slope, under a heavy canopy of banana leaves and ripe avocados, placing red flags in the dark soil wherever I found human remains. Let's put it this way: I ran out of flags. I went back to my room that night and wrote in my journal about the realization of a dream. And I kept on writing.

PART ONE

—

KIBUYE

January 6–February 27, 1996

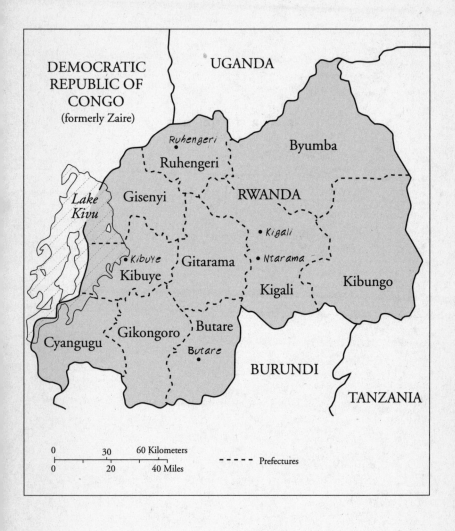

On April 6, 1994, the president of Rwanda, Juvenal Habyarimana, was killed in the sky over Kigali when a missile shot down the airplane in which he was traveling. The identity of those who launched the missile is still argued over, although most evidence points to extremists within the president's own political party. Within an hour of the downing of the plane, the Presidential Guard began killing people whose names appeared on lists created months earlier—anyone from political opponents to university professors and their students, "regular" people, their families, and anyone who had ever associated with them. Within one hundred days, more than 800,000 people—about a tenth of the population of Rwanda—were murdered, not by automatic weapons but by machetes and clubs wielded by soldiers, mayors, police, and neighbors, all urged to "do their work" by twenty-four-hour hate radio incitements. The organizers' intent to expunge particular groups—even if those "groups" were mythical—is what defined these activities as genocide. It is also estimated that in this time, 70,000 women were raped and 350,000 children witnessed the murders of family members. The first massacre site marked for forensic investigation by the United Nations International Criminal Tribunal for Rwanda (ICTR) was in Kibuye, on the western border of the country.

1.

THE BLOOD'S LONG GONE

IT TOOK TWENTY-FOUR HOURS TO FLY FROM CALIFORNIA TO Rwanda. I crossed ten time zones and ate two breakfasts, but there was one constant: my thoughts of Kibuye church and the job I had to do there. Most of the facts I knew were bounded by the dates of the genocide: the church was in Kibuye town, within the *préfecture,* or county, of Kibuye. During the three months of the 1994 genocide, this one county alone suffered the deaths or disappearances of almost 250,000 people. Several thousand of those had been killed in a single incident at Kibuye church.

According to the few Kibuye survivors, the *préfet,* or governor, of Kibuye organized gendarmes to direct people he had already targeted to be killed into two areas: the church and the stadium. The *préfet* told them that it was for their own safety, that they would be protected from the violence spreading through the country. But after two weeks of being directed to the "safe zones," those inside were attacked by the very police and militia who were supposed to be their protectors. This was a tactic typical of *génocidaires* all over Rwanda: to round up large numbers of victims in well-contained buildings and grounds with few avenues of escape and then to kill them. In fact, more people were killed in churches than in any other location in Rwanda. Some priests tried to protect those who had sought refuge in their churches; others remained silent or even aided the killers.

I read the witness accounts of the attack on Kibuye church in "Death, Despair and Defiance," a publication of the organization African Rights. Reading them was like having the survivors whisper directly in my ear: they describe how the massacre took place primarily on April 17, a Sunday, on the peninsula where the church sits high above the shores of Lake Kivu. The attackers first threw a grenade among the hundreds of people gathered inside the church; then they fired shots to frighten or wound people. The small crater from the grenade explosion was still visible in the concrete floor almost two years later, along with the splintered pews. After the explosion, the attackers entered the church through the double wooden doors at the front. Using machetes, they began attacking anyone within arm's reach. A common farming implement became, in that moment, an instrument of mass killing, with a kind of simultaneity that bespeaks preplanning.

The massacre at the Kibuye church and in the surrounding buildings and land, where more than four thousand people had taken refuge, continued for several days, the killers stopping only for meals. The hairs on the back of my neck stood up when I learned that the killers fired tear gas to force those still alive to cough or sit up. They then went straight to those people and killed them. They left the bodies where they fell.

People living in Kibuye after the genocide eventually buried the bodies from the church in mass graves on the peninsula. The UN International Criminal Tribunal for Rwanda had requested our forensic team to locate the graves, and to exhume the remains and analyze them to determine the number of bodies, their age, their sex, the nature of their injuries, and the causes of their deaths. The physical evidence would be used at the trial of those already indicted by the Tribunal on charges of crimes against humanity, to provide proof of the events and to support the testimony of witnesses.

Every time I read the accounts of Kibuye survivors, I ended up crying because they described a type of persecution from which there appears no escape, followed by a shock survival stripped of joy due to the murders of parents, children, cousins—and family so extended the English language doesn't even have names for them, though Rwandans do. Reading those accounts one last time before the plane delivered me to Kigali, my reaction was no different, but I tried to hide the tears from people in the seats around me and that gave the crying a sort of desperation, which in turn made me wonder how I would handle working in this crime scene.

As I stepped out of the airplane and walked across the tarmac of the Kigali airport, my concerns faded because my immediate surroundings occupied me. The first thing I noticed in the terminal was that many of the lights were out and the high windows were broken, marred by bullet holes or lacking panes altogether: cool night air poured in from outside. Just inside the doors, the officer at passport control inspected my passport and visa closely.

"How can you be a student and also come here to work?" he asked. I told him I was with a team of anthropologists.

"Who?"

Would he have a negative reaction to Tribunal-related activities?

"Physicians for Human Rights," I replied nervously.

His face lit up. "Ah! Well, you are very welcome."

Relieved, I walked downstairs to the baggage claim. The carousel was tiny, squeakily making its rounds, and I could see through the flaps in the wall to the outside where some young men were throwing the bags onto the carousel. My bags came through, but two teammates I had just met on the plane, Dean Bamber and David Del Pino, were not so fortunate. The baggage handlers eventually crawled inside through the flaps in the wall and stood in a group, looking at the passengers whose bags hadn't arrived as if to say to them, "Sorry, we did all we could."

While Dean and David went to find help, I walked past the chain-link fence separating baggage claim from the lobby, pushed past the crowd of people there to meet this twice-weekly flight, and met Bill Haglund, our team leader. I recognized Bill because I had met him a couple of years earlier at the annual meeting of forensic anthropologists in Nevada. He was a semi-celebrity at the time, from his work as a medical examiner on the Green River serial murder cases in Seattle, but the reason he made an impression on me was his slide show from Croatia: he had just returned from working for Physicians for Human Rights (PHR), exhuming the remains of Croatian Serb civilians killed by the Croatian army in 1991. Now here he was in Kigali airport, just as I remembered him: wearing glasses, tie, and hat, his multicolored beard (white, gray, blondish) a bit straggly. In a hurried but low tone that I came to know well, Bill immediately started to brief me on the team's logistics and plan of action, both for our two days in Kigali and the first stages of the mission in Kibuye. It sounded like an enormous amount of work—or was that just Bill's rushed-hushed delivery?—but I was excited and felt ready for anything, particularly because Bill emphasized that no forensic team had ever attempted to exhume a grave of the size we expected. We would be pioneers together, learning and adapting as we worked.

By now, Dean and David had arranged for Bill to get their bags when the next flight came into Kigali in a few days, so we walked outside. Our project coordinator, Andrew Thomson, was waiting for us in a four-wheel drive.

As we drove into Kigali town, I could not believe I was there. You know it is Africa: the air is fresh and then sweet—strongly sweet, like honeysuckle. Kigali's hills were dotted with lights from houses. On the road, the traffic was rather chaotic. Drivers did not use turn signals; they just turned or jockeyed for position as desired. Our boxy white Land Rover was one of many identical vehicles, though the others had the black UN insignia marked on their doors.

We checked in to the Kiyovu Hotel, but left almost immediately to have dinner in a neighborhood of ex-embassies. The manicured tropicality of this area exuded another kind of African beauty, like a postcolonial Beverly Hills. Before dinner at a Chinese restaurant we met two more people who worked for the Tribunal; their high front gate was opened by a guard named God. The doors of the house lay open as though surveying the garden arrayed down the hill below. Standing there at that moment, I was at ease with my companions and tremendously happy to be in Rwanda. I was finally back in East Africa, a place I remembered from my childhood as exuding an abundant vibrancy of epic proportions.

UPON WAKING THE NEXT morning, I saw that at least the outskirts of Kigali did not dispel my memories. The suburbs consisted of a multitude of green hills lined with unpaved roads, and valleys filled with low, red-roofed buildings. Flowers bloomed everywhere, and the contrast of green grass against orange earth was as saturated and luminous as a scene from Lawrence Durrell's Alexandria. Even the grounds of the modest Kiyovu Hotel inspired awe: climbing vines with massive purple flowers; huge hawklike birds nesting in the trees. The birds swooped out over the valley and came into view as I looked through my binoculars at the city, wondering how it would compare to all this.

We spent the next day and a half in town, gathering our exhumation equipment from the Tribunal's offices to take to Kibuye by car. The roads of central Kigali were in excellent condition and allowed Bill to drive fast, roundabouts providing an extra thrill. When I wasn't sliding across the backseat, I could see that Kigali's hills seemed to create neighborhoods through topography. People walked along the road, some carrying pots on their heads, while others tended the oleander bushes in the median dividers.

The Tribunal's headquarters were in a small multilevel building that provided only the barest respite from the growing warmth and humidity. We set about unpacking the many boxes of equipment that had been shipped to Kigali in the previous weeks. As we sorted and inventoried the contents, it became clear that much of the equipment was either inadequate or simply absent: we had office supplies and rubber boots of various sizes, but the surgical gloves were three sizes too large; the scalpel handles were massive and their accompanying blades were so big I wondered if they were meant for veterinary pathologists; the screens were all wrong, nothing like the mesh trays needed to sift small bones and artifacts out of bucketloads of soil. There was no time to remedy the situation. We would simply have to be creative once we were in Kibuye.

We ate a late lunch at the Meridian Hotel, Bill challenging Dean, David, and me to think about our purpose in the work for PHR and the Tribunal. He reminded us that our priority as forensic anthropologists in Kibuye would be to determine age and sex, gather evidence of cause of death, and examine for defense wounds. The conversation was as yet removed from reality because we hadn't begun the exhumation. It was more about expectation and had an almost academic distance—Bill even asked us what sort of bone remodeling we might expect in people who had regularly carried heavy weights on their heads. When the conversation turned back to human rights and the right to a decent life, David told us about retrieving human remains from a mine in Chile, where he had helped found the Chilean Forensic Anthropology Team. He talked of how it took hours to just climb in and out of the two-hundred-meter-deep pit on a rope, retrieving the skeletons bone by bone, and of having to deal with the grief of the families sitting on the edge of the mine shaft. Although it was the highlight of the day to talk together like this, as we sat in the shadow of the hotel I began to feel chilly.

I couldn't shake the feeling even during dinner, which we ate at an outdoor Ethiopian restaurant set among other houses on an unpaved back road. At one point, four men dressed in different styles of Rwandan military uniforms strolled into the restaurant. They were carrying machine guns. I don't know what I expected to happen—were they there to eat or to arrest someone?—but everyone just looked at them and they looked back and then strolled out. Whether out of tension or jet lag, I suddenly lost my appetite; Dean and David weren't eating much, either. We watched Bill tuck into his dinner, but on the way back to our hotel, David said to me, "You didn't eat much. You are still hungry." It wasn't a question.

After a fitful night of being awoken by small lizards taking refuge in my room and the sound of the linoleum peeling up from the floor (it conjured up visions of a caterpillar the size of a small dog chewing through dry leaves) I joined Dean and David to go to the UN headquarters to get our UN driver's licenses and identity cards. This was my introduction to the true international character of the UN and a glimpse of the bureaucracy for which it is infamous. The HQ, the old Amohoro Hotel, was buzzing with activity: cars passing in and out of the guarded gate, armed soldiers from all over the world escorting us, people charging around apparently getting things done, everyone wearing the blue beret of the UN at a rakish angle.

While our IDs were being processed, Dean, David, and I walked around the corner of the building to the transport office for our driver's licenses. The test consisted of driving up the street, around the roundabout, and back again. We all passed. The examiner went over the rules for driving a UN vehicle, but he spent most of the time berating us about the frequency with which these were disregarded, as though we had already transgressed.

Drolleries aside, those two bits of identification were essential: our identity cards and licenses gave us immunity, free passage, and protection from personal or vehicle search. We were to wear them on a little chain around our necks at all times. With our newly laminated cards sticking to our sweaty chests, we walked back to the Tribunal building and loaded up the Land Rover and trailer for the drive to Kibuye. Bill was staying in Kigali that night, so he had arranged for two ICTR investigators, Dan and Phil, to escort us to Kibuye. Although Kibuye was only about ninety kilometers to the west, it would be a four-hour drive, slowed by periodic Rwandan Patriotic Army (RPA) roadblocks and sections of unfinished road.

MY FIRST IMPRESSIONS of Rwanda beyond Kigali came through a soundtrack by ABBA, pouring loudly out of the car stereo via Dan's Walkman. The initial forty minutes of the drive were on paved road; the latter three hours began on an unfinished graded surface and ended on potholed dirt, so those of us in the backseat could only see out of the windows only when we weren't airborne. But as we drove, I felt so light, anticipatory, and excited at what was to come that I believe I hardly blinked, and I couldn't stop smiling to myself. The scenery was encouraging these feelings: being in East Africa made me think gratefully of my parents, and I was happy to see Africans again; their proud carriage made me want to sit up straight. Out the window, all was majestic beauty: I could see the transition of the land from the flatter parts near Kigali to the uplifted, mountainous region toward the west, where we were headed. The hills were cultivated with tea, bananas, and coffee plants in vista after vista of patchwork slopes sprinkled with thatched-roof huts and mud-brick houses. The people walking along the roads between the villages carried pots and harvest food on their heads, and babies on their backs. Children waved at us as we passed.

Each town had a roadblock where we had to stop the car. A young soldier would then emerge from a small building and indicate that we should reverse three feet or pull over or whatever he felt like making us do, before coming to the window to inspect every person's identity card and ask in French where we were going, where we had come from, and what we were doing. Once he had established that he was in control by having us keep the car idle for several minutes, he would indicate to another soldier to drop the rope barrier so we could drive on.

When we finally got a first glimpse of Lake Kivu, it was breathtaking because the road dropped out of the mountain to flatten down along the water's edge, like a roller coaster, before climbing again into Kibuye town. When we drove past Kibuye church, it was very different from what I had envisioned, but when I saw more of the country, I recognized the architecture as typical of a Rwandan Roman Catholic church built in the 1960s by Belgian priests: tall and cavernous, with a stone finish, stained-glass windows, and a bell tower. However, reading the Kibuye witness statements hadn't prepared me for how isolated it seemed: from the road, the church appeared to be the only building on the crest of a peninsula in Lake Kivu, accessible only by water or the one road.

Farther down that road, we left the equipment trailer with our UN military guard unit, already based at the Eden Roc Hotel, before we continued on to the Kibuye Guest House. This had a main building containing the lobby, restaurant, kitchen, and a lakeside veranda, with gravel pathways leading to nine or ten circular, thatched-roof huts spread about well-kept grounds of lawn and nasturtiums. The setting was idyllic, which was fitting as the guesthouse had been a water-skiing resort before the genocide. I'd never stayed in anything close to a resort so I was bowled over by its luxury—the palm and pine trees amid lush grass (cut by hand with something like a panga, a few blades at a time), bordering a small beach, and the sound of lapping water from the vast lake stretching to the horizon created by Zaire's mountains in the great distance directly to the west.

As soon as those of us from Kigali walked past the driveway, we were met by five teammates. Ralph Hartley, Melissa Connor, and Melissa's husband, Doug Scott, were from the U.S. National Park Service Midwest Archeological Center in Nebraska and had been living in Kibuye for the past month, mapping the church peninsula. The fourth person was Roxana Ferllini Timms, an anthropologist from Costa Rica. I looked at her with interest because Bill had told me that he thought I would get on particularly well with her. She had arrived a few days before with Stefan Schmitt, one of the founding members of the Guatemalan Forensic Anthropology Team. They all made a good first impression—particularly Ralph, who quietly carried my ridiculously heavy suitcases to my hut, neither asking whether I needed help nor waiting around to be thanked. Each hut had a wall down the middle, dividing it into two semicircular rooms, each with its own bathroom. Though the bathroom left a lot to be desired—the shower didn't function, the toilet lacked a cistern, and there was no running water most of the time—I loved my room for its French doors facing the lake. There was a narrow bed, a reclining deck chair, a desk with another chair, and a lockable closet.

Once I had settled in, I felt I needed to correlate my first impressions of Kibuye church with what I'd read in the witness accounts. But as soon as I started to read the familiar accounts, I became acutely aware that I was now just down the road from where the events had taken place less than two years earlier. In fact, I began to wonder what had happened at the guesthouse in 1994. Did people hide here? I started looking around my room and feeling odd.

I learned that night not to read witness statements from massacre sites while I'm in the field. I have an active imagination as it is, and have no difficulty picturing how events might have looked and sounded even if I haven't been to the site. After I'd worked on several missions, I could picture how people had looked in the last moments of their lives, down to the details of clothing, hair, fingers, and house keys. The danger is that when I am then working in a grave, I am not able to easily maintain my anthropological stance of seeing remains as a puzzle that I need to solve. Instead, I see the remains as people who experienced great fear, loss, and pain before they were violently killed. I identify with them in their last moments. Yet there I am, very much alive, scraping soil out of the folds in their clothes, holding their scalp to their skull with my gloved hand, gathering into a bag the fingernails that have sloughed off and attached themselves in an orderly scatter to the clothing of the corpse next to them in the grave.

I need distance from the bodies themselves to learn about their lives, or I can't restrain my own sadness, fear, empathy, and despair enough to do the bodies justice. And doing the bodies justice is my job, my duty. That first night in the guesthouse, I put the Kibuye accounts into a flap in my suitcase and I didn't look at them again until after I left Rwanda.

2.

THEY KILLED THEIR FRIENDS AS IF
THEY DIDN'T KNOW THEM

BILL HAD TOLD ME IN KIGALI THAT OUR FIRST JOB IN KIBUYE would be to retrieve and analyze surface—unburied—skeletons from the hillsides around the church. Before we started this task, Doug gave us newcomers a tour of the church, the priests' rooms just behind the building, the privies down the slope, the periphery of the peninsula, and, at the far end of the peninsula, the Home St.-Jean and the former house of the Belgian nuns. Then we teamed up in pairs to locate skeletons in the undergrowth on the slopes, except for Ralph, who, as photographer, had to shuttle between our pairs to document the stages of our excavations.

As we began clearing vegetation wherever we found bones on the hillside, it became clear that these were the remains of people who had tried to escape from the killings in the church and were murdered as they either hid in the banana groves or brought water at night to wounded survivors in the church. Remarkably, they still lay where they had fallen, all over the hillside, all exhibiting sharp force trauma to their heads. As I worked with Roxana on one skeleton whose postcranial elements put its age at under twenty-five years, I felt sad in the way that one does at the loss of a young life, but my sorrow was tempered by a thrilling awareness that I was really there, doing what I had longed to do, and, dammit, we had a chance to identify these people and help make meaning out of all this death.

I'VE OFTEN THOUGHT back to that first day on the hillside at Kibuye church. Even now, I use the memory for a jolt of positive energy, because I experienced a kind of elation. I know that sounds strange, given the context of festering death and abandoned hope. But I knew I could contribute there. Initially, I could recover people's remains from a resting place that was temporary at best and unrestful at worst, what with animals free to scavenge among them. Then I could examine the remains to help determine whose they were and what had happened to them; this process would also involve assembling their parts into anatomical position (the head at one end and the feet at the other and all the bones in between in their proper places), thereby restoring an aspect of their humanness, if not their identity. Finally, even if we couldn't positively identify certain remains and return them to relatives, the remains would at least be able to speak in the collective voice of the victims of the Kibuye church massacre.

All of these elements were coursing through my veins that first day in Kibuye; I think that is when I started smiling a lot. Many people have asked me how I could smile so much in the midst of a mass grave or a field of scattered bones. It is because I see not just death—about which I can do *nothing*—but bones and teeth and hair, which I *can* do something about, something that serves the deceased and possibly a greater community, not just theirs but other communities around the world.

The way the bones fueled my awareness of my job assured me that the fears engendered by reading the Kibuye witness accounts would not come to fruition while I was working on these bones. Strangely, what affected me more than the skeletons were the bloody handprints (tiny hands) in the priests' rooms, the machete cuts in the doors of the outdoor privies, the blood splatters on the ceilings—the *ceilings*—of the church anterooms, the machete slash to the middle of the clay Virgin Mary statue, and the lower extremity of an angel lying on the windowsill. Those remnants of violence were evocative in a different way than the bones.

We spent days searching for surface skeletons, placing red flags in the soil as we worked until we had located so many that it was more helpful to ring whole areas in crime scene tape wrapped around tree trunks. Bones from multiple people were scattered across several meters through taphonomic processes: mostly water runoff down the slope, but also disturbance by animals and perhaps by people, as they collected bananas and avocados from the trees. We recovered around fifty bodies from the hillside and began analyzing them on tables we set up along one side of the church, on a sort of widow's walk that was at the level of treetops and birdsong and afforded glimpses of sunlight reflected off Lake Kivu far below. Anthropological analysis of the skeletons consisted of laying the bones out on the table in anatomical position, then determining age, sex, stature, and cause of death, following our standard procedures.

One day, most of the skeletons we worked on were children with massive sharp force trauma and blunt force trauma to the head. I was mentally thanking my Stanford adviser Lori Hager for all the work we had done with mixed dentition—that is, when juveniles' adult teeth begin to erupt while some baby teeth remain. Repetitive analysis of such dentition now allowed me to age the Rwandan kids with relative speed, though I felt I could use a refresher on "siding" (determining left and right) immature tibiae and fibulae (lower leg bones), which can look just like smooth sticks if the child is very young.

Farther down the widow's walk, Ralph had set up a table with a black velvet cloth as a backdrop: a photography section. Here, all the surface skeletal remains were photographed in anatomical position, and then the trauma was photographed in detail. I walked up as he photographed one person with a stabbing gouge in the back of the distal tibia, a wound we'd seen a number of times already. We began theorizing that the perpetrators had cut the Achilles tendons of the people we'd found on the hillside to prevent them from running farther. The murderers would have returned to kill them at another time. The tibia cuts weren't a cause of death, we realized: they had been accompanied by sharp force trauma to the heads.

Of the adult skeletons I analyzed that day, I particularly remember that of a man wearing a dark blue outfit in the style of an American gas station attendant. The embroidered name tag on the jacket read MATT and underneath, in partially destroyed white letters, was FRAU——— [or FRAN———] AUTO PARTS and a phone number. One child was wearing a baby outfit. Stefan held up a machete of the type named in the Kibuye indictment to the trauma on another child's cranium: there was a perfect fit between the curved blade and the two defects on opposite sides of the head. I had Stefan's characteristic catchphrase down by then: "I mean, Jesus."

The more we worked, the more jumpy I felt whenever I was alone in the church. Now that I had held the bones of people killed there, I found I couldn't stop glancing at the blood on the very high ceiling even though it was horrifying me to pieces. Ralph said that he had experienced a similar sensation when he was at the other end of the peninsula in the Belgian nuns' house, where he had to photograph the crawl space above the ceiling where people had tried to hide. There were holes in the ceiling from the sharp instruments the killers had used to flush out those in hiding.

On another day, Willie, one of our logistics technicians and a Ugandan, came around to where I was analyzing a skeleton. Willie and I had become friends since I had told him that my mother's mother—my *jaja*—was from Kampala. Every time he saw me, he would exclaim, "Ha HA! The *jajas*! Ho HO! The *jajas*!" doubling over with laughter at my use of a Swahili word. This time Willie was more serious, contemplating the skeleton for a few minutes before saying, "There is a man, first he has a car and he is complaining, even though the other man cannot even afford a bicycle. And then he wants a second car, and he is complaining, and he wants a third car, and then *this* is not enough, and he must have a plane. And still the other man cannot afford a bicycle. You look at this body here, and you see this person who was very rich or very poor, but when this happened, they are all the same; no one is left with a penny in their pocket. These people killed their friends as if they didn't know him."

DURING THE FIRST FEW weeks of the mission, I became sleepy earlier and earlier, until I was hardly able to keep my eyes open past nine P.M. The fatigue was directly related to working on a steep slope or standing all day at the anthropology tables, my neck getting sunburned. Down at the guest-house, we were "showering" in very cold lake water we carried to our huts in buckets, rushing to get it before night fell so as to reduce the number of minnows, or whatever the squiggling lake life was, having a shower with us. When I emptied the bucket over my head, I would think of Jaja saying, "This is a real business," indicating unsatisfactory things and actions per-formed under duress, said while shaking her head ruefully. The cold water did nothing for the back pain I had developed from working on the hillside, but the firmness of the little bed did its part. Sometimes water came out of the taps, but usually brushing one's teeth involved dissolving tablets into lake water to reduce the diseases it was alleged to carry, then making sure one didn't swallow any of it.

The team became used to waiting a long time, sometimes in actual paroxysms of hunger, for dinner, which was orchestrated by the over-worked concierge/maître d'/waiter, Ephrem. Dean had told me that Ephrem had been away in Kigali during the genocide, but his entire family had been wiped out. He asked Dean what we were doing in the church and Dean had replied, "Studying what happened." Although Ephrem became quite emotional he only said, *"C'est bon. . . . C'est bon."* ("That's good. . . . That's good.") As for Gistav, the junior concierge who had welcomed us to the guesthouse when we first arrived, he wouldn't talk to Dean about the genocide. I hadn't been able to bring myself to ask either of them about it but I had talked to Gistav about how he had been in school in the south, studying French and English. His life Before.

When Bill arrived in Kibuye, we began a tradition of eating dinner as a group on the veranda of the main building. When I looked around the table at the team, I felt special, in part because there were so few of us and in part because it was an impressive group of scientists, all of whose personal characteristics I liked: Ralph's equanimity, Stefan's gruffness,

Melissa's gung ho–ness, Doug's tendency, when asked a question, to set-
tle down into the answer as though snuggling into an armchair with a
pipe and a good book. I found myself laughing perhaps too much at Bill's
rendition of picking up Dean and David's baggage from Kigali airport
customs:

Customs: "Open this up!"

Bill: "I don't have a key!"

Customs: "Open this up!"

Bill: "I don't have a key!"

Customs: "Open this up!"

Bill: "I don't have a key!"

Customs: "Okay, go!"

It was so African somehow; I could picture the customs official irritably
waving Bill away, and Bill being amused rather than frustrated.

Eventually, we ate at the white plastic tables set up around the lawn,
next to the lake. After dinner, I would usually retire to the veranda to sit
with Dean, Ralph, and Roxana, where we talked and made each other
laugh and watched the lake become as choppy as the sea when the rains
blew in. The veranda evenings were marred once when a man we knew as
Captain Eddy, of the local Rwandan Patriotic Army unit, imposed himself
on us while his entourage of young soldiers took up positions around the
veranda and the lawn. I knew Captain Eddy had tried to come up to the
church a few days earlier but had been barred by our UN soldiers. I could
smell alcohol emanating from him that night; he seemed drunk, and that
made me nervous because he was carrying guns. I kept my gaze averted
from him at all times but at some point he turned his attention to me and
tried to arrange a marriage between me and one of the soldiers in his entourage. This same young man kept trying to get Captain Eddy to leave the
guesthouse but was waved away more viciously each time. I finally looked
at Captain Eddy directly and saw that his eyes were terribly bloodshot.
Then he said his mother was in the grave at the church and he wanted to
come up to see her. I saw his drunkenness in a new light, but I also wondered why he was telling us about his mother now, of all times, and
whether, somehow, we were in danger.

Theoretically, any danger for our team would be mitigated by the presence of almost thirty UN soldiers, all from Ghana, and twelve of whom were on the church peninsula at all times. But I didn't know how much of a deterrent they could be. While they carried machine guns, they had agreed not to use them in accordance with the cease-fire and had put cotton wool in the muzzles to keep the dust out. The little white puffs jutting out of the barrels looked incongruous. The soldiers were only there to protect the grave from tampering by people or animals but once we had exposed the bodies, one of the soldiers told me they were uncomfortable on duty, particularly at night, because they believed the spirits of the people in the grave were wandering around; having been murdered and not buried properly, they were not at peace.

Most of the soldiers were professional and friendly. When the captain of the unit asked me if I'd been to Africa before and I explained that I had, when visiting family, he responded, "Oh! So you are a *true* sister! Ha ha!" There was hearty laughter followed by lots of shaking of hands every time I saw him, and I enjoyed that connection. Some soldiers, on the other hand, were a bit of an annoyance, regularly turning up in the foliage when I was off having a pee. When I discovered I was being watched and told them to go away, they responded by saying, "I love you." Melissa and I took to going together, taking turns to pee while the other kept a lookout. But one of the soldiers seemed aggressively intent on making an amorous advance. He appeared almost every time I was alone on the hillside with a skeleton, and he made it clear that he was not above using force to get me into an embrace. I used the most formal French I knew to rebuff him, and I wasn't frightened of him until the evening I was told that a soldier had actually come looking for me. This was unheard-of; the soldiers never came to the guesthouse. I didn't know whether my visitor was that particular soldier, but I stayed in Roxana's room for a few nights anyway. So when Bill said he was considering having some of the UN soldiers live at the guesthouse to provide protection from anyone unhappy about the evidence we were unearthing around the church, I was worried. What do you do when you want protection against someone who is supposed to be protecting you? How seriously do you treat such a threat after you've spent all day excavating the bones of people who have been murdered—by *their* supposed protectors? Compared to their murders, your situation is trivial, and yet it looms.

UP AT THE SITE, I could tell that Bill was really enjoying his position as team leader; the working of the cogwheels I had perceived in his mind back at the Kigali airport manifested itself in constant action, mostly hurried, as he supervised the unloading of equipment that kept arriving in various states of distress. The water pump fell off the back of the delivery truck and broke, the body bags were twice the necessary size, the tire came off the trailer bringing the big generator, the prefabricated Italian toilets weren't chemical though they did have toilet seats, and the prefabricated showers had yet to arrive. Even in our second week, we had no food for lunch other than what we could purchase at the market in Kibuye town: tomatoes, carrots, onions, and avocados. We couldn't get bread and, without water, we couldn't wash our hands before eating. But Bill persevered, fitting in helicopter rides to and from Kigali and receiving unannounced visits from church officials who were asking him to pay for the right to exhume any graves for the Tribunal. Inside the church and priests' rooms, he divided the spaces into "Evidence," "X-ray," and "Archaeological Equipment," then designated a flat area of ground for the inflatable tent due to serve as an autopsy suite.

On January 15, when we were close to finishing the recovery of skeletons from the church hillside, Roxana and I discovered the skeletonized remains of a baby off by itself with a miniature pink pacifier near its body. The bones were only slightly buried but the thin layer of soil had been enough to hold the body intact and in anatomical position. When Roxana and I notified Bill of the completeness of the remains he reserved the exhumation for himself, saying that he could work on it slowly and use the time to relax. He instructed me to work with him on this case so he could spend more time training me on body recovery, since my experience was primarily in analyzing remains in a laboratory.

I recorded in my journal only one word about working with Bill: "Excellent." We exhumed the baby slowly over several hours, and as we sat there in the quiet banana grove, we speculated about how such a small child—maybe two years old—came to be separated from adults or older children. Our discussion wasn't emotional. Something about talking with Bill insulated me from picturing the horror of what might have happened: the relative who was holding the baby becoming separated from it, being attacked and knowing they couldn't save the child; or the baby alone on the hillside, hungry or cold or hot—for how long? Instead, Bill and I noted that the skeleton was only covered by soil eroded from higher up the hill and thus had not truly been buried, so we searched the surrounding area for artifacts and other bones whose location might suggest human behavior. I learned a lot about body recovery during those hours with Bill, and it was good quality time alone with him that I wasn't sure I would get again.

3

THE GRAVE

WHEN WE HAD ARRIVED IN KIGALI, BILL TOLD US THAT FOUR forensic pathologists would be arriving in a few weeks. They would be conducting autopsies on any fleshed bodies and, for any case, they would determine cause and manner of death while the anthropologists would provide age, sex, stature, and trauma analysis for both fleshed and skeletonized bodies. We would only have the pathologists for three weeks, during which we would have to exhume the entire grave, estimated to hold up to one thousand bodies. As for now, we had to sufficiently excavate the grave so body removal could take place immediately upon the pathologists' arrival. On January 17, after completing our recovery of the surface remains from the hillside, we began exposing in earnest the mass grave itself.

Since the bodies had been buried by people in Kibuye after the genocide, the general location of the main grave was known: a large, somewhat sunken area of dirt and grass below the priests' rooms and on the cusp of the northern slope down to the lake. With Stefan at the controls of the backhoe over the previous day or two, the surface layers had already been lifted away and four of us began working with picks, shovels, and trowels to expose the human remains closest to the top of the grave. Doug was setting up and running the electronic mapping station that would chart the contours of the site and provide a three-dimensional outline of each body and its location in the grave. The production of highly detailed and trial-friendly maps was Melissa's specialty. Ralph was running between the grave and the analysis areas by the church, photographing both processes.

While Dean and Roxana finished the analysis of the surface skeletons, the rest of us were trying to delineate the edges, or extremities, of the grave. This is done primarily on the basis of distinctions in the soil. The trained eye can see the difference between the sterile, unturned soil outside the limits of the grave and the "backdirt," soil that has been removed, then piled upside down, as it were, on top of the grave opening itself. Some graves don't present one with a clear delineation; others do: we encountered a very nice one later that year at Ovčara in Croatia, complete with color differentiation.

It is important to "clean" a flat surface near the suspected grave edge with the side of a trowel, scraping away a level of soil and then standing back to note any change in soil color. You can also use a probe, which is a long metal rod with a pointed tip that you insert into the ground wherever you suspect there are buried human remains. If the probe suddenly sinks into deeper levels of soil as though encountering no resistance, this suggests an air pocket or simply loose soil—that is, backdirt—which could indicate an anomaly. An anomaly could be a grave location but it could also be a rodent tunnel or the location of an organic object, such as a tree limb, that has since disintegrated. Also, when the probe is removed, you can sniff the metal: if you smell decomposition, bodies may be nearby. Of course, if the probe strikes something soft, you've got a find down there. It is important to use a probe with moderated force, or it can inflict postmortem trauma. By probing systematically in an area you may get a sense of the grave's edge.

Looking for edges and using a probe are most effective when you already have an idea of where a grave might be. You can't just walk into a field and probe every foot in every direction, unless you have a lot of time and security. In the case of the graves at Nova Kasaba near Srebrenica, we were able to use satellite photographs that showed areas where significant amounts of earth were moved in a short space of time during the 1992–1995 war in Bosnia. Although we knew more or less where the Kibuye grave was, we still had to locate the edges. Once we did this, we could dig outside the edges with the backhoe, saving the work of digging with hand tools for exposing the top of the grave itself.

As we opened the grave, the first bodies we encountered were skeletonized and mummified; they were clothed, and some were wearing jewelry. In these upper levels, the bodies did not lie side by side but were separated by soil. We used the soil as walkways to move around in the grave without stepping on human remains. Many bodies were fully extended, some with their arms flung out to the sides. But the pathologists who were on their way needed fleshed bodies, as well, to conduct their autopsies. Bill wanted to reach deeper levels in the grave as soon as possible, in the hopes of encountering more whole bodies. As we worked in the grave with our picks and shovels, Bill reminded me of the father talking about the transport of frozen lettuce in the film *East of Eden*, constantly muttering to himself, "If we can just get past this level . . . I know we'll be peeling them off every two minutes . . . just past this level."

Bill's concerns regarding the pathologists' arrival meant he repeatedly shaved half days off the four-day holiday we were due after working for ten consecutive days. We ended up with two days off, during which some of the team went to see the gorillas at the Parc des Volcans in Ruhengeri, about a two-hour drive north from Kigali. We returned for a half day of work that was to entail simply being present while the U.S. ambassador to the UN, Madeleine Albright, visited the site. By that time, the grave was mostly a deep excavated crater with red flags stuck in the soil wherever human remains were exposed.

The morning of Ambassador Albright's visit, we got up for a 6:30 breakfast of the samosas we had brought from Kigali and then drove up to the site to prepare for the UN entourage. Bill instructed those of us in the grave to keep working while he showed the visitors around. To make the site easier for a layperson to understand, we cleaned up our footprints in the grave and used plastic numbers to denote body parts exposed so far. Then we awaited the convoy. The helicopters came in from the east and I saw one fly directly over the site. Eventually we heard cars, then people advancing toward the grave.

I kept working, following Bill's instructions, and exposed the scarf and cranium of a woman on my edge of the grave. She was lying on her left side, her back to the wall of the grave, and the radiating fractures from a hole on the left side of her head reached around her cranium like fault lines. Her body was more fully exposed than most, and it was becoming clear that she was on the grave's western extremity. To the east of her, red flags marked legs or heads just beginning to jut from the flat soil of the top of the grave; I began to sense many bodies, just like this woman, below the surface of the ground over which I was crouched.

The flies were relentless—they had been since remains were first exposed—but the whole time we had an audience, I ignored them and they landed first on the bodies, then on my mouth, hat, and arms. I could faintly hear Bill about six meters away, at the southern edge of the grave, explaining what we were doing, and other voices talking about the importance of this exhumation for evidence and corroboration of witness statements. Then I heard camera shutters clicking and people asking Bill questions, and realized there were reporters present as well.

I was finding it hard to work in a crouched position because of the heat and the stench: normally I would be alternately standing and crouching, picking and troweling. But I forgot my discomfort when I found pink necklaces around the skeleton's neck vertebrae and some hair. Now I was totally focused. This woman had been alive once, not so long ago, and had fastened the necklaces herself. Ralph wondered later if the smaller of the two necklaces would turn out to be a rosary like a plastic one I had found on a surface skeleton. But as I crouched over this body, I couldn't know what the pink necklaces had meant to her.

The next thing I knew, Melissa was giving us the signal to get out of the grave if we wanted to. I stood up, but I had to quickly crouch back down as I felt a head rush come on from the sudden movement after being bent over for so long. I looked at the grave before walking away and it held a new poignancy because of that woman and her necklaces. That moment forever changed the way I look at the ground. It was no longer simply something solid that we all stand on. Now I was aware that its depth could harbor hundreds of bodies. Ever since I was a kid, I'd thought the ground could be full of interesting things but I had never pictured it like this. I think that affected what happened next.

I walked up the slope past the priests' rooms to the Anthropology area along the side of the church. I could see that some reporters remained, and since we were to "keep working" while they were there, Roxana and I began analyzing the teeth of one of the surface skeletons. The age came out to eight years plus or minus two years. While we worked, a crew filmed us and a Swiss journalist asked us what we were doing (examining stages of) and what it would tell us (the ages and sexes of all those found). Then Bill walked up with a Reuters journalist, Elif Kaban, who asked us mostly personal questions, for instance about how we dealt with death and the families of the dead. We all responded that we were scientists, there to do a job while also trying to provide a service, and that the place for emotion is away from the site. Bill pointed out that we'd never get anything done if we thought about the tragedy while we worked because it would turn us into "blubbering idiots." At that stage, we hadn't actually interacted with bereaved families; that would come later. But when Kaban asked me what I was thinking about when I was in the grave, the pink-necklace woman was foremost in my mind, particularly the way she had given the grave character by individualizing its "contents." Then I remembered how each time I had used a pick to break through the soil on top of the grave, I heard the thud and felt the vibration through my boots, and sometimes I had wondered if the bodies could sense us above them. So I responded to Kaban's question by saying something like "I'm thinking: 'We're coming. We're coming to take you out.' " My teammates, who were standing nearby, nodded in agreement.

Apparently my remark made it into Kaban's article in the *Irish Times*. Physicians for Human Rights told Bill that the quote had garnered a fair amount of attention, with people calling the organization in Boston wanting to speak to me. I didn't know any of that at the time, but I did know that I was being teased mercilessly about what I had said. Bill first joked that I was thinking, "We're coming . . . we're coming to take you out to dinner." At first, I laughed, too, but when the teasing was still going on weeks later (Bill even made up a song: "Clea, Clea, with her Pepsodent smile, hearing voices all the while!"), I wondered why my teammates had agreed with me if my statement was so laughable. For me, the conundrum was that I was capable both of scientific detachment and human empathy, but when I revealed the latter, I was made to feel I had revealed too much.

I peeked into Kibuye church that day after Ambassador Albright had left, and saw that she had brought a massive wreath—of freesias, I think. I don't know whether she's aware that the *bourgmestre* (mayor) of Kibuye town placed her wreath with the body bags after we completed our work there. Of all the nonlocal dignitaries who have visited grave sites where I've worked, Madeleine Albright was the only one to bring something to mark the occasion.

For my part, unless I've been the one giving the tour, I have always followed my team leader's instructions to ignore visitors. I now wish I'd looked up more often, because I'd like to have seen the faces and heard the words of nonforensic people when their feet came within inches of so much death. I don't think my own words and sentiments would lack company.

THE DAY MADELEINE ALBRIGHT visited, the forensic pathologists and autopsy technicians arrived in Kibuye, so we began exhuming bodies from the grave the next day, creating a schedule that the team stuck to for several weeks. I described it at the time in a letter to my parents:

We wake up at about 6:30 A.M. to the sound of the crows that live in the palms around the guesthouse. Upon getting out of bed, we hope for running water in the bathroom and have a nice surprise if anything comes out of the tap besides the groan of the pipe. By 7:30 at the latest, we sit down for breakfast on the lawn, looking across the lake to the distant mountains of Ijwi Island and Zaire. It is invariably beautiful, in part because the lake is massive, clear, and undeveloped. Ephrem, the concierge, eventually brings out tea, powdered milk, some form of coffee, sugar, and one or more of the following (depending on who's paid their room bill, thereby enabling Ephrem to buy more food): toast (homemade bread), margarine, jam, bananas or pineapple, and when there's no bread: crêpes. We never know what we'll get. Occasionally, there is no food at all. Only drink. We try to finish breakfast by 8 A.M. and go back to our rooms to brush our teeth and gather our things. By 8:20 or so, whoever has a set of keys to one of the three Land Rovers opens a vehicle and we pile in. We drive the five minutes up the road to the site; the road is dirt, very bumpy and rutted, all uphill. Waiting at the turnoff for the church are locals looking for work, but we only employ seven people to assist with digging and laundry. We drive past yellow crime scene tape lowered by our Ghanaian guards, up to the church where we park next to the soldiers' tents.

Those of us going to work in the grave or doing autopsies change into our smelly-from-use protective gear: coveralls and rubber boots. Those of us going to the grave also grab our buckets, shovels, picks, machetes (to cut through tree branches), trowels, brushes, knee pads, body bags, and paper bags (for small bones, loose clothing, and artifacts) and walk to the far side of the church to descend to the grave. Some time is spent deploying the diggers, greeting soldiers, and setting up the video camera (we are videotaped by a stationary video camera for several hours a day to record the overall exhumation progress).

Three of us—excluding Bill—are in the grave each day, and we each have our own area of the grave that we work on independently, with occasional consultations. Body numbers are assigned by cranium only, to help us determine [the] minimum number of individuals (everyone has only one head) but you don't get a number for your body until you have exposed enough of it to actually exhume it without being blocked by the entangled body part of another corpse. Once the body is exposed and numbered, Ralph is called in to photograph the body with a ruler, north arrow, and number label. Doug runs the Sokkia [mapping station] from a location outside the grave while we map in "points" on each body, calling out "Left shoulder" or "Right knee" as we hold the mapping rod in that position and Doug electronically captures its coordinates. Then, we make a joint effort to remove the exposed, numbered, mapped, and photographed body. Once a body is exhumed and placed in a waiting, numbered body bag, the bag is carried up to the church on a stretcher either by local workers or by one of us with a local.

The rest of the time, the locals are carrying and emptying the buckets of soil that we removed from on top of the bodies. Most of them only speak Kinyarwanda, but one young man named Robert speaks Kinyarwanda, French, and English and so is a sort of foreman, communicating between all of us in the grave. This communication includes an ongoing, lively discussion of what bride price my father would require for me to marry one or more of them. [I thought this was a joke until I said five hundred cows and a week later, they came back with an offer of $250 and 250 cows. It was not a joke. I raised the price to one million cows and they exclaimed, "Un million de vaches?" immediately asking how I could be worth that much. I responded, in French, "Wouldn't you like to know?"]

We work until noon, when we break for lunch: the workers leave on foot to eat in town, while we eat in the breezy spot on the side of the church that used to be the Anthropology area. We need to be in a breezy spot because we stink like hell. Most of us just roll down our coveralls to the waist so we don't have decomposing tissue within reach of our food but the stench lingers, even on the undergarments. From where we sit, at tree-canopy level, we can look down to the lake and see the town of Kibuye and the one road back to Kigali. We can also hear everything, even though it is far away: the fishermen singing on their boats, the people walking on the road, and any car or truck coming along. For lunch we eat staples brought from Kigali by whoever passes through there: peanut butter, Digestive biscuits, cheese like La Vache qui Rit, and apples. This is supplemented by groceries from the outdoor market located next to Kibuye prison.

The workers return around 1 P.M. and we go back to work in the grave until about 5 P.M. if Bill's in Kigali, or 6–7 P.M. if Bill's in Kibuye. (Doug and Melissa instituted the five o'clock departure, based on their experience of running teams on long-term digs: people work better with more rest.) After securing a tarp over the exposed bodies (to protect them from rain and dogs), we trudge up to the opposite side of the church from where we have lunch, and take showers in lovely Italian prefabricated units with blessed hot water that has been trucked in by our British logistics chief, Geoff Bucknall.

When we eventually get back to the guesthouse, people generally take a minute for themselves, then go to the back veranda and order dinner. Dinner takes upward of an hour to arrive. I think there is only one cook. Andrew Thomson, our project coordinator and a New Zealander, had joked that the guesthouse has a choice of four dishes, two of which are permanently unavailable, but it's not quite that bad: there are goat kebabs, spaghetti, and filet de boeuf. The menu is actually two pages long but the majority of it doesn't exist anymore. If you're lucky, you get tilapia, the local lake fish. If you want to eat light, there's grilled cheese on toast. You eat any of these with either rice or French fries—except cheese on toast: Ephrem doesn't believe this goes with fries, so if I order both, he accordingly never brings the frites. Invariably, something is wrong with your order, but you take whatever you get on your plate because it takes so damn long to get anything. To drink there is Fanta (orange or citron), Coca-Cola, or beer. No dessert even though it's on the menu: for example, "Gâteau." You say to Ephrem, "S'il vous plaît, je voudrais de gâteau." ["I would like some cake, please."] You point to it on the menu, just for clarity. Immediately, you receive the Response: Ephrem gets a pained expression, tilts his head to one side, points to the same thing, repeats, "Aaahhhh . . . le gâteau . . ." and then he rocks his hand back and forth and sucks in his breath, exhaling to say, "Kigali." That is to say: "There's cake in Kigali, but not in Kibuye. We have cake if someone brings it from Kigali. No one has been to Kigali in two years, however."

There is a team rumor that we're going to receive some outdated (and therefore, free) military rations to supplement our diet but until then, we share within our own "food groups" or with someone who has something to share back, like cheese or chocolate. We used to all eat together at one table when we were a smaller group of eight, but now we sometimes break off into groups, unless Bill wants to talk about work and then we all feel obligated to sit together. After dinner, some folks stay on the veranda to talk, others go off to read or work on their computers. It is very, very beautiful here

*with the tranquil clear water, the clear sky—at night almost as starry as in
Dar es Salaam—the lapping water, and the occasional bleat of a baby goat.
You wake up the next morning for the same routine. The only thing that
seems to change is the condition of the bodies in the grave itself.*

As we uncovered the deeper layers of the grave, the state of the bodies
progressed from skeletonized to mummified to simply decomposing. The
direct sunlight during our workday sped up decomposition, creating stench
and a sense of stillness. As the number of bodies went into the hundreds,
there was barely any soil left between them, they were so tightly pressed together. The reduction in the amount of backdirt that had to be removed
meant faster exhumation. This was important, because we had no idea
how many more bodies lay below: would it be the one thousand we had estimated on the basis of witness reports? The less skeletonized condition
also sped up exhumation, because a body could be lifted out almost whole:
we no longer had to carefully gather more than two hundred individual
bones. However, we were delayed by the way in which the bodies were entangled with each other. It seemed that some of them had been pushed by
a bulldozer or other machine in order to make more space in the grave, and
this had twisted the bodies and blurred the layers. Another problem was
that bodies in the state of decomposition known technically as saponified
have a tender skin. If you punctured it, something not dissimilar to cottage
cheese came foaming out, and then you had to clean away that as well.

Soon, Bill was concerned that we just weren't working fast enough.
One day, it was hotter than usual and even though we usually took a water
break at 11:30, I was parched by ten. The grave was generally emitting two
decomposition scents, one being sharp and ripe, the other thick and
"hairy," and waves of the latter, which I find less manageable, kept coming
over me. I stopped early for lunch, aware that the cold I'd recently picked
up was wearing me down, but proud that four or five of us had exhumed
nineteen bodies in several hours despite such difficult conditions. By the
end of the day, we'd exhumed a total of thirty-two. This was two bodies
more than the goal Bill had set in the morning. At the time, reaching daily
goals seemed important: they enabled us to feel we were progressing in

a massive job that presented unpredictable challenges in every subsequent layer of the grave. However, the morning's impressive body count prompted Bill to raise the quota at lunchtime to forty so we actually ended up eight bodies short. It was frustrating to find the goalposts were suddenly moved downfield. We got tired of running, and instead thought, "We may as well walk, since it's so far to go."

That afternoon, everything about the way we were doing the exhumation frustrated me: the sense of feverish activity Bill created every time he wielded a pick or yanked one body's legs out from under another's; the inefficiency of stacking filled body bags in groups of three between the pews in the church (I could see we were going to run out of space, besides which the arrangement struck me as awful since we were returning these people to the place where they were killed); the discomfort of having to wear oversized gloves and coveralls all day long; and then the insult of our chief pathologist objecting to those of us working in the grave using the coveralls ("They're for the pathologists!" he had yelled, as if we weren't handling the exact same decomp they were); the dreams I kept having of dismembered legs in the bed with me, or trowels scraping through saponified flesh; the way Bill's stress infected Melissa and Doug with a dictatorial approach (yelling, mostly) toward the local workers; the fact that my body was totally confused and had saddled me with a second period in one month. And, finally, I was tired of the stench of death and how it pervaded everything.

A few days later, things had not improved. I wrote in my journal:

Thursday (though who'd know it), 25 January '96
Kibuye Guest House, 9:17 P.M.

Well, what a day. Yesterday morning we were totally civilized, clearing and cleaning as Bill followed his own path, but the afternoon deteriorated when Bill "helped" the rest of us exhume the bodies we'd freed earlier. We just ran around after Bill all afternoon. Well, not David, because he's on the far edge where the bodies are pushed up into a wall, but Melissa and I. Bill basically went at a fever pitch, removing parts and tugging on things and making me shove my hand along clothing tracks, feeling out bones and so on. He calls this the birthing of the body. I ran after him, mapping (though not fast enough by his standards, but I'm not going to skip points); troweling; getting buckets (ndobo—my specialized Kinyarwanda vocabulary) while Melissa ran around assigning numbers and labeling body bags. It was absurd. Thank goodness for the method of the morning—all of the preparation. The first couple of bodies were fine because they'd been mostly exposed and were "ready to pop," as Melissa puts it. But after that, instead of going back to method, Bill suited his actions to the rapidity of his thoughts. Bam, bam, bam. I was almost embarrassed, wondering what the workers thought. They already refer to us as wazungu [Swahili for "foreigners" or "white men"]. Most of the time Bill seems like the mad professor from a fifties B movie, but this time I was helping him. He would exhume a child and then actually rip its mandible off to get a look at dental age for our grave form. It reminded me of the first time I observed Walt saw out maxillae at the ME's office in Arizona; it's really shocking. I mean, it is horrific that we have to do things like extract pubes for sexing, or saw out bits of femur for DNA sampling, but the goal is about restoring personal identity, and it comes at that price. Intellectually, I know that Bill isn't ripping the mandibles out with force because he wants to look possessed but rather, it's the bones adhering with just the last bits of mummified temporal muscle, and a bit of elbow grease is what it takes to get a look at the teeth and thus, preliminary age. And is our process more horrific than the actual cause/manner of death? After all, we wouldn't even be here if these people hadn't been attacked by machete-wielding assailants while they prayed to some god for protection.

By January 29, we were calling the grave the nursery because we had found so many children. Stefan took charge of it at this point, having dug a drainage trench around the entire area to deal with rain runoff and provide a place to throw backdirt (the walls of the grave were now so deep that we couldn't just hurl it out ourselves). It was a new era for us because Stefan instituted breaks during the day. Yes, breaks. He'd step out into the drainage trench, lean against the dirt wall, and hand out cigarettes to the workers before lighting one for himself.

Initially, I kept working, and he'd say, "Clea, you gotta take a break. Take a moment to step back."

And I'd say, "That's fine for you, you have something to do—smoking a cigarette. It's hard to stand here and just look at the grave when there's so much to do."

"Maybe you should start smoking," he'd say with a grin.

Stefan was teasing me, but he had a point. It *is* important to pace yourself, especially when you're working hard and sweating a lot in a place with stenches so strong they can make your eyes water. At this depth, the bodies still had more or less intact intestines, which would emit strong, ammonia-scented fumes when prodded or exposed.

Those fumes were just some of the odors permeating our clothes, despite the protective coveralls. Underwear was no exception. I used to own only a couple of bras: one to wear while the other one was washed, and maybe another one for exercising. I took three to Rwanda, and that didn't cut it. One was for wearing to work—my "grave bra," which I had to keep in its own plastic bag because even after I soaked it in Woolite, it stank. Then I had to have one bra to wear after work in the early days when we couldn't get a proper shower. That left one bra that was sacred, to be used only after a hot shower with full, exfoliating, scented scrub-down. I soon made a mental note that if I ever went on another mission, I would take plenty of bras. (Indeed, on later trips I packed not just several work and downtime bras, but also day-off bras, going-to-civilization-for-the-weekend bras, relaxing-in-my-room-by-myself-don't-need-as-much-support bras, and so on.)

As for periods, I learned after having two in one month that time that the key was to do as much physical labor in the graves as possible—swinging a pick, shoveling, running a wheelbarrow—anything to lower my body fat and thus make my periods as light as possible. That meant less painful cramps and less hassle when there was no hope of a proper bathroom until the end of the day. This need to do physical labor later became a problem when I worked on teams with macho types who were pained to see women swinging a pick. Some guys would leave their part of a grave to come to my area and pick it down, despite my protests. Little did they know I was trying to become a hard body for a very specific reason. Anyway, I feel very protective of my work area—my part of the grave is my part and I want to take care of it from using a pickax to remove topsoil at the beginning, down to the end when I'm using a chopstick to dislodge the dirt between the buried person's finger phalanges.

I find it inordinately satisfying to lift bodies I've excavated out of their grave. These are people whom someone attempted to expunge from the record, the very bodies perpetrators sought to hide. I particularly cherish helping to carry my bodies on their stretchers away from the grave. It is as though I've seen the bodies through, from initial uncovering to liberation. As a laboratory-trained anthropologist, I gain significant satisfaction in analyzing remains for the biological information that provides the primary descriptors of postconflict mass graves. How many men, women, and children? How old were they? Were they executed or killed in combat? These statistics are important in demonstrating a crime against humanity, for example. But in later missions for the UN, I often requested that I at least start in the field, removing people from the graves. The grave site provides a context for the bodies, and that context enables better understanding of the details that are revealed through examination in the morgue.

4

THE MAN WITH THE PROSTHETIC LEG

WHILE WE WERE EXCAVATING THE GRAVE, THE PATHOLOGISTS had been receiving the bodies up in the church and conducting autopsies in the tent. The chief pathologist was Bob Kirschner, director of PHR's International Forensic Program. Dean had been working with the pathologists to determine each decedent's age, sex, and stature. One morning at breakfast, however, Bill said he was rotating me into the tent, while Dean would go down to the grave. Bill asked me twice whether I was ready for the task, saying, "The reason I haven't had certain people in there so far is I only want the fast people, you know, doing analysis in ten minutes." Since Dean was the only anthropologist who had been assigned to the tent so far, the implication was that Bill didn't think anyone else was fast enough. But I was thinking, "If there's one thing I know, it's lab analysis—I was trained by Walt Birkby, for heaven's sakes!" Sure, forensic anthropologists in the States usually have several *hours* to analyze just one case, but the condition of the bodies from this grave favored speedy casework because the decomposing tissue would come away from the bony surfaces with relative ease, thus leaving you to get down to the business of analysis. Still, I went up to the church that morning feeling as though I had something to prove, and needing to remind Bill why he had made me a part of the team in the first place.

The autopsy tent was just a large inflated nylon arch over a floor of grass. It was located just outside the back doors of the church, between the church and the priests' rooms. After the radiographer X-rayed each body in the church and developed the X rays in the darkroom he'd created in one of the prefabricated Italian toilets, the bodies were brought by the autopsy techs into the tent, where there were three metal benches set up for the autopsies, as well as a table for the anthropologist and a table for cleaning equipment. There was also a table for storing the autopsy equipment, such as extra scalpel blades and handles, medical scissors, and tweezers. On the anthropologist's table were the wooden osteometric board (for measuring long bones), scalpels, blades, heavy-duty pinching tweezers (for removing muscle and flesh from bone), and calipers (for measuring the diameters of bones). Our paper sheets of anthropological standards were also on the table, encased in protective plastic, so that after noting the stage of tooth eruption in the mouth of a youngster, for example, we could pick up the standards while still wearing dirty gloves, check the age range for that stage of dental eruption, and enter the range into our log. (Of course, in determining the final age range, we would take into account all the age indicators from the rest of the body.) When the pathologist finished with each autopsy, he or she could simply turn to the anthropologist and ask, "What's the age for 291?" and fill it into a line on their report.

When I was in the tent, we autopsied about thirty bodies each day, with more external examinations taking place inside the church. For the anthropologist, that meant inserting oneself into the autopsy procedure at the right moment to examine particular bones. In some cases, when the body was so fleshed that you had to extract bones to examine them, an autopsy tech might expose the surfaces of those bones, then just hand you the bone saw. They might even saw out the bones for you if they had time (both technicians, Peter "the Great Dane" and Alex "the Unintelligible"—a Scot—were efficient as well as cheery, so they were easy to work with). Then you'd take the bones to your table and remove enough tissue to make the various determinations. A high-pressure water hose was set up outside the tent. Here you could put the bones into a fine mesh screen, then hose them down to remove more tissue. This was also the area where we could clean autopsy equipment en masse by the same method. The anthropologist would copy case reports onto clean paper during the lunch break or at the end of the day, then hand the clean copies to the pathologist to attach to the autopsy report.

By late afternoon, the pathologists would be working on their reports inside the church while the autopsy technicians cleaned the pathologists' stations and equipment, and the anthropologist finished cases and paperwork, then cleaned the anthropology equipment. By the time everyone was done, the people exhuming the grave were just arriving up the hill, and a shower rotation started, the pathologists having showered first to be out of the way.

That first day in the autopsy tent, I was up to Bill's ten-minute standard by lunchtime. Nizam Peerwani, the genial chief ME from Tarrant County, Texas, said, "Clea, you picked this up fast!" I just laughed and didn't tell him that I'd been studying human osteology for four years, and doing forensic casework and osteological analysis since 1993. It also helped that most of the adult bodies were under the age of forty, so their pube and rib phases were as clear as day, and of course, the children had plenty of markers for aging. I loved the speed and efficiency engendered by being the only anthropologist in the tent with three pathologists and I thrived on the constant pressure to make decisions. Dean told me that the pathologists had run him ragged, but I found that I was less tired after working in the tent because it produced less physical stress than the grave. Here, most stress was mental. And I was only dealing with three bodies at a time, whereas the grave presented what seemed like a never-ending, interlocked puzzle.

There were also fewer live people to deal with in the tent: just three or four pathologists and maybe two autopsy technicians, who were regularly in the church retrieving the next body from the X-ray table. Sometimes I was the only one in the tent, cleaning and analyzing bones in the relative quiet. Everybody I worked with in the tent contributed to a sense of bon-

homie: Peter Vanezis, a well-known Scottish pathologist, smoked cigars between cases and beamed from beneath his bushy eyebrows as he worked
out the nuances of some trauma. Nizam actually sang show tunes as he
prepared for the lunch break. After lunch Mitra Kalelkar, from the ME's office in Chicago, always said, "The sooner we get back to work, the sooner
we'll be finished." I think their positive attitude was possible because they
hadn't been in Kibuye during the setting-up stage, when everything seemed
to break or go missing and there were neither toilets nor running water. I
wrote in my journal that it was probably easier for the pathologists to see
the light at the end of the tunnel because they were only in-mission for
three weeks. Whatever the explanation, joining them in the tent after being
absorbed by the enormity of the grave helped me to see that although the
grave was the source of all our activity, exhumation was just one cog in the
wheel. Given that we were a small team, it was important for people to
wear many hats. Roxana, for example, was actually doing a completely different job from the one she had come into the mission to do.

Roxana had volunteered to log the clothing and artifacts carried on the
bodies. I heard about the process every evening, particularly since we'd
started sharing a room at the guesthouse (Bob had said that the pathologists "couldn't" share rooms, so some of the other team members had to
double up to make space). But in early February, it was clear that Roxana
was coming down with a serious illness. Bill and Bob diagnosed her with
malaria, and it seemed to me that she should be taken by helicopter to the
hospital in Kigali. One morning, I woke up from yet another night of
dreaming that there were body parts in the bed with me and found Roxana
unable to stop coughing. She was trying to pack her things, saying that Bill
and Bob had arranged for someone to drive her to Kigali. She was too weak
even to close her suitcase, so I helped her, feeling angry about her having to
take a four-hour ride over bumpy roads. I was selfishly sorry to see her go.
I was going to miss talking with her about life and listening to stories about
the beauty of San Jose, her hometown in Costa Rica; in fact, I was going to
miss her whole attitude, which I could sum up in her statement, "Look, just
because I'm out here digging in dirt and bodies all day doesn't mean that I

can't put lipstick on after I've had a shower—not to impress anyone, but just for me, you know?"

At breakfast, Bill said I would take over from her on Evidence.

WHEN I ENTERED what I thought of as Roxana's room behind the church, I studiously avoided looking at the bloody handprints on the walls and prepared to receive clothing. From working in the autopsy tent, I already had a good idea of what I would be seeing: clothing, passports, baptismal cards, books. These items might be our only leads on people's identities—dental X rays wouldn't be of much use: we had barely seen any cavities, let alone dental work—so each artifact needed to be cleaned, documented, and photographed. Bill told me that we might be able to stage a Clothing Day, when survivors of the Kibuye attacks would come to the church, look at the clothing recovered from the grave, and make presumptive identifications. With any luck, we would be able to take blood samples from maternal relatives of the victims so that a mitochondrial DNA comparison could be made with the body found in the clothing. The idea of Clothing Day energized me so much that I persevered in making sense of all the bags that Roxana had left seemingly at random in the middle of the Evidence room. Then I remembered she had told me that a lot of clothing hadn't dried because of the rain. How she remembered these details in her malaria haze, I don't know. Once I figured out that the bags contained these damp clothes, I consulted the protocol list she left for me and got to work.

Before Ralph got too busy with autopsies, I put out for him the clothing not photographed from the previous day. I set a new backdrop cardboard on the outdoor table where the clothing was photographed, pre-labeled the bags "KB-G1-__" to receive clothing removed from the bodies autopsied that day, and dropped off the bags in the autopsy tent. It seemed to take ages to lay out all the clothing that needed to dry (or "go under the sun," as Roxana had put it). Each of the thirteen bodies seemed to have been clothed in many layers. I was thankful for my face mask as I inventoried the clothing and artifacts, because they gave off a lot of dust and their odor had a pungency that rivaled decomp. Meanwhile, bags from four or five new cases were already piling up.

Roxana had warned me that things could get really hectic in Evidence, that it was difficult to get Ralph for the photographs, and that the whole job was very tiring. At first, it wasn't as bad as I feared, probably because the speed of the autopsies was reduced since both technicians had left, and that in turn slowed down the arrival of new bags of clothing. However, by lunchtime, I was beginning to see how working with clothing built fatigue: it was the sharp stench from the material combined with the knowledge that the decomposing tissue adhering to it was actually lifting off in air-borne particles, alternately bothering your throat, nostrils, and stomach as bleach does. This particulate stench was omnipresent as one went through the day, bending and standing and crouching and spraying, all in the hot sun.

By the end of my first day, I was standing with relief in my lukewarm shower behind the church, listening to the local workers come up from the grave to clean up and socialize with the women who were washing the team's clothing just outside my door. Kinyarwanda sounded beautiful, with lots of "eh"s and clicks. I regret that I never had Robert say something into a tape recorder for me to listen to after I left Rwanda. Now I treasure the memory of his daily greeting to me—"Hello, my sister! *Bon travail!*" As I listened to the conversation, I thought about my shift into working with evidence. The items themselves were interesting—identity cards, pins featuring President Habyarimana's portrait hidden on the inside of pockets, tax receipts, church donations, records of house sales, house keys—but it wasn't until I had seen more of these artifacts that their significance dawned on me.

As I laid out the clothing from KB-G1-33__, a man with a prosthetic right leg, I found myself thinking about my mother. In particular, I was thinking about her interest in people with disabilities in Rwandan culture, and about how this man was the first person with a noticeable disability we had exhumed so far. Indeed, he was one of the few disabled folks I'd seen in Rwanda. My mother's interest in them arose from her own experience: when she was four and living at home in Kampala, she contracted polio, which paralyzed her left leg. Before I left for Rwanda, she asked me to look out for disabled people and then characterize for her their mobility and support culture. So I looked at KB-G1-33____ closely. I noticed the added material he had worn related to this massive, heavy, cumbersome prosthesis: cloth wrappings where it joined the thigh, and a piece of padding, which probably sat inside the cavity that held the well-rounded stump of his thigh. He was in his forties and quite hefty. He must have been strong to support that brace. Then I thought about the fact that he was wearing two pairs of underwear, two pairs of shorts, and pants on top of all of that. Many of the bodies were dressed this way—even children. I thought about people leaving their homes, not knowing when they would be able to return, and how they must have figured that wearing a couple of changes of clothes would be their best bet. They took their important papers with them. Why? Because they expected to survive, perhaps in another town, perhaps after returning from a refugee camp. Many bodies had keys—the old-fashioned kind, worn around their waist on a string. I had heard that a string tied tightly around the waist reduces the sensation of hunger. These are the signs of life in a grave, like the woman's pink necklace, all speaking toward individuality and identity, if only the right person can listen. Clothing Day had been set for February 17. I hoped there were enough survivors out there to recognize these small but important signs.

With all the bodies now exhumed and Clothing Day approaching, the team was on track. Then Bill learned that he would be leaving on short notice to probe for graves in Bosnia. We had three hours before the helicopter arrived for Bill to delegate responsibility for the closing down of the project, get particular evidence from me for official transfer to the investigators in Kigali, and discuss the logistics of the rest of the team's departure on February 25. We had to fit this in around Bill's media interviews and meetings with the *préfet*. So the entire team got caught up in the vortex (Melissa's term for Bill's world), trying to finish and print documents not slated to even be reviewed until a week later. In a group effort, however, we completed all the tasks and then piled into a Land Rover to take Bill to the "helipad" (a clearing up the road) with Stefan driving maniacally over the rutted road and all of us holding on for dear life. Then no chopper! Apparently Kigali was stormed in.

We sat with Bill at the helipad for over an hour before the helicopter arrived. He had been asking me to join him in Bosnia, and I had agreed, so we discussed logistics. But at that moment, my mind was fully occupied with the more immediate future: Bill had delegated Clothing Day to me.

Bill had decided that Clothing Day should take place in the front yard of the church and include only clothing with identifiable characteristics and artifacts. However, the clothing should be drawn from both bodies autopsied and those that had received external examination. This meant that I couldn't simply use Roxana's and my clothing log to select material that was still conveniently located in the Evidence room. I would have to review over 450 autopsy reports to learn whether the pathologists had done an autopsy or an external examination (on the whole, they didn't check the convenient box denoting this), then discern from their description of the "externals'" clothing whether there was anything remotely identifiable about it or whether it was associated with jewelry or other artifacts. Then I would have to go through every body bag stacked in the church annex rooms (they had been moved from between the pews), looking for the case numbers of those externals so I could remove the clothing. To make matters worse, the body bags were in random order and I was faced with two rooms of body bags piled four feet high.

When I got down to it, my job was much easier because I corralled four of our best workers: Robert, Ignace, Macombe (his nickname; his real name was Bernard), and another fellow whose name I never knew. We tackled the body bags together: Ignace called out the numbers on the bags in either Kinyarwanda or English, whichever tumbled out first, then Robert and I would scan my list of targeted cases and yell out, *"Yego!"* (Yes!) or *"Oya!"* (No!), and Macombe and the fourth worker would hoist the bag and sling it (yes, I'm afraid it's the only way) onto the finished pile. We did this with all four-hundred-odd cases. Many of the bags were heavy, leaking body fluids and maggots.

Each time we got a hit, the guys would bring the bag out on the floor and stand back—way back—as I opened the bag. Now, this really was something—this was a *real* business. I'd practically get knocked over by the chemical decomp stench, and the sight of the maggots and flies hatching and cavorting on the remains. Then I'd remove the clothing and put it in a numbered and labeled bag I had prepared earlier. This job was much worse than exhumation because the bodies had taken on an almost unnatural horribleness since the flies had been able to lay their eggs when we uncovered the grave; some of the bags were actually hot to the touch.

We worked at a steady, reasonable pace, pausing relatively often to discuss my bride price (apparently, Bill, as my "father," had said he'd trade me for just one decent chicken dinner at the guesthouse); gun ownership in the States (they wanted to know, "Is it true anyone can have a gun?"); the refugees in Zaire; and the prisoner who'd tried to escape from Kibuye prison the day before and been shot (we had seen this unfold from our vantage on the widow's walk of the church, the prisoner's pink uniform visible even from that distance). Robert, Ignace, and I spoke mostly French, but they taught me Kinyarwanda equivalents, while Macombe and the fourth guy (two of the naughtier ones when it came to discussing my value in cows) always spoke to me in Kinyarwanda and I spoke back in English and we just went on like that, with lots of laughter and eyebrow raising on both sides. It is a funny business, communication.

The whole task took four hours, less time than I had expected but long enough. It was frustrating to know that the job had been made more difficult by our own lack of planning, but who knew we would need to open particular body bags again? We kept this in mind on later missions, piling body bags in groups of ten or twenty consecutive numbers because it seems one always *does* need to get back into at least one bag for some reason.

The next morning eight workers and I washed and dried all the clothing and artifacts I'd selected from the pathologists' reports. By late morning, Jose Pablo Baraybar, a Peruvian UN anthropologist who had just arrived from a mission in Haiti, arrived on-site to help. Three things were remarkable about this: he spoke fluent French, so he communicated much better with the workers; he fit seamlessly into our routine without questioning my system; and he took off his shirt. His skin instantly reminded me of caramel and I wished Roxana were still there so we could have girl talk about it later. Nonetheless, I was glad of Jose Pablo's presence, because I had just learned there had been a snafu in Bill's travel plans and he was on his way back to Kibuye. I needed all the help I could get to finish our tasks, shower, and get back to the guesthouse before he arrived and assigned me to another hellish project.

That evening, I was feeling confident and organized. I knew exactly what I would be doing the next day: Ralph and Jose Pablo had said they'd help me lay out all the potentially identifiable clothing and artifacts (fifty-plus cases) in the front yard of the church and then cover them with tarps in case of rain. The following day, Saturday, the seventeenth, was what I thought of as the Big Day, Clothing Day. Then the team had only site clean-up to do until the proposed reburial date of February 25, after which we would return to Kigali. As we approached the end of the mission, I was relaxed and felt good. Then it all changed. I changed.

On the night of February 15, the team was down at the guesthouse, waiting for dinner to arrive. At my request, we were sitting closer than usual to the water's edge for a more al fresco feel. The water near us was in darkness and we were chatting. Then we heard some quiet moaning and splashing coming from the lake. I thought the noises were unusual and sinister, but others thought we were hearing locals out for a swim. I had only seen people fishing in the lake, not swimming, and only during the day. I persisted in saying that I thought something was wrong, but again my concerns were dismissed. Someone said it was probably the Rwandan army doing training exercises at their camp across the water. The sound of moaning stopped abruptly when the spotlight from a speedboat was turned on, illuminating the faces of two men, treading water.

A second or two passed in silence and then the sound of machine-gun fire blasted through the night air. The water around the men's heads spurted and puffed up as bullets entered the lake. Except for one bullet (maybe there were others, but I wasn't aware of them) that ricocheted off the water, across the short expanse of grass, and down the middle of the table where we were sitting. I heard a whistle or a hiss pass in front of my face from left to right. Several of my teammates ran to shelter behind the wall of the nearby gazebo and I ran up to the veranda, ducking, as though that would help. After perhaps one minute that felt much, much longer, the shooting stopped.

The men's heads were still visible in the lake, but half submerged or on their sides. I was horrified, not knowing at this point if, on top of killing those two men, the shooters were going to spray everyone at water's edge with bullets; I couldn't conceive of which "side" they were on, or which side *we* were thought to be on, or, indeed, if there *were* any sides. Those of us who had left the table returned and Ephrem even came out with our dinner, just as usual, though with a furrowed brow. I was still staring at the lake, and then the shooting started again. I remember thinking, "That's *it*!" and running back to the veranda. Somehow I had brought my food with me and I remember that my eyes were open wide, one hand clutching my plate and the other involuntarily held tight to my chest. A Rwandan soldier came over to me, put his hand on my back, and said, *"C'est normal, c'est normal,"* in a soothing tone, smiling. Smiling, as the two men were further mutilated by bullets just yards from where we stood. I noticed, then, that the guesthouse had an unusual number of diners that evening, most of whom were wearing army uniforms—the women were in evening wear—and all of whom were watching the execution with interest.

I rarely lost my appetite in Rwanda. That night I did. I remember trembling as I stood just inside the doors of the brightly lit main lodge. I sat down at a dining table feeling like I was in some alternative reality: outdoors, two men had just been murdered, but indoors, I was being encouraged to eat something by people who seemed to be smiling. I remember not being able to understand what people were saying to me, not even Geoff and Ralph, who were both there. I don't remember anything else that night, but every night in Kibuye after that, I experienced an exhausting, darkness-induced, boat motor–triggered fear.

The next day, we worked nonstop on the clothing and tarps up at the church, but the whole time, I was preoccupied, wondering about some of my teammates, those who were brushing off the execution because "we didn't even know who those guys were." I couldn't see how that mattered:

whoever they were, they'd been murdered in front of people who had traveled to Rwanda to help remedy human rights violations. I couldn't understand their blasé attitude. Forensic scientists like us necessarily deal with people who are already dead; we aren't usually (ever?) there at that indefinable moment when a person—*a real, live person!*—is shot in the face, inhales lake water, and stops breathing. If those two men had been brought to me in a body bag, my reaction would have been quite different. I wouldn't have been in a psychological wind tunnel; I wouldn't have been looking at some of my teammates as though I had only just come to know them. Of course, not everyone reacted that way. Geoff, for example, earned my warmest and most unwavering loyalty when he walked up to me the next day, proffering something I hadn't seen since arriving in Rwanda: a Cadbury's chocolate bar. All he said was, "Here, after last night, you need this." He didn't try to psychoanalyze anything, didn't try to talk, but by that act of kindness simply indicated: *I know that was awful and we all need comfort.*

Although we reported the shootings to the Swiss ambassador to Rwanda—the only person available nearby—he could only elicit an "apology" from the army and the *préfet* that we had to witness what were called defensive actions taken against "insurgents from Zaire," meaning they were Rwandans who had supposedly taken part in the genocide, fled to Zaire in July 1994, and tried to reenter Rwanda from Lake Kivu. I hated the impotence of not being able to do more than just report the killings and I hated the fear I now felt for my own life, even though the bullets hadn't been directed at me or my teammates. And, insult upon insult, I hated the fact that I got to leave this place so easily. When I came to Rwanda I had been so certain of our mission's goal, but seeing people killed muddied that certainty. Now I wondered how we fit into the Rwanda of 1996.

The episode and its aftermath underscored my concern that we weren't doing enough to help the living people associated with the bodies in the grave, something I became keenly aware of when we unearthed a body clothed in the robes of a priest. The priest's niece had repeatedly asked Bill for permission to come and see his "probable" remains (she recognized that they might be the remains of someone who had simply donned the priest's robes in an attempt to save his own life). Once Bill finally agreed, we put the remains in a fresh body bag on a table in the widow's walk, carefully opening the zipper of the bag to show only his head, which, in this case, was fully skeletonized. Before the niece came, I tried to look at him as though he were someone I knew and got a shock. You can prepare yourself to see someone you know dead by picturing them asleep. You might be able to imagine them wounded. But you can never prepare yourself to see someone you know as a skeleton. I mean, how can you? There he was— just his cranium, not even a lower jaw, his entire head resting on his upper teeth in a ghastly truncation of normalcy.

I was standing at the far end of the widow's walk when the niece came around the corner of the church and started walking toward the table with the body bag but she didn't make it all the way because as she caught sight of what was in the bag she suddenly collapsed against the wall, turning away, sobbing. A woman with her, a relative maybe, sat down and cried. Just sat there, bolt upright, tears streaming. Bill and Jose Pablo could only stand silently, hands clasped behind their backs. The women left, clutching their purses and barely able to put one foot in front of the other. We had given them nothing. Not even the assurance that it was really her uncle. We didn't know that yet. They didn't get his bones, they didn't get his clothes. And now the memory of him was replaced by this skull in this bag, and these *wazungu* scientists. Seeing them at their nadir. It made me sick and I wanted to know how it could be done better. I felt there had to be a better way. There had to be.

5

"THANK YOU VERY MUCH
FOR YOUR WORK"

CLOTHING DAY AND ITS LEGACY RESTORED SOME OF MY EQUI-
librium. I was up early on February 17, and I had lots of help to set up the
clothing. Milling around the church were tribunal investigators and translators who had arrived from Kigali with Bill. They had been tracking down
the relatives of people whose identity cards we had recovered from the
grave. Over the previous two weeks, the UN had been making a radio appeal for the relatives' help. Relatives who came to view the clothing would
be interviewed by these investigators. Norwegian nurses from the Red
Cross field hospital set up a station where they could draw blood from any
willing maternal relatives for DNA comparisons. Then we waited for the
families, whom we expected to arrive on foot as well as by the truck that
had been sent out to more distant villages.

But the first people to arrive were the international media. We hadn't
expected so many of them but eventually Bill had to set up crime scene
tape as a perimeter line so the families could have some space as they
walked down the rows of clothing. Bill circulated among the reporters, giving interviews and tours of the now empty grave.

Then family members and survivors started to arrive. The first woman, wearing a long white T-shirt over trousers, strode quickly up and down the rows of clothing and exclaimed, "These clothes are so dirty, how can you expect us to see anything?" I was a bit hurt—it hadn't been easy getting the clothing even that clean, as we'd had few supplies and the cleaning had required careful modulation of the high-pressure hose to remove mud and saponified tissue with minimal tearing. Despite her words, this woman stayed all day.

There were only thirteen documented survivors from the killings at Kibuye church, yet more than thirty survivors turned up, some of whom the Tribunal knew about but had been unable to track down. The investigators didn't have enough staff to take all their statements so I asked Willie (our Ugandan logistician) to help with translation, and I began helping to take the statements myself. By doing so, I gained some decidedly unscientific insight into how survivors cope. With Willie's help, I filled out the Tribunal's witness statement form as I interviewed a woman who had stopped in front of a set of clothing. The woman looked to be in her fifties, wearing a *kanga* (a large piece of cloth with a colorful print) wrapped around her body, and a knit shirt. She had the air of someone to whom one should accord respect, as do many older African women. She told me that she recognized the jacket on display. I asked her whether she would be willing to answer some questions about the person whose jacket she thought it was. She assented, but looked as though she didn't really want to be involved in such a dirty business.

The first questions on the list asked for her name and where she lived, and she answered those. I then asked her to whom she thought the jacket belonged and what she knew of where he had lived. She responded with the name of a person and of a town in the Kibuye *préfecture*, adding that she didn't know whether the presence of his jacket meant that he was in the grave: he could have lent the jacket to someone else, and then *that* person was killed at Kibuye church. I just nodded, to show that I understood, knowing that it's true: anything is possible. Clothing really does provide just a presumptive identity—especially in places where there is prolonged war, fighting, or refugee movement. People will take clothes from dead relatives—or dead strangers, for that matter—to help them survive the dire conditions they still face.

I then asked the woman whether the jacket's owner had any living relatives, especially any maternal relatives. She responded that she did know of one, that he had had a sister. I asked for the sister's name and where she lived. Without looking at me, the woman gave me a name and location. The name seemed familiar so I flipped to the front of the statement form to check. Sure enough, the name she'd just given was her own. She was speaking as though she were someone else. Instead of answering, "I'm his sister," she was saying, "His sister's name is _____."

Understanding and discomfort hit me simultaneously. Whereas before, this woman wouldn't make eye contact with me, I now couldn't look *her* in the face; my eyes went to the jacket, which now looked empty. Thoughts of my own brother, Kimera, flooded into my mind: "What if that was Kimera's jacket and it had come out of a grave?" I knew that, yes, it was conceivable that this woman's brother wasn't the one wearing this jacket at Kibuye church, but she had come, hadn't she? She had an idea, or actual knowledge, that he had been killed there; otherwise, why would she be at a Clothing Day for the Kibuye church massacre?

I dragged my gaze up from the jacket to the woman's face. She was looking into the outer distance and her eyes were brimming with tears. She was showing just a hint of the emotion I'd been expecting to see so much of that day. A lump rose rapidly in my throat when I saw her restrained tears because she had been so together, so tightly together. I didn't know what to do. My first thought was of comfort but, honestly, I didn't know how to give any. I couldn't think of anything that was good enough; all my ideas fell short. I finally put my hand on her arm and was surprised to find her smooth, soft skin cool despite the blistering heat. We stood like that for several minutes, and then she agreed to give a blood sample to the Red Cross nurses, as she was the maternal relative necessary for a DNA comparison. I later wrote that, as I held her arm, "I had a true sensation of being on the continuum of history for the Rwandans affected by the genocide. Working with these remains we are irretrievably part of the survivor's process of healing."

I really feel this concept of continuum. I don't even have to meet the relative of someone whose body I've exhumed, let alone touch the relative's arm. It's more metaphysical than that, as though in the whole grand scheme of things, there is a thread between me and the living relatives of people I've exhumed. In my mind's eye, looking at the world from outer space I can see these great long silvery strands between me and my teammates and lots of points in Rwanda, Bosnia, Croatia, and Kosovo. I've developed this idea further, into the area of individual and collective memory, because forensic anthropologists affect people's memory of events through exhumation and identification: the existence of a body disallows a relative from maintaining that the person is being held in a prisoner-of-war camp or that the person survived but can't get in touch. Similarly, in places where government or military propaganda continually denies that certain people were killed, the exposure of graves and the analysis of remains refutes the "official story."

There was also a girl at Clothing Day—maybe she was thirteen. She was shepherded by a middle-aged man and she didn't seem to touch the ground when she walked, she seemed to glide. Adults whispered when they spoke to her, leaning down to her level, as though seeking her permission or approval. When I looked at her face, I saw an expression that I'd never seen before. It wasn't grief or sadness. She was neither pleased nor scared. It was as if she was in another world and something private occupied her. All this made her seem wise despite her apparent youth.

A Canadian crew who had interviewed Bill earlier that week also filmed Clothing Day. Several years later, Bill sent me their finished film, *Chronicle of a Genocide Foretold*. Part of the story followed a man whose wife had been killed at Kibuye church. Their daughter had witnessed the murder and had hidden in the church, escaping death and being reunited with her father some time later. In the film the father and daughter walk slowly among the clothes laid out on the tarps. As they walked toward the church steps, I suddenly realized that the girl in the film was *that* girl—the gliding, regal girl. Now I knew why she had seemed unreal, otherworldly: it was because she had survived an event where not only hundreds of other people were killed, but where the killers were doing their utmost to murder everyone. It wasn't as though she had survived a freak accident, like a tornado that sucks up some houses and not others; she had escaped a deliberate attack that by all rights should have taken her life.

Later in the film, the father shakes his head, saying that he and his daughter didn't find his wife's clothing, but they know she was killed there; the daughter saw it. And the second realization hit me: the only reason they didn't find her clothing was because it wasn't in the group I had selected to display. We hadn't been able to display all the clothing, only as much as could fit in the churchyard, so we'd given priority to particularly identifiable garments in good condition and ideally with associated identifiable artifacts. And the clothing of this man's wife—this girl's mother—was not in that group. Even though they knew she had died there, they still came to Clothing Day, still wanted that bit of proof or that bit of memory. I had to stop watching the film as all of this washed over me. I sat with a feeling of utter dejection, wanting to apologize to them for not having her clothing out, bitterly regretting that the churchyard had been too small to handle five hundred sets of clothing, and crying.

Someone whose clothing *was* recognized on Clothing Day was the man with the prosthetic leg. He was the only person with a prosthesis in the whole grave, so I suspected someone would remember him, even if he had no surviving relatives. Sure enough, almost every survivor who came to the viewing recognized both the prosthesis and the man's clothing. I was told that he had one living relative whom people knew of, a young niece last seen on Ijwi Island with other Rwandans who fled ahead of the brunt of the killing in April 1994. Even though she wasn't in Kibuye to provide blood for an eventual DNA comparison, there was very strong evidence to assign a presumptive identity to this man. He was well known, distinguished in death as he had been in life.

WE WERE DUE to leave Kibuye in less than a week, but, despite the positive outcome of Clothing Day, I still felt scared as soon as night fell and I trembled whenever I heard the motor of the Rwandan Patriotic Army boat chugging in the darkness of Lake Kivu. I woke up terribly excited one day because I thought it was Wednesday when it was actually only Tuesday. I wanted to get to Kigali as soon as possible, admitting to myself that the executions in the lake added a sense of danger that made the usual things—like the attentions of the aggressive Ghanaian soldier, or the possibility that the local RPA soldiers would try to obtain some of our UN supplies (like our cars) for themselves—feel worse. Simply waiting for dinner (now back on the veranda) for up to two hours was an ordeal because the veranda light could have served as a convenient target for the crosshairs of the M-16 on the RPA's U.S.-donated speedboat.

On February 20, I arrived at breakfast just as the RPA boat roared into view and came to a sudden stop. The bodies of the men killed on the fifteenth had floated to the surface and the soldiers began pulling them onto the boat. Members of our team had actually placed bets on when the decomposition gases would send the corpses to the surface. Those who predicted five days were the winners.

Some of the soldiers retrieving the bodies were wearing regular street clothes: slacks and button-down shirts. Not exactly floater-retrieval garb, and I laughed inwardly as they almost fell overboard with the effort of grabbing the no doubt bloated corpses. After fishing them out and leaving them on their backs on the deck, the boat sped away toward Zaire. When it came back, we couldn't see anything on deck. Whether the soldiers were hiding the bodies or had dumped them farther out in the lake, hoping they'd float toward Zaire as a warning, we didn't know.

CLOSING DOWN THE SITE required the return of all the clothing to the proper body bags and then making sure all the bags were stacked in the priests' rooms, which would be secured with a lockable door and bricked-up windows. Geoff was handling the logistics of removing all the equipment. With only those tasks ahead of us, Bill gathered the remaining team for a debriefing of sorts on the lawn of the guesthouse. It was a sunny afternoon, and the turquoise lake formed a backdrop to the group: Ralph, Jose Pablo, Dean, Stefan, Geoff, Andrew (just flown in), and Melissa. We covered what had worked well. For example, we had completed the job in the allotted time, the evidence we had recovered supported the witness statements, and the staging of people—bringing the pathologists in later than the rest of us—had been successful. We also discussed what hadn't worked well. The equipment should have been examined in London before the wrong stuff was sent to Rwanda; the logistics chief needed to precede the anthropologists by two weeks so he could finish setup first; we needed more autopsy technicians, another archaeologist with electronic mapping experience to work in the grave, and elbow-length gloves. We talked about what to do in the future, like organize the pathologists to do their own data entry every night, and we talked about our role within the Tribunal as independent gatherers of information. In the end, we asked ourselves how much forensic evidence is enough. Is it necessary to dig every grave in Rwanda to prove the genocide happened? We didn't know. It was up to the Tribunal judges, and *they* didn't know because this was the first time such forensic evidence would be used in an international court. This exhumation would set the standard.

I was interested to discern a divide between those who felt that the goal of our work on behalf of the Tribunal was to provide evidence in the prosecution of cases, and those who took the human rights perspective, which is to tell the whole story and get the facts on record. I didn't think these goals were mutually exclusive. I was also interested to learn that many of the investigators had initially felt that the forensic evidence was unnecessary: "Everyone knows there are graves here, that a genocide happened." Unfortunately, physical proof *is* necessary: there really *are* people who don't believe there was a genocide.

As we sat together that afternoon, we felt satisfied with what we had accomplished. But I was still coming to terms with our role in the Rwanda of 1996. Then, on one of our last days, Bill and I were driving through Kibuye town to take some of the workers home when the woman who had complained at Clothing Day that the clothes were too dirty saw us and came over to the car. She leaned in the open window and kissed me on both cheeks, twice. Then she said, *"Merci beaucoup pour votre travail."* ("Thank you very much for your work.") She called over the women she had been standing with and told them who we were and what we were doing up at the church; she didn't let go of my arm as she talked, patting it possessively. She changed everything for me, because she put our time there into some perspective.

A FEW DAYS LATER, I was on a flight home to California. I had spent two days in Kigali databasing the remaining 112 autopsy reports on behalf of the pathologists. My head was filled with their language, for example, Nizam's oft-used phrase "putrefied, smelly mass of residual unidentifiable viscera." Reading these autopsy reports had caused me to consider why so few of the Kibuye bodies exhibited defense wounds. We had expected to see more injuries such as trauma to radius, ulna, and hands. The realization washed over me that, on the whole, these people hadn't fought back. Forget about fighting back, actually: they hadn't even raised their arms to protect their heads.

Of the first seventy cases I entered into the database, the vast majority were women and children whose death was caused by blunt force trauma, while the others had died of either undetermined causes or sharp force trauma. One person was an exception, with "shrapnel" given as the cause of death. Beyond those facts, I knew that the amount of force used to hit adults and children wasn't modulated, if that's even a valid expectation. I mean, some of these kids' skulls hadn't even fused yet, and the outer *and* inner tables of the cranium had been cut clean through, just like the adults'.

Now here I was on a plane, just three days away from Kibuye and those bodies, eating my in-flight dinner. I looked around at Dean and Stefan sitting a few rows apart from me (Bill was up in first class), thinking about the relationships we had developed during this mission. We had rejoined the rest of the world, but we shared the experience of exhuming almost five hundred bodies from a single grave. Over half of the dead were children; two thirds of them were women or children. All had been murdered. We had gone from recovering surface skeletons whose bleached bones and scattered ribs nestled in soil and undergrowth—as if this was most natural—to accepting the grave's offerings: first, the skeletonized and mummified bodies, their hair adhering in chunks to their skulls and the colors of their clothing faded by stuck-on soil; then, beneath those upper layers, the well-preserved bodies with almost no soil between them, arm against arm, eyelashes and stubble, babies strapped to their mothers' backs—the bright colors of the cloth slings still visible. We took this in stride while we worked in the grave, but now, in the bright, pressurized cabin, I felt overwhelmed by the details of those bodies, the loss they represented, the sadness, and the resounding, irretrievable finality of death.

BY THE TIME I was on my next flight and finally over the United States, I felt a bit more balanced, and was still smiling over Bill's last words to us when we had parted in Brussels some hours earlier: "You're good workers. Buy some warm clothes. Your number's not going to change, is it?" As I settled into my seat, I looked up at the film playing on the movie screen several rows ahead of me. The film was *Get Shorty,* and I had no prior knowledge of the story. I saw a man backing up against a railing at night. Another man is facing him. The second man shoots the first, who falls backward over the railing to the ground. Even with no sound and no context I actually jumped in my seat. I immediately felt a sense of outrage. I kept thinking, "This isn't right . . . they shouldn't be allowed to show that!" I looked around the plane at my fellow passengers—surely they would share my outrage—but only saw people absorbed in their glossy magazines, wanting half-and-half instead of "just milk" for their coffee. Now these innocent people were aggravating me, and I didn't know why exactly. Then I started to cry—not because the scene startled me but because my reaction to it was involuntary. I didn't like feeling as though I couldn't control my body. But my anger at the film scene and my frustration with other people's complacent insularity were just side effects of the mission. Only much later did I understand how much the mission had changed me. In fear of more disjunction, I curbed my tears and sat back in my seat, avoiding the movie screen and feeling like an outsider.

6.

AFTERLIFE

I PARTICIPATED IN SIX MISSIONS AFTER MY FIRST ONE TO RWANDA, and each time I flew home, I experienced a reentry phenomenon. It starts on the plane, or while I'm waiting for my departing flight. Invariably I feel like an alien, even if I'm surrounded by military personnel on leave from the same place I've been working. Then I arrive at the first stop. I am always shocked at how modern the next airport appears, how automated and clean things are because they haven't suffered recent war or conflict. The duty-free shops stand out—golfing socks and gold-plated pens seem absurd when the previous day I've seen a crowd of otherwise dignified people taking with great alacrity the outdated rations we've left for them. On top of all of this, airports are the places where people from all over the world pass through at once, whereas the countries I've worked in have comparatively homogenous local populaces, multiethnic foreign aid workers notwith-standing. When I get home, I am always struck by street lights that func-tion, roads not worn down by tank treads, and the fact that people aren't keeping well clear of the road shoulders for fear of land mines. I appreciate all this and feel safe, even though for about the first week, when I wake up in the night I wonder where I am. I don't unpack for a few days and mean-while I continue to wear "mission clothes." It's hard to let go.

The slow transition is compounded by culture shock after taking on routines and ways of life in a postconflict region. I'm also coming down from the mission, remembering the feeling of being on deadline with a seemingly insurmountable task, being cautious about my surroundings, careful about saying who I am and why I'm there, and above all, feeling as though I'm doing a Good Thing. But there is more: when I wake in the night now, I lie rigidly still, thinking about what would happen if I was in Rwanda and the genocide was starting, or in Bosnia and the shit was really beginning to hit the fan. I imagine neighbors hurriedly coming to wake me up to warn me that people are heading to our street wielding guns, and we have to hide now. It could happen, "even" in the States, and my windows won't keep an assailant out any better than those in Kibuye or Brčko did. Where would I hide? What about my cat? Could I fight? What if I was with my mother? Could I carry her if we had to move in a hurry? The first time these questions erupted in my head, I tried to quash them, but they were ir-repressible. The effort of trying to answer them made it hard for me to breathe, so I just lay there, trapped by the darkness and the questions until daylight and exhaustion led back to sleep. My life After had begun.

PART TWO

—

KIGALI

June 3–June 24, 1996

7

"EVERYONE KNOWS A GENOCIDE HAPPENED HERE"

ON MY FIRST MORNING BACK IN RWANDA, I WOKE UP TO DISCOVER that the irregularities in the cloth wall-covering of my Kigali hotel room were bullet holes. The night before I had thought they might be machete slashes but I hadn't looked closely because it was dark and I was jet-lagged. Fatigue also prevented me from noticing the copious amount of blood higher up the wall. No doubt the hotel staff had made valiant efforts to clean this room, but this was what you got when you were assigned to a street-side room at the Meridian Hotel in 1996. Two years earlier, people had hidden in the Meridian during the genocide and were shot at by attackers stationed mostly on the street side of the hotel. Poolside was a better bet for an unscarred room, although the poolside room across the hall from me still had the equivalent of crime scene tape across its door. I was told major remodeling would be undertaken before that room was available to guests again.

I was back in Rwanda three and a half months after leaving the country so eagerly, on another forensic mission organized by Physicians for Human

Rights for the UN International Criminal Tribunal for Rwanda. It was to be a short mission, carried out one month before a contingent of us began the first exhumations in Bosnia for the International Criminal Tribunal for the former Yugoslavia. If this second Rwanda mission had meant four weeks in Kibuye, I might not have joined. Though my first mission had been a profound experience, witnessing the murders in Lake Kivu in February made me think of western Rwanda as a place where not only anything *could* happen, anything *did* happen. So when Bill Haglund said the mission would investigate a site in the capital, Kigali, my participation was assured: I saw this as working in quiet, eastern Rwanda.

Accordingly, when I arrived at the Kigali airport, I felt like a relaxed old hand, particularly when other passengers from the flight marveled at the terminal's bullet-scarred interior. Bill met me, Melissa, Dean, and Dean's graduate adviser, Owen Beattie, as though we were long-lost family, waving madly at us in the lobby. He launched into a business meeting as soon as he began driving us through the cool humid night into Kigali. He had to yell over the engine and the wind, so everything he said sounded really urgent but we could barely hear it. All systems normal.

But three events coinciding with our arrival put me on edge: three Swiss humanitarian aid workers were killed in Zaire; a bounty on American heads was declared in Burundi; and a child in Kigali found an antipersonnel mine at a bus stop. Now that I was recognizing the bullet holes in my Kigali hotel room for what they were, I was reminded of what I should not have forgotten: vigilance can't be regional.

Intellectually, I knew there was a limit on how much money the Meridian could or would spend to refurbish their rooms, but I didn't want to live in one crime scene while we investigated another. Fortunately, the hotel's location turned out to be too peripheral for our daily excursions, so the whole team was in favor of moving. We had to stay in the Meridian one more night and it was a problematic one for me: even when I avoided inspection and forensic interpretation of those physical remnants, I wondered about the spirits still trapped in that otherwise unobjectionable room.

WHY HAD I thought Kigali would be so different from Kibuye? After all, we were in Kigali to investigate the deaths of people murdered during the genocide. And, as in Kibuye, the deaths were the result of coordinated activities. But in rural areas like Kibuye, organizers of the genocide had herded people into sports stadiums and churches before killing them en masse, whereas perpetrators in Kigali had used roadblocks to stop both pedestrians and people in cars to inspect their identity cards. The national identity cards, carried by every Rwandan at that time, listed a piece of information crucial for the killers: the holder's "ethnicity." Every Rwandan was classified into one of three "ethnic" groups—Hutu, Tutsi, or Twa—and the politicians who planned the genocide had made it clear that April 1994 was the flag-fall for the murder of all Tutsis—and anyone married to a Tutsi, *and* anyone whose politics could be described as moderate.

The extremist dogma of the planners held that a mutually exclusive combination of physical features betrayed each ethnicity. In particular, Hutus were described as stocky, dark-skinned, and broad-nosed, while Tutsis were stereotyped as tall, with straight noses, and lighter brown skin. Ironically, these descriptions were a legacy of late-nineteenth-century European colonization of Rwanda. When Germany finagled the first colonial administration (1897–1916), Rwanda had a monarchic culture of both agriculturalists and cattle owners, and the terms "Hutu" and "Tutsi" were descriptors of social standing among a people who spoke one language and practiced one religion. What is more important, those descriptors were fluid: one's standing altered as one acquired (or lost) cattle or married into a family. In a move that facilitated the colonial program of divide and conquer, the colonizers eventually transformed those traditionally fluid descriptors into rigid classifications based on beliefs about racial superiority popular in the late 1800s.

The next colonial administration, held by Belgium, introduced the mandatory identity cards in 1934, generally awarding Tutsi "ethnicity" to those who owned more than ten head of cattle. The Belgians also lionized the Tutsis as people whose "almost European" features clearly meant they were superior to other Rwandans and deserved employment privileges within the colonial administration.

But I have often wondered why it was necessary to state ethnicity on a card if it was so obvious who was, for example, a Tutsi. To me, the "ethnicity" field on the identity card belied both the colonial pronouncements and the extremist dogma that led up to the genocide. Listing ethnicity suggests that it must have been difficult, to tell who was who by looking at their features. Even if "ethnic" assignment *had* been based exclusively on physical features, Hutu-Tutsi intermarriage has been documented since precolonial times, for different lineages historically sought to strengthen their ties in this way. Certainly in 1994, it must have been impossible to describe "Tutsis" as only tall, light-skinned, thin-nosed people and "Hutus" as the opposite. Thus the need for cards to identify "ethnicity," cards crucial even for those inciting genocide—despite their broadcast instructions to the killers that "you will know them [Tutsi] by their thin noses."

The identity cards were especially necessary in Kigali, because people's social groups were less known in the relative anonymity of the city. Between April and June 1994, if you were in Kigali, were stopped at a roadblock, and your identity card read "Tutsi," you were detained, then killed on the spot.

THE SITE WE WERE investigating was located behind a garage in one of Kigali's hilly business districts. Our team drew a few curious looks as we drove to the bottom of the garage driveway and parked in a flat, walled courtyard almost completely filled with waste: mostly rusting car parts, paint cans, and rubber, but also shoes and clothes. By climbing over all of this, we reached a doorway that opened onto a hillside sloping down to the right. Out here, we were behind the businesses fronting the main road. We could see down to a ravine with some small trees in it and, skirting the bottom of the ravine, a dirt path.

Standing at the top of this hillside and looking outward beyond the ravine, I had a sense of being above the world because the crows were flying by on our level, the sounds of the town drifted up from some-where below, and the only other features at our elevation were two distant deep green hills, perhaps bulky enough to be mountains, seen as though through mist. Bringing my focus close again, I could look directly down into a latrine pit. Bill had located bodies in the upper levels of this latrine and, working with Pierre Heuts, one of the Tribunal investigators for this site, had been struggling to climb in and out of the pit on a rope. As soon as we arrived, Dean used his hiking skills to rig up a pulley-and-harness sys-tem with materials Bill had specifically asked him to bring to Rwanda. The pulley allowed Bill and Pierre to reach the bottom of the latrine, eight me-ters down, and to resurface, with the rest of us pulling on the rope together to winch them back up. Bill and Pierre took turns descending into the pit for a couple of hours each while the other leaned over the top edge, taking notes and throwing bottled drinking water down the shaft. Several pathol-ogists were on standby to fly in and conduct autopsies, but so far all the bodies in the latrine were skeletonized. The rest of us had to investigate the other areas of the garage in search of graves with less decomposed bodies or it would be too late to cancel the pathologists.

An informant had allegedly seen body parts in several pits in the garage courtyard, but before we could dig, we had to clear all the rubbish off the ground. It was hard going, what with the ticks, the stink of the functioning latrine right next to us, and dishwashing gloves as the only protection against rusty metal. We strained our backs moving an entire truck chassis from spot to spot to expose different bits of ground. Even if we could have moved it more than a few inches at a time, it was too big to remove from the courtyard altogether. We dug lots of test trenches, while Melissa mapped and took Global Positioning System coordinates. We found noth-ing. We essentially cleaned up the entire rubbish dump, an idea that proba-bly occurred to the garage employees about halfway through the day when they saw what a lovely job we were doing.

We finally left the garage after five P.M., hungry (there had been no lunch), fatigued by jet lag and strenuous activity, and demoralized. If we didn't find more human remains, or evidence of their presence, by the next afternoon, Bill decided, we would analyze the skeletons he and Pierre had already recovered from the latrine. After that, we might travel the country, assessing sites. This didn't seem like such a safe prospect. We had just learned that mines had been found on the road to Kibuye. Bill said he felt safe but didn't want to impose his comfort level on anyone else. He added that he thought staying on main roads would be sufficient. I just looked at him, thinking about how the road to Kibuye *was* a main road.

After a second fruitless morning at the site, where we were mostly food for mosquitoes, Bill called off the pathologists. But before we began analyzing the latrine skeletons, a group of us went to Ntarama, a village about thirty or forty kilometers south of Kigali. Ntarama is rural, with red earth and inviting side roads, and its church is an unusual memorial for victims of the genocide. Inside, victims' bodies have been left exactly where they fell in 1994. The church complex was guarded by two old men. Once they let us into the dirt courtyard, we fell into silence.

The main church building was smaller than Kibuye's but there was a large outdoor area where platforms were lined up under a tarp canopy. The platforms were covered in dry bones collected from the surrounding area. The bones were organized by type—all limbs together, all skulls lined up together, as one sees in photographs from Cambodia. As I approached the church itself, I didn't know what to expect, but the gatekeepers gestured for us to go right up to the window openings and doorways and look inside. I saw backless pews just like those in Kibuye church, but these were draped with the mummified and decomposing remains of *a lot* of people, their clothes both sticking to them and falling off, and everything sort of melting down onto the floor between the benches. It was difficult to see where the bodies ended and the floor began. It was difficult to see the floor at all. There was a mattress jutting up from the fray halfway down the room— perhaps a remnant from when people had taken refuge in the church.

The two guards encouraged us to take photographs. I couldn't even take my camera out of its bag, couldn't imagine how I would ever forget how that room looked. I felt I was seeing a time-warped image of Kibuye church—how that cavernous main room might have looked before the bodies were removed and placed in the grave we exhumed. Yet we were on the other side of the country from Kibuye. I envisioned a string of churches between Ntarama and Kibuye, all scenes of violent death; I saw the enormity and felt weighed down by it.

Ntarama is a memorial but it is also proof. Proof of the stories from the genocide, which are so often set against a backdrop of churches; proof that the killers couldn't be bothered to hide the evidence (arrogance? laziness?); proof of the systematic nature of the killing (people from disparate, rural areas were brought to collection places); and the scores of bleached bones on the platforms are proof that even those who escaped the church were killed outside and their bodies lay where they fell.

Ntarama is not the only memorial in Rwanda that incorporates the display of human remains. Other memorials are in clearings and include bones that have been collected from a wide area, layered on large outdoor platforms. Forensic anthropologists would call this mixing of bones from multiple people commingling, and it is avoided by forensic investigators because it complicates the positive identification of individuals. Does that mean Rwanda puts less emphasis on the identification and return of remains, and is that due to a dearth of survivors? Are there not enough people left to press for identifications, as they do in Bosnia and Argentina? Or is it that, despite the majority conversion, in the early twentieth century, to Catholicism with its custom of burial, Rwanda is now employing a variation of one of its ancient funeral practices where bodies were left exposed on deserted hills, in swamps, or in caves?

I gained another perspective on Ntarama from a documentary in which the grown children of a man who was killed at Ntarama meet up with a man who thinks he knows where their father's bones lie. He leads them through some scruffy grass beyond the church to a clearing but there weren't any bones. The children just stood there, crying, trusting that their father had died in that spot, believing that there just wasn't *any* trace left of him. There was a hopeless emptiness to their grief. Those children must have walked past the platforms covered in bones, but still they searched the clearing. Their behavior tells me that while the church at Ntarama provides proof of one kind, it may not be the holding-on-to kind, which relatives of missing persons often state they need, whether they're missing someone after a war, a natural catastrophe, or a baffling abduction from a local park.

THE DAY AFTER visiting the church in Ntarama, our team was called back to resume the search for proof behind the garage in Kigali. When we arrived at the site, investigators came running up, all out of breath: their witness had pointed out another area down the hill from Bill's latrine; could we check it out? We did and, sure enough, we uncovered one body. And another. And another. There is a saying that every hillside in Rwanda has bodies on it: it felt true on that day.

The first grave was more than halfway down the slope from the latrine and therefore quite close to the public footpath at the bottom, so a security unit was deployed. In contrast to the Ghanaian soldiers who had guarded the site in Kibuye, these were skinny young men wearing dark blue uniforms and carrying billy clubs. They were from KK Security ("For All Your Security Needs"), also employed by the Tribunal at the gates of the Amohoro compound (the new HQ since the UN departed Rwanda). Although there was a constant stream of people walking below the site, they displayed only restrained curiosity about our activities. *Everyone knows a genocide happened here.*

Within a day, we detected more graves, running almost the whole length of the hillside, so we were able to spread out and become organized: Dean and I took on a grave at the bottom of the hill, Bill and Pierre took the grave above us, and Jose Pablo worked above them. Each of us had two workers (including Robert, our multilingual foreman from Kibuye) digging and hauling backdirt while several workers cleared the entire hillside of vegetation so we could easily test trench if necessary. Owen photographed and videotaped, while Melissa worked the electronic mapping station we had used in Kibuye. A new member of the team had just arrived from Somalia, Dave Buchanan, a physician's assistant from Alaska, and he "ran the rod," allowing Melissa to chart each body and the grave outlines. Dave was lively and went all-out with twenty-minute body outlines that would have been impossible in Kibuye, but now we had the time. The results were excellent, particularly after Melissa used the computer program to round off the edges and establish proper body contours for the legs, arms, and so on. The whole mapping process had improved since Kibuye. Melissa had brought voice-activated microphones mounted onto headsets so that she and the person running the rod could call out the coordinates without yelling. In Kibuye, every day had been punctuated by "Top of head!" "Got it!" "Neck!" "Got it!" all the way through about twenty points on the body, for perhaps thirty bodies per day, all at a decibel level intended to be heard over the backhoe engine or other people's voices.

While we exhumed the Kigali graves, we parked on the street in front of the garage and I saw that we were just up the way from a large and busy market. The *bourgmestre* had asked us to keep the eventual transport of body bags "discreet" as we would be driving past shops and cafés, but there is just something about body bags that is inherently indiscreet. Even the combination of dirt and scent carried on our clothes betrayed our daily occupation. At the end of the day, we attempted to walk as quickly as possible through the lobby of our hotel to make it to our rooms before any staff or guests had to see or smell us. I always felt a sort of desperate and inappropriate humor at these times because the hotel staff, unfailingly polite, would be trying to say, *"Bonjour,* hello, how are you?" and we would be trotting past, calling out, "Fine, thank you," over our shoulders without breaking pace, in a most rude fashion, only able to exchange pleasantries when next in the lobby after a shower.

Working at this site was also very different from working in Kibuye. In part, this was because we were nearer Tribunal headquarters, so investigators came through often to see our progress and what, exactly, we were doing. Pierre was an excellent liaison between the team and the investigators because, as a scene-of-crime officer with the Dutch police, he was good at explaining the value of forensic evidence. Thus their visits weren't just interruptions by onlookers. One time, several Australian journalists who were following the path of an Australian Tribunal investigator followed him all the way over to our site. The word quickly passed around the team from grave to grave that one of the journalists had the last name Bone. This made us want to laugh but even though the journalist looked horrified by the site as she courageously made her way down the slope.

From our perspective, the journalist was seeing "just" a few bones: the graves each held two or three bodies, fully skeletonized. They were therefore classified forensically as "multiple graves." In Kibuye we'd had several discussions about how many bodies need to be in a grave for it to be classified as a "mass grave." I think we decided that more than three bodies is "mass," while two or three is "multiple." We also decided that the debate was one of semantics only.

The skeletonized condition of the Kigali remains was due to the relative shallowness of the graves and the fact that were only a few bodies in each one. And it was immediately clear that some of these exhibited gunshot wounds. I was interested to see what we would find during analysis.

8

THE HOSPITAL FOR THE DEAD PEOPLE

WHILE WE HAD BEEN WORKING BEHIND THE GARAGE, OUR LOGIS-
tics chief from Kibuye, Geoff Bucknall, established an anthropological
analysis area on the outskirts of the Tribunal's Amohoro compound, consisting of a large tent inflated by a generator that hummed all day, with tables and lights set up inside. But our first day of work in the tent was
delayed when representatives of the *commune* arrived at the garage site as
we exhumed the bodies. They said they'd heard we were taking the bodies
to Arusha (in Tanzania, where the Tribunal courts are located) and that we
had brought illegal workers from Kibuye who had been sent by the Kibuye
préfet in order to throw bones into the street. After some discussion, Bill
and Jose Pablo gave the officials a tour of the site to reassure them of our
intentions, and they arranged to come to the Amohoro the next day to visit
"the hospital for the dead people" and establish for themselves whether the
laboratory was an acceptable place for the bones.

Before they arrived the next morning, we cleaned the tent and assem-
bled all the tables. There was lots of space, so the osteometric boards,
calipers, cameras, and computer could all be arrayed properly. The representatives included a man named Viateur, who walked with a cane, and a

middle-aged woman who had been looking for her son since the genocide. She had heard rumors that he might have been buried on the hillside we had just excavated. They arrived at the Amohoro to be met by Bill, who was in his vortex as usual but wearing a clean tie and flanked by Tribunal staff, while the rest of us were beginning our analyses inside the tent. I remember the visit as very quiet—we could hear only murmurs while they examined the setup—but they were satisfied with the conditions and made an appointment to return several days later for a longer visit.

We didn't have a lot of time to complete our analyses of the skeletons, because both Bill and Jose Pablo were due in Bosnia within the week. We followed the standard procedures of anthropological analysis to determine the age, sex, stature, and cause of death; then we photo-documented the overall skeleton and took detail shots of the bones we used to age it (for instance, the faces of the pubic symphyses and the sternal tips of ribs 3 and 4), as well as of any trauma and individualizing features that family members might recognize. After only a few hours, the atmosphere in the tent would become oppressively humid and hot and I often felt nauseated. I think this environment, combined with the changes Bill sometimes made to our agendas after we had started working, led to strain during the workday that eventually spilled over into downtime.

One morning, I was finishing up the analysis of a skeleton I had begun the previous day. I'd given the skeleton a preliminary age of between ten and thirteen years based on the teeth and was starting the analysis of the postcranial elements (those below the head) when Dean walked over. He said he thought the age was eight to fourteen years, because several of the postcranial elements were open. Now, let me explain about creating age ranges and why that difference of two years was worth discussing. Children present more age indicators than adults because, in addition to all the postcranial indicators, teeth form and erupt in the mouth at generally predictable ages (except for the third molars, or "wisdom teeth"). The formation of crowns and roots can generate an age range, which can be further informed by the state of fusion in the long bones, pelvis, hands, feet, and even fingers and toes. So where forensic anthropologists often give five- or ten-year age ranges on adults who appear to be over the age of thirty-five years, for children a narrower age range can usually be assigned. You might find one indicator that a child is no younger than five, for example, and then another three indicators that put him under eight. With this information, you can safely record an age range of between five and eight years at death. Similarly, for a young adult male, you might find that the sternal epiphysis of the clavicle is unfused, putting him roughly under twenty-five years, but that his distal femur was still fusing, putting him older than fourteen but under nineteen. Now you can begin to form an age estimate, one that does not have to be as broad—perhaps sixteen to twenty years. Then you look at the other bones to refine or adjust the age range further. The goal is to improve the chances of finding a match with a missing person, and the forensic anthropologist must take into account the variation he or she has seen in cases where the actual age of the decedent became known after a positive identification.

I agreed with the upper end of Dean's age range of fourteen for the Kigali skeleton, because the pubic elements were not fused yet. But on the younger end of the range, the dental arcade exhibited fully erupted second molars (as well as canines and premolars), which indicated to me that the body's age was at least ten years regardless of whether it was a male or female. I felt there was no need to go as low as eight. Dean was concerned that I was putting too much stock in the teeth. I responded that I was just now taking into account the postcranial and that since the finger and toe phalanges were fusing, I thought we could definitely go older than eight.

Then Dean told me that it had been "decided" in Kibuye that skeletons with "discrepancies" between teeth and bones were all younger than their teeth indicated. I didn't remember us making that decision—and anyway, it would have been impossible. We didn't yet have a single positive identification of a youngster from Kibuye, so we couldn't know who had young bones and old teeth, or vice versa, if at all. I said as much, but Dean replied that he'd looked in the mouths of kids around the Kibuye guesthouse and seen that their teeth were older than their chronological age. "How many mouths did you look in?" I asked. He replied, "Well, only two, but . . ." Two didn't constitute a representative sample, and Dean, as a doctoral student doing his own research on prehistoric DNA, would know that. I pointed out that while he might have seen some live kids' teeth he couldn't have seen their bones, so only half the problem had been investigated. Dean replied that that was true but then he said, "Well, I don't want to get in on your case, I'm just saying." I exclaimed, "Dean! It's not 'my' case! We're all working here together," but he was already walking away.

I was a bit hurt by this sparring because I didn't come from a background of giving irrationally small age ranges—in fact, when Stefan Schmitt had created our anthropology databases in Kibuye he had said, "I like your lab, Clea," because he felt I was giving appropriately large age ranges to allow for population variation. Plus, I had come out of the collaborative tradition Walt Birkby had created at the Human Identification Laboratory at the University of Arizona. There, even though one student wrote up the case, she or he canvassed the opinions of several other people in the lab. If there was a difference in opinion, we would discuss the issues (sometimes with great animation) and we always came to consensus (even if it meant widening an age range), perhaps because the same person trained us all. Those cases were often identified through comparison of antemortem and postmortem dental records, so we had the opportunity both to check the accuracy of our age estimates and to learn if we could narrow those estimates any more. This information was exactly what we didn't have yet from Kibuye. Sure, we were able to provide the age ranges necessary for the Rwanda Tribunal to determine which bodies in the grave were those of children, but we had not yet established through positive identification that those children's teeth were unreliable indicators of their ages.

By the time Dean walked away from the table, I was already adjusting the age range in light of the postcranial skeleton and was prepared to compromise on the bone-versus-teeth age "discrepancy" because it couldn't be resolved without positive identifications on young skeletons. What was really steaming me up, though, besides the infernal heat in that tent, was that Dean didn't appear willing to discuss the issue, to also make compromises and to admit what he could not possibly know. Jose Pablo came over to me, muttering that he "trusted" the teeth and was going off to dig up an article on the point, but this didn't make me feel much better.

The atmosphere was tense and strange, and it was going to stay that way through a long evening, because we were to have a good-bye dinner for Bill, who was about to fly to Bosnia. On our way out of the Amohoro compound, I passed Steve Myall, an investigator I'd become friends with. I bitched cryptically to him and he replied in his clipped British accent and through his nicotine-stained teeth, "My motto is: Don't let the buggers get you down." He made me laugh and I went to dinner in a slightly lighter mood.

After dinner, Jose Pablo and I discussed the importance of having team members who are team players, who look to each other for backup and can double-check each other's work without bristling. Four years after that discussion, Jose Pablo was the Tribunal's chief anthropologist and I was his deputy. We were in the Tribunal mortuary in Kosovo, no longer working in a dusty inflated tent but in a proper building with running water and electricity. But we were still heeding the lessons we had learned that day with Dean in Kigali: the four anthropologists in the Kosovo morgue were all instructed to consult with at least one other anthropologist for a second opinion on age range. Age estimates were singled out for this extra attention because they are the result of biological indicators *and* a given anthropologist's experienced opinion. No matter what, we looked upon our teammates as just that. The Kigali mission would provide further confirmation of the importance of being able to rely on your teammates, both professionally and personally.

PERHAPS FORTUNATELY, WE RAN out of space for analysis in the tent, so we set up tables outside where we finished laying out the remaining nine skeletons in anatomical position. This created the ideal field conditions: fresh air, clear light, and my teammates working nearby. Pierre was logging artifacts and photographing clothing, and just beyond him, several workers were washing the skeletons. Odetta and Beatrice, two local women, did our laundry amid big tubs of water and a clothesline. (We had had no way to do laundry before this time and had been rotating clothes carefully. I had been washing my underwear in the sink at the hotel; the gift my mother had given me before I left for Rwanda—an elasticized miniature clothesline with attached pegs—was getting good use.) As I worked on skeletons and collected associated pupa casings, I would look up at the tall boundary fence to see the children who had clambered to the top to watch us; they usually smiled at me. These were the best days, working quietly outside, the tranquillity only disturbed by occasional visits from Tribunal investigators asking serious questions about how we reconstruct crania that have been broken into pieces by gunshots, or by animated conversations with Jose Pablo about music in Italian films, punctuated by questions like "Would you describe this GSW as a keyhole entry?"

Meanwhile, the skeletons were telling their stories, and they were different stories from those that came out of the Kibuye church mass grave. The second skeleton I analyzed, that of an adult male, exhibited all manner of trauma: a fractured mandible, a fractured clavicle, a fractured sternum, bilateral rib fractures, both humerii fractured, and a fractured right foot. That is, this person was beaten to death and had tried to defend himself in the process. In contrast, the trauma on the Kibuye bodies had made it hard to picture the violence in the church: how was it that so few people had raised their arms to protect their heads as their assailants approached with upraised blunt and sharp instruments? The absence of defense wounds gave my image of that massacre an eerie calmness; did people take the blows as though taking the sacrament? Or had so many people been packed into the church that they couldn't even raise their arms to protect themselves? But here in Kigali, this skeleton was telling the story of a person struck on the chin, defending himself from blows to the body and chest and, probably, blows even after he fell to the ground. Buried next to him were another man, beaten, and yet another, shot.

I was conscious that one of these men might be the son of the woman who had visited the analysis tent with Viateur from the *commune* office earlier that week. When she returned for the second visit, she was again accompanied by Viateur, who had noticed my middle name, Msindo—also my mother's name—on my UN identity card. He had recognized it as an African name and was very pleased about this. Now he greeted me as simply "Msindo!" and ignored my first name altogether. He pronounced it as my jaja does, with an emphasis on the "sin," which is hissed, rather vehemently, through the front teeth. He grasped my identity card and pointed out "Msindo" to his companion while he slapped me on the back in a rather boisterous fashion. I felt as I had in Kibuye when the Ghanaian captain would say, "So you are a *true* sister!" It was as if I was viewed as more concrete, more real, than other members of the team because I had a name that was familiar and therefore memorable, a name that suggested I was connected to Africa in a meaningful way. This discriminatory enthusiasm in my favor made me feel I had to give my *personal* best, not just my professional best, because there were people who might hold me personally accountable.

WE PREPARED FOR our Kigali Clothing Day without Bill, who had departed for Bosnia, leaving Jose Pablo as team leader, a role closer to his proper (though belated) designation as chief anthropologist. The analyses were nearly complete and we had even recovered a driver's license from the clothing on one of the bodies. The license allowed us to make a presumptive identification until a relative could confirm the person's identity. As at the Clothing Day in Kibuye several months earlier, if potential maternal relatives recognized anything, they would be asked to supply a blood sample for future comparison with mitochondrial DNA drawn from the bones. We had decided to use our old autopsy tent from Kibuye with tables set up around the edge and the clothing displayed on the tables. We would have to arrive early in the morning to set it up before the family members arrived. But by the time we got to the Amohoro compound at ten to nine the next morning, some relatives were already there. We moved fast, and I was glad that Bill wasn't there to distract us with his vortex. With the help of two workers, we brought the clothing into the tent, used our yellow plastic numbers from the field to mark the clothes' case numbers, and were ready for the relatives by 10:30.

We chaperoned the relatives through for the next hour and a half; potential identifications regularly cropped up. The mothers, brothers, wives, cousins, and employers of the dead were there. By the afternoon session, we had four preliminary but strong identifications, with ages matching our age ranges. In the case of the body with the driver's license, the man's brother recognized his clothing. His brother's age at death was thirty-five; we had estimated between thirty and forty years.

Three relatives of one missing man thought they recognized a set of clothing, but they weren't positive. We asked whether their relative had had any lasting, identifiable physical features—had he broken any bones, lost any teeth, walked with a limp? They told us he had an obvious chip in one of his upper front teeth. This presented us with a challenge. We didn't want to show the relatives the skull because, apart from potentially upsetting them, it could distract them from focusing on the teeth. Even putting a skull behind a board with a rectangle cut out to show the mouth seemed too unpleasant. Finally, we decided to make still video images that showed only as much dentition as you might see in a smile. We filmed four people's teeth, including the man whose clothing the relatives thought they recognized.

As we took the Kigali relatives to view the images inside the Awohoro building, I thought about what an improvement this was over the incident in Kibuye, when the priest's niece collapsed with shock upon seeing the cranium resting on its upper teeth. Now, in the semiprivate office, we explained what the relatives were about to see and showed them each "smile" in succession. The relatives unanimously recognized the chipped left maxillary incisor in one of the images. The skull was from the body that had been wearing the clothing they recognized. There was relief all around.

Dean took blood samples from maternal relatives and I assisted with Band-Aids and moral support. Since Jose Pablo was flying to Bosnia that evening, we had to arrange the repatriation of the remains to the *commune* office the next day. We wrote to the *bourgmestre* explaining that some of the remains had been presumptively identified and might be claimed by their relatives. The following day, I had the letter translated from English to French by François, one of the Tribunal translators. As he translated, he said he admired us for the work we were doing. I felt the same for him, and I told him so; after all, he had to hear the words of the survivors and witnesses. Outside the building, we put the remains in wooden coffins and loaded them onto a trailer, suffering many cuts to our hands from the large staples that were holding down the identification labels we had attached to each box.

There was no ceremony with the elegant *bourgmestre,* M. Ruganbage, but I felt a sense of closure as I sat in the *commune* office with the three investigators from Clothing Day and a translator. This was the only mission at which I was present for such a handover, and I took solace in it. But whenever I see a copy of my memo to Bill about the Kigali Clothing Day, I am reminded that the woman looking for her son didn't recognize any of the clothing or artifacts as his. This still saddens me. Then, when I read the memo's "nota bene" informing Bill that she left her blood for a DNA sample anyway, I feel more than sadness. It's as if the closure I felt at the time is a knitted garment that is being unpicked, unraveled into a shapeless, unfinished difficulty.

9

RWANDA, LIVE

WITH THE KIGALI REMAINS REPATRIATED, THE MISSION WAS completed with a week's time left in Rwanda. Bill had given permission to assess sites for future exhumations, but this initially only led to a team argument about how to define "assessment." Meanwhile, multiple Tribunal investigators were clamoring for actual *exhumations* of their sites. They were tired of having to share their forensic team with the Yugoslav Tribunal and didn't understand why a week wasn't enough time to complete one.

One investigator quickly moved beyond this conundrum and used us to his best advantage within our "assessment only" mandate: this was Pierre, the Dutch investigator for the garage site. We spent a day in the rural areas north of Kigali with Pierre and another investigator, Henny Koele. We drove down numerous dirt roads flanked by fields of tall corn; whenever we reached a town, children would come running after the Land Rover. About six of them would jump onto the back bumper, climbing onto the roof rack and holding on for a ride, yelling with glee. When we stopped the car, Henny would get out and inflate balloons he had brought with him from Europe, fascinating the kids—you couldn't buy balloons in Rwanda then. Henny would let the air out while holding the mouth of the balloon to make it whistle, and the kids were delighted. Then Henny gave them the balloons as gifts.

One of our destinations was a mine that reportedly held remains. Dean rappelled down the shaft to investigate, while several women came to lie on the grass and watch us. One of them had a terrible swelling in her leg, encompassing the top of her foot and traveling up her shin and calf. She explained to Pierre that during the genocide, her husband had paid five thousand Amafaranga (Rwandan francs) to her would-be killers to save her from being thrown alive into the mine. The aggressors took her husband's money but cut her Achilles tendon before they left. The ankle had been trying to heal itself for almost two years. She sat on the grass while she talked quietly, and I thought about Kibuye, just as I had at Ntamara. Here we were, on the other side of the country from the church whose grounds yielded skeletons with deep cut marks on the backs of their ankles, talking to a woman who survived the same kind of assault because her attackers were open to negotiation. I imagined thousands of such women—and men, and children—across Rwanda, walking with canes or crutches, their skeletonized counterparts half buried in the ubiquitous verdant undergrowth.

A beautiful younger woman stood with me, holding her baby, who had the sniffles. The young woman said her parents were in the mine. Then, out of the vegetation behind me, a little girl materialized, holding a ball. She seemed to take a liking to me, coming up close behind me and grinning, then hiding in the bushes, only to return a moment later, smiling and looking at me with the sweetest, most expressive eyes. Maternal feelings of a strength I'd never experienced enveloped me every time I looked at this girl. I tried to take her photograph, but she disappeared into the bushes every time I lifted my camera, only to sidle up to me when I lowered it. For some reason, she stood still when Melissa took a shot of the two of us together; I treasure this photo, which has captured the girl's mischievous innocence. Despite the attention the girl gave me, she wouldn't speak; I could only hope her parents weren't in the mine.

It was a real team effort to get Dean out of the mine shaft: we had to winch him up on a rope tied to the back of the Land Rover, whose tires became stuck in the mud. I was trying to catch Dean, who was swinging on his harness over the mine shaft, and then everyone started laughing because we realized that if I lost my grip, *I* would fall in, while Dean would just keep swinging. I didn't know it then, but that was the last "team moment" we would have on the mission.

That evening, we had what I described in my journal as a "breakdown in team goodwill." In the absence of both Bill and Jose Pablo, communication quickly deteriorated. One person would report, "I spoke to Bill and he said to do this." Response: "But I just talked to him and he said to do *that*." And so on. I remember there were raised voices. Okay, there was yelling. I remember that two people stopped talking to each other altogether—and we were a team of only five by then, so it made a difference.

I was disappointed. Team identity was a major part of what makes this work bearable for me. In the graves, it is crucial because none of us works in a vacuum. The archaeologist needs to read the soil and make the maps before the anthropologist can begin making sense of the bodies and exhuming them, for example. We cannot be renegades in the grave, working to our individual paces and plans. Then, there is the time outside the graves. When I'm sitting in a vehicle at the end of a long, hot day and I reek of decomposing tissue and my back is aching from lifting bodies and I'm trying not to think about everything I just saw wrenched from the ground that day, I feel better looking around me and seeing my teammates, just as grimy and absorbed in their thoughts, people who have just gone through everything I've just gone through. Even if we never talk about it, we understand one another's experiences that day as no one else could. Given that we can't go home at the end of the day, we need support from each other, even if that support is unspoken.

In Kigali, the five of us were living in three separate locations, and we didn't all have telephones. I have noticed that the missions with the weakest team identity were those whose members lived in separate accommodations. As much as any of us moaned and groaned in Kibuye when Bill came to the dinner table with his crumpled notebook to discuss work, that activity maintained our team identity even during downtime. Though we lived in separate huts at the Kibuye guesthouse, we all lived there together, ate there together. The same situation was created on the military bases in Bosnia and Croatia. But in Kosovo, team members found their own housing, and ate on their own, and information the team needed to know would be passed around from house to house instead of team meetings being called. People felt more like contract workers for the UN than members of the Tribunal forensic team.

Despite the importance of Tribunal forensic investigations, if a team's system has a breakdown in it—even something as harmless as a personality clash—the work cannot progress efficiently, as communication and morale drop to dangerously low levels. The Kigali breakdown was resolved through a couple of late-night phone calls with Bill, who was both father figure and mediator—perhaps more so than he ever was in person—but the damage was never fully repaired. And we still had one important task to carry out.

Bill had promised the Kibuye *préfet* that we would put two skeletons on display at the church as a memorial. Two preparatory tasks were crucial: to obtain an appointment with the *préfet,* and to secure a vehicle with a communications radio. The former was resolved through a telephone call: M. Kabera, the *préfet,* was most obliging. The latter took some more effort, but it was important that we have the ability to communicate with the Tribunal offices: we had learned that the roads around Kibuye were indeed dangerous. I had been talking with Koos Barten, a Dutch investigator, during a party at Jose Pablo's house a few days earlier. Koos informed me that the land mines being found on the road to Kibuye were not the same as those set during the genocide but were new American antitank mines. That is, they weren't leftover dangers, but fresh ones. Koos and I were dancing when he said that the road between Kibuye and Gisenyi was very bad for mines—the sticks and leaves used to repair potholes in the dirt roads were ample cover. "Don't be the first to drive it in the morning," he advised as the music ended.

WITH GEOFF'S HELP, Melissa, Dave, and I secured Jose Pablo's old Land Rover, so we had not only a "comms" radio for security but also a cassette player for proper road-trip music. And we had some backup. Ovind Olsen, whom we had met at the Kibuye Clothing Day, would be on the road with his investigation team a few hours after us. They would be equipped with a satellite phone. Ovind's crew would also be staying at the Kibuye guesthouse. Once on the road, we made good time, getting through all the roadblocks easily. I had learned that it helped to pretend you couldn't speak French.

At the Kibuye guesthouse, Ephrem wasn't there but we were met by the new manager, George, who enthusiastically listed the improvements he had made: we could have hot water brought to the rooms if we wanted it, most of his staff now spoke English, and there would soon be phone extensions in every room.

The guesthouse was as beautiful as I remembered, and we had cold drinks on the lawn before choosing rooms. Dave had my old room, Number 8; Melissa had Jose Pablo's old room; and I had Bob Kirschner's old room. I had coveted that one because of its position away from the hotel driveway, which I used to fear because it could deliver that one aggressive UN soldier directly to my bathroom window. Everything was more or less as I remembered but it was good to have a different room and there was a new item on the edge of the sink: a Jack Daniel's bottle filled with lake water (for brushing one's teeth?). The nicest surprise was seeing three hotel staff who recognized us from before; there was beaming on all sides and many repetitions of *"Bienvenue!"*

Since it was still just midafternoon and the *préfet* had been out when we arrived, we decided to walk up the road to his office. His staff showed us from the waiting room into the outer office, where I filled in an "audience form." After waiting some time, we were finally shown in to his office, where we were invited to sit in massive, faux-leather armchairs, a long way across the huge room from the *préfet*'s desk. M. Kabera was wearing a jacket and tie, glasses, and a nice watch. The setting was both intimidating and surreal. Kabera began telling us in French about the housing project he had just visited: the houses still needed doors, windows, cement. (What *did* they have? I wondered.) The *préfet* then called M. Nkurunziza, the *bourgmestre,* to have him take us to the church with a key.

At the church, M. Nkurunziza directed us to drive all the way up the first set of steps into the courtyard where we had held Clothing Day. Inside the church, everything seemed very clean and there was no smell left from when we had had the bodies stacked in the annex rooms. Against one wall were the display cases: two roughly finished pale wood boxes on legs, with glass lids. We walked through the church and outside to the priests' rooms where we had left the bodies. The bricked-up windows looked good, as did the door, spray-painted silver. Nkurunziza unlocked the door. Inside, everything was as we left it except that Madeleine Albright's wreath had been placed with the bodies, along with other, smaller bouquets.

As I stepped inside I realized there was hardly any smell coming from the body bags. We found the two bags marked "Display" and the child Bill and I had exhumed together on the hillside, still laid out in anatomical position as we had left it. We took the two body bags out of the room to ascertain the contents and Melissa was arranging the black velvet cloth to be draped at the base of the display cases when Nkurunziza told us that when we were finished, we'd have to put the cases back into the storage room because the church wasn't lockable. This wasn't part of the plan; we had understood that the displays were supposed to be inside the church where people could visit them freely. I suggested locks for the cases, but the *bourgmestre* thought vandals would just break the glass tops. So we checked to see whether the display cases would fit into the storage room; no, they were too big. After much discussion, we decided to put the bones back in storage and talk to the *préfet* the following morning about a solution.

Once we were in front of the church again, Dave took two Polaroid photos: one for the *bourgmestre* (he seemed very pleased to have it) and one for Bill, as a photo-document of the visit. Another Polaroid was taken when Concessa, one of the local women who had done our laundry during the old mission, turned up, truly surprised to see us. We drove Nkurunziza back to his office, watched by what seemed to be the town's entire population. I could hear the prisoners in the jail singing; they seemed to be perpetually cooking a meal out in the front yard, just as when we were there a few months earlier. Then we returned to the church so we could look at the grave. There was a lot of new plant growth—crazy-looking purple weeds and white flowers—plus a deep pool of water in the bottom of the grave. We photo-documented the pool for Bill so decisions could be made about whether we should arrange to have the water drained. I walked back to the nuns' house: everything was very clean and weed-whacked, and there were new doors—but still there were the bloody handprints on the walls, and blood splatters on the ceilings.

Overall, there was very little evidence of the forensic team's time there, I was happy to see, except for a few stray kneepads under some of the trees and our crime scene tape, now being used ingeniously behind the Home St.-Jean and also down at the guesthouse to mark out borders for new flower beds.

A less welcome reminder of our last mission occurred during dinner, when a Rwandan Patriotic Army speedboat motored up to the beach. I was momentarily very tense but recovered enough to eat all of my brochettes. Even though the speedboat was the strongest possible reminder of the murders in February, I slept well that night.

The next morning, we had another audience with the *préfet,* who called Nkurunziza about options for finding locks and locksmiths in Kibuye. There were none. They would have to get someone, someday, to come from the next biggest *commune* over to do the work. Kabera and Nkurunziza both were quite relaxed about the timing of this, so the issue was tabled until Bill's return in November. We parted with good wishes on all sides.

Before leaving Kibuye, we stopped by the stadium just past the center of town. The stadium was the other main area in Kibuye where people were collected and killed in 1994. The bodies there had since been buried in the soccer field and enclosed by a brick wall and flowers. The ground looked uneven. A large sign explained in Kinyarwanda, French, and English what had happened there. Perhaps the *préfet* of Kibuye had been less concerned with the glass display cases at the church because he already had this memorial.

THE NEXT FEW DAYS were occupied partly with writing reports for Bill but mostly with downtime. We visited the Rwandan Artisans' Cooperative, which sold local art, and investigated the jewelry stands that we'd never had time to stop for before. We finally experienced a traditional Rwandan dinner: baked chicken, barbecued fish, *pommes frites,* a type of tabouli, a creamed legume dish, potatoes, and peas—a massive meal that the restaurant's owner ate with us and for which he would not let us pay. Melissa and I also spent a lot of time with Pierre and Koos, who took us to the Kigali market, where pangas were used to cut the meat and where I bought "African" cloth (made in the United Arab Emirates, mostly) for my mother. We had drinks in a local café where, for the first time, we were the only "internationals." We even experienced a very late night (or early morning, really) at the Cadillac, Kigali's hottest nightclub at the time, which pulsated with Zairian and Algerian music while locals, UN personnel, and NGO staff all danced together. I could see why internationals who were in Rwanda for a year or more needed the Kibuye guesthouse as a holiday retreat, how their weeks needed weekends, and how someplace raucous and relatively uninhibited like the Cadillac was just what some of them wanted on a Saturday night.

One evening when the team was on its way to dinner at the American Club, I noticed with surprise that Ephrem, the concierge from the Kibuye guesthouse, was with us. As we walked, I asked him whether he had married, as was the plan when we had last seen him in Kibuye. No, he replied: when his fiancée saw that his house had been "broken" during the genocide, she refused to marry him. Without property of some kind, Rwandan men cannot wed. He told me he had no friends, no family, and no money. I didn't know what to say.

Inside the restaurant, I realized that Ephrem was essentially working the room, which was full of Tribunal and NGO internationals, most of whom had been to the Kibuye guesthouse at some point for a holiday and knew and liked Ephrem. Despite his skills as a maître d', he was having to ask for any available job. Brenda Sue, a Tribunal prosecutor, said she might be able to get him a job as a guard at her house.

Many private houses in Kigali had guards, as I had noticed when Jose Pablo invited Melissa and me to move into his house when he left for Bosnia. He shared accommodation in the suburb of Kicukiro with Humbert de Biolley, a Tribunal legal officer from Belgium. The first time Melissa and I went there, we had driven behind Pierre and Koos, wending our way past little bistros and shops, all seemingly packed with people, until we entered a residential neighborhood of deeply rutted roads where the dwellings were barely visible behind tall gates and walls. There was a guard at Jose Pablo's house. Even in the dark night, I could see that he was just a very old man with a big stick. I didn't see how he could protect any property, except by raising an alarm. When I moved in, however, I was grateful for his presence.

Indeed, when Melissa and I lived in the house, we used to joke, "Now *this* is the life!" as we sat on the long rear veranda looking out over the garden. Inside, the furniture was carved from wood and the cushion covers were made from dark-yellow-and-burgundy-patterned *kanga*s. We basked in Humbert's hospitality; every morning, he would lay out our breakfast before going to the Tribunal offices. The whole experience of living in a neighborhood and driving home in the evening made an impression on me. But more than this, peering into lit doorways and thus into people's lives— even for just a moment—gave me a perspective on Rwanda beyond what I had learned from its graves. I saw people laughing, people having their hair cut, small businesses selling bottles of Fanta and Coca-Cola from apparently unmarked windows. Unexpectedly, Humbert was responsible for one of the lasting memories I have of Rwanda.

When I first met Humbert, I thought he was a cross between a well-bred schoolboy and an earnest bureaucrat, with his conservatively cut blond hair, cornflower-blue eyes behind civil-servant glasses, and ruddy cheeks. His carefree and loud singing during his morning shower did nothing to dispel that image. So I was surprised when, one day, he took Melissa and me on a drive whose destination he wouldn't reveal but which could only be reached by following a warren of unmarked side roads. We finally arrived at a house surrounded by a high wall. Inside, there was a well-swept dirt courtyard. Two women met us and invited us into a small room where children of all ages passed through, greeting Humbert; the littlest ones vied to sit on his lap. He finally explained to us that this was an orphanage, but not just any orphanage. We went back into the courtyard, where three chairs waited for us. Once we sat down all the children, from little ones to teenagers, arranged themselves in two lines and, after a shy start, danced and sang a long song in Kinyarwanda. Their delivery was beautiful, lilting and professional. My cheeks ached from smiling nonstop.

When our enthusiastic clapping died away, Humbert started to pull something slowly from his pocket. The feistiest kids ran to him while the shy ones stayed back, eyes trained on Humbert's hands, which emerged holding multicolored balloons. There was an eruption of sheer, visceral delight as the children converged on Humbert just as the children by the mines had when Henny's balloons appeared. Humbert had exactly one balloon for each child: I realized that he had been to this orphanage many, many times before. He told me later that he liked to bring balloons, a better treat than tooth-rotting sweets. What Humbert had unwittingly revealed was that even back home in Belgium, he was thinking of Rwanda. Rwanda was with him, in him, all the time, as it was with me.

It was a documented phenomenon in postgenocide Rwanda that young orphans, of whom there were more than 100,000, were "adopted" by families that then used the children as servants. To guard against such entrapment, the two women who ran this orphanage raised the children until they were eighteen and could earn their own living. By performing songs at weddings and other events, the kids earned the money to help keep the orphanage going. They were like a Rwandan Von Trapp family, except they had two "mothers" (the children called them both Maman).

The children spent the afternoon teaching us hand-clapping games; then we drove one of the mothers to the Kigali hospital to see one of her charges. The girl had a terrible cough but she was glad of visitors, smiling shyly at us all. The hospital smelled not of antiseptic but of oranges and beef stew.

When Humbert had told us back at the house that we were visiting orphans from the genocide—a genocide whose dead I had already met—I had expected to find it saddening, but as we drove away from the high wall of their yard, I felt lonely without them and their energy. They were orphans, yes, and the older kids were quiet and serious, but they each had two mothers, mothers who both protected them from and prepared them for the world outside.

When I left Kigali the next evening, I felt lighter than I had after my first mission. I was "full up"—my Jaja's phrase—with the Rwanda Humbert must have known: the living Rwanda, the going-on Rwanda, the take-care-of-others-who-need-you Rwanda, the future of Rwanda. I didn't want to leave. This was in direct contrast to how I'd felt when I left the Kibuye mission: I had been practically aching with relief then, only to have the relief overtaken by feelings of guilt. If I hadn't joined the second mission to Rwanda, I wouldn't have learned that my guilt was misplaced. I wouldn't have seen how people survive in a place like postgenocide Rwanda, and how most of them wouldn't trade their uncertain futures for my plane ticket or my own uncertain future. It was as though I had been looking at an image with only the foreground in focus and then someone who knew how the image was supposed to look adjusted the focus to bring in the background and my picture became more balanced. I had had a tantalizing, lingering glimpse of Rwandan people as they live, not just how they died.

—

PART THREE

BOSNIA

July 4–August 29, 1996

Kalesija

SERBIA

Cerska
Nova Kasaba

Milici

Vlasenica

Srebrenica

CROATIA

Sava River

Brčko
Tuzla

BOSNIA
AND
HERZEGOVINA

Vlasenica

Srebrenica

Sarajevo

SERBIA

Split

Brač Island

Montenegro

Adriatic Sea

ALBANIA

ITALY

0   50   100 Kilometers

0   50   100 Miles

Republika Srpska

Less than a year after Slovenia and Croatia declared their independence from Yugoslavia in June 1991, the war within Bosnia, the third of Yugoslavia's six republics, began. Fighting started after Bosnia-Herzegovina voted for independence from Yugoslavia; the cause of the war is usually attributed to the Bosnian Serb leadership declaring that they wished to remain a part of a federal Yugoslavia and, to that end, were creating a Serb-only republic made up of regions scattered throughout Bosnia-Herzegovina. The war was fought between regular troops of the Bosnian and Croatian governments, Yugoslav People's Army troops sent from Serbia, and more than a dozen paramilitaries and irregular forces. The fighting lasted for three years and was marked by war crimes and crimes against humanity on all sides: detention camps, shelling of civilians, forced migrations of millions of people, systematic rape of more than 20,000 women, the deaths of 200,000 people, and the disappearances of tens of thousands of military-aged men. The United Nations International Criminal Tribunal for the former Yugoslavia (ICTY) subsequently sent forensic scientists to multiple mass grave sites, but the first exhumations concentrated on the events that took place in 1995 along the border with Serbia.

10.

ALMOST PICNIC

SIX DAYS, SEVEN NIGHTS. THAT'S USUALLY LONG ENOUGH FOR a vacation but short enough not to disrupt your life. The six days and seven nights I was home in California between returning from Kigali and departing for Bosnia were enough for me to do laundry, find my thermal underwear, and buy more toothpaste, and for my mother to mend my lucky travel socks. But it wasn't long enough to get out of mission mode.

Nonetheless, I wasn't entirely sure where the Bosnia mission would take me. I knew that our team would be living on a NATO military base in a town called Vlasenica. We would be conducting the first ICTY exhumations of mass graves suspected of holding the bodies of people missing from the town of Srebrenica. We would start digging almost one year to the day after eight thousand men and boys left on foot just hours before a Bosnian Serb army takeover. The men never made it to Tuzla, their destination, then in Bosnian government army territory. To discover what happened to them, we would set out from Tuzla and travel south, to Srebrenica. Somewhere along the way, we knew we would find the missing men.

. . .

I ARRIVED AT Zagreb airport on July 4, 1996. Jose Pablo, Stefan Schmitt, and David Del Pino, all friends and teammates from Rwanda, were waiting for me at the Hotel Dubrovnik. There was only one new person, Fernando Moscoso, a Guatemalan anthropologist. We would be driving four hours to Tuzla the next afternoon to meet Bill Haglund, but first we had to obtain mission-appropriate IDs and driver's licenses at UN HQ, Camp Pleso.

Pleso was just beyond the airport, guarded by extremely serious Finnish soldiers. The compound was so big, it had its own villages, restaurant, and gas station. At the Transport Office nestled in an evergreen wood, the Finnish testing official had an animated face and a way of moving that reminded me of actor David Suchet's Hercule Poirot: lots of little steps. He bounced happily around the office, apparently reveling in the minutiae of the UN driving protocols. The testing vehicle, a pickup truck, had a loose gear shift. Poirot gave directions, cracked jokes, and at last boisterously exclaimed to each of us: "Well, I am sure it is no surprise that you have passed your test!" Like the tester in Rwanda, he even hectored us about the transgressions of previous drivers, but here the focus was on speeding violations and a little device named CarLog.

The CarLog was a small box mounted on the dashboard. You swiped your identity card through it, and if you were registered to drive that vehicle, the ignition would start. Inside his office, Poirot insisted that we practice swiping our cards ten times through a wall-mounted mock CarLog while he tutored us on its features: it would record our identity, what UN sector we were driving in, and our speed. He said these measures had been introduced because UN employees had been speeding around the former Yugoslavia, offending locals and endangering lives. Now the CarLog beeped until the car slowed to the sector speed limit and, supposedly, sent the driver's ID number to the Transport Office for disciplinary action. The CarLog has appeared in my nightmares when an evacuation under gunfire is impeded because teammates not registered to use the CarLog can't get the cars to start.

We were ready to leave Camp Pleso a few hours later, in convoy with several vehicles and a massive drops truck loaded with a refrigerated

My brother Kimera and me with our parents, David and Msindo.
Even when they traveled to make their documentaries,
our parents took us with them. *Author's collection*

Kibuye church sits on a long peninsula in Lake Kivu, Rwanda, a country known as the Land of a Thousand Hills. *Physicians for Human Rights*

Outskirts of Kibuye town, near the shores of Lake Kivu.
Author's collection

UN vehicles outside Kibuye church, where several thousand people were killed during the genocide in 1994. Some of their bodies were later buried in a mass grave that we were asked to investigate. *Physicians for Human Rights*

The interior of Kibuye church, with body bags between the pews. Whenever I carried in body bags, I was more disturbed by the remains of violence—like blood splatters on the ceiling—than by the human remains.
Physicians for Human Rights

Part of our work at Kibuye was cleaning and documenting clothing and other personal belongings that could help identify bodies. Later, we held a "Clothing Day," on which survivors came to help identify the dead, who were often relatives. Clothing Day allowed me to see our work in a humanitarian, rather then solely forensic, context.

Physicians for Human Rights

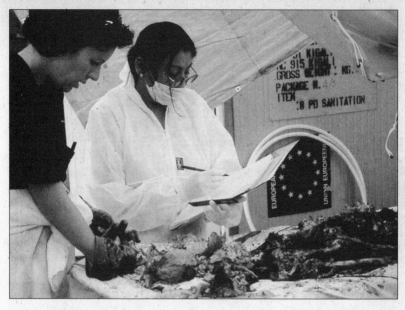

Roxana and Mitra working in the autopsy tent in Kebuye. Pathologists, anthropologists, autopsy technicians, a radiographer, and a photographer worked on about thirty bodies a day. *Physicians for Human Rights*

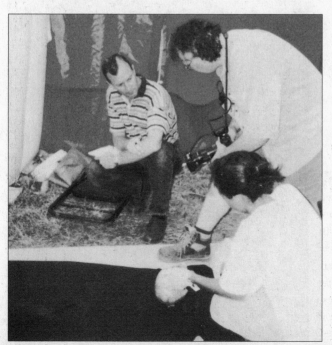

Working with Pierre and Owen in the analysis tent in Kigali. *Author's collection*

Sitting with Melissa Connor where we ate our meals at the Kibuye Guest House. Lake Kivu was a beautiful backdrop, but also central to the only harrowing memory I have from Kibuye.
Author's collection

When I visited orphans from the genocide in Kigali, they taught me their hand-clapping games.
Melissa Connor

Melissa's photograph of me and the little girl near the mine north of Kigali.
Melissa Connor

Working with Bill Haglund in Kigali. *Pierre Heuts*

Cerska, near Srebrenica. A place that would have been good for a picnic once, it was our first site in Bosnia, and the exhumation of more than 150 bodies was made more difficult by the steep slope. *Physicians for Human Rights*

"Cleaning" the surface and finding the edge of the grave at Ovčara, near Vukovar.

Physicians for Human Rights

The morgue team at Kalesija, outside Tuzla, Bosnia. Standing, from left: second is Bill Haglund, sixth (partly hidden) is Juerena Hoffman, then me, Geoff Bucknall, Kamble, and Dorothy Gallagher; in the sunglasses is Jose Pablo Baraybar, then Peter Knudsen, Mike Warren, Fernando Moscoso, David Del Pino, and John Gerns, and far right (in white shirt) is Bob Kirschner. Sitting, from left: third is Shuala Martin, fifth is Angela Brkic, seventh is Patrick Myers, and eighth is Molly Ryan. *Author's collection*

In Croatia, following our military police escort through Vukovar, which had been severely shelled in 1991. *Author's collection*

We frequently had to cover the grave against rain at Ovčara, until the UN administrator for Eastern Slovonia, General Jacques Klein, saw us and ordered a tent. The tent that arrived was massive and well constructed, a big improvement over the few tarps we had to stretch over the grave in Kibuye.

Physicians for Human Rights

More than two thousand people were missing from Vukovar, as the names on these walls outside UN headquarters in Zagreb attest. Some of their families didn't want us to uncover bodies—they wanted to find their relatives alive. *Ralph Hartley*

An aerial photo of the site at Ovčara. It was believed people taken from Vukovar hospital were shot and buried in a mass grave here at the edge of the woods. *Physicians for Human Rights*

At one of the mass graves in Brčko, Bosnia.
Timothy Loveless

In Erdut, Croatia, at the Belgian military base we called home. It had been a difficult day "at work," but I was trying to focus on the bigger picture: determining what happened to the people in the grave and helping to return them to their families.
Ralph Hartley

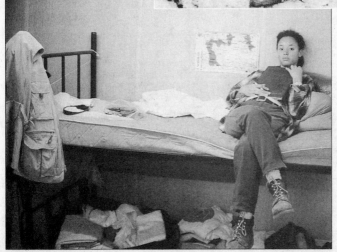

In Kosovo, on a lunch break with my housemates Derek and Barney in a cemetery where we were exhuming unidentified bodies. People often said they were surprised I could smile so much during missions, but I was happiest when I was doing this work. *Justine Michael*

With Justine Michael and Sam in Skopje, Macedonia. My friendships on missions provided me with the "debriefing" I never received from the UN.

Author's collection

When I uncovered this body of a young boy in Kosovo, I could see a handful of marbles in his trouser pocket. *Justine Michael*

Ute and I "taking down" the backdirt at another mass grave in Brčko, Bosnia. *Timothy Loveless*

Holding a
tape measure at
the start of a
workday in Kosovo,
still smiling.
Barney Kelly

container—filled for now with our exhumation equipment and the wine we bought for Bill from the UN store. But then, in familiar and almost comforting UN style, the Finnish soldiers at the gate wouldn't let us out without proof of ownership of the contents of the truck. Jose Pablo, a bona fide UN employee, was furious, but the more he gesticulated and raised his voice, the more stubborn the Finns became. Eventually, a higher-ranked military police officer was found, and he let us out. We were on our way to Tuzla.

Cosme, our Filipino backhoe operator, led the way in the truck because he had been to Tuzla before. The first leg of the journey looked promising, the highway wide with two lanes on either side of a metal divider and roadside stops with cafés and fuel stations. This was the former Brotherhood and Unity Highway, linking Zagreb and Belgrade, which had been reopened only a few months earlier after being shut down during the war. The UN vehicles were the only odd note on the highway, which otherwise had little traffic. Most of that was traveling in the opposite direction and consisted mostly of civilian sedans with large piles of belongings strapped to their roofs. I presumed some of these were families on their way to holiday on the Adriatic coast. After several hours, it seemed that we were making a lot of wrong turns, including U-turns on the undivided highway we'd joined. At the five-hour mark, we hadn't even reached the border with Bosnia yet, and our convoy pulled over to regroup, tempers running high. A very apologetic Cosme confessed he had only been to Bosnia once before and he hadn't been driving, so it was very difficult for him to recognize the nonsignposted landmarks that were supposed to indicate turns that led to the river crossing into Bosnia. I endeavored to make the supply of beef jerky and chocolate that David and I had pooled last longer.

I didn't have a map so I thought we'd finally reached Tuzla when we crossed a narrow temporary army bridge over a beautiful wide river I later learned was the Sava. American soldiers were guarding the bridge and controlling traffic flow, instructing us to drive very slowly (three kilometers per hour) and not tailgate. Bosnia was indeed on the other side, but the town wasn't Tuzla. It was a ghost town of rutted streets, buildings reduced to rubble, and a few people braving the choking dust storms created by the oversized and ominous U.S. Army Humvees roving the tiny streets. We saw all this on yet another wrong turn. I got angry at this point—we were barely making forward progress—and David was glad of the company: *he* had been angry for the past two hours. I came to know this ghost town the following year: it was Brčko.

We reached Tuzla a couple of hours later and looked for our hotel by circumnavigating the town. Three sides were bordered by mountains; a hulking factory spewing foul-looking smoke marked the fourth side, from where most traffic entered. The main drag was flanked by tall apartment buildings with shops below. When we finally found the Bristol, on a narrow side street, I was surprised to learn that only Jose Pablo had a room here, while the rest of us were a few blocks away with a woman named Laurie Vollen, who worked for Physicians for Human Rights. When we got to Laurie's house, we found out that Bill was staying at yet another hotel—the best one in town. I thought about this as I watched Fernando, Cosme, and David find space in the one room they had to share. As the only woman, I had a room of my own in the attic with a sofa pulled out into a bed and lots of books (*Tito the Hero* was one I noticed). The landlady's dog slept on the other side of the door.

During dinner with Bill at the Hotel Tuzla, Laurie told us she was an American medical doctor who used to work for Doctors Without Borders and had just been hired by PHR to develop an antemortem database for the sites we would be excavating that summer. Antemortem databases are usually used by forensic scientists attempting to identify large numbers of human remains from mass disasters, plane crashes, and bombings. The purpose of the database is to gather all the identifying information on missing persons in one searchable computer record and then compare that with anthropological and odontological information gathered from dead bodies.

It was already known that most bodies in Bosnia could not be identified through dental records: either the majority of the dead had not had lasting dental work, or their records had been destroyed during the war. But there was one great hope for making successful identifications: unlike the genocide in Rwanda, the war in Bosnia often saw captors separate women from men. The men were disappeared, but the women "benefited" from the laws of war and were bused to safe territory. On the way, they were often imprisoned and raped systematically but many survived even this. Bosnia-Herzegovina was a land of bereft and traumatized women, some thousands of whom are the wives, mothers, sisters, daughters, aunts, nieces, and grandmothers of the men from Srebrenica. It was to these women that Physicians for Human Rights would turn in order to fill in the antemortem database. Consequently Laurie was designing the database with fields for information about their missing relatives that could be elicited from the Srebrenica women during an interview: age, approximate height, weight, eye color, hair color, beard color, a description of his clothing and personal belongings, and where he was last seen. Laurie's journey with those women was just beginning when we met her in Tuzla.

The next morning, I woke up at 4:30 with the call to prayer wafting in the window from a nearby mosque. The call sounded as though it was coming from a cassette, but it was still pleasant. I went downstairs in search of breakfast and discovered that two new teammates had arrived in the night: Becky Saunders, an archaeology professor from Louisiana State University, and one of her graduate students, Dorothy Gallagher. We walked over to the old town, a village of narrow streets, small parklike squares, and roundabouts. It reminded me of Italy, but a worn-down version. The young people were stylish and the old people reminded me of those I've seen in Greece, particularly the women: solid and all wearing black. It didn't take long to find a coffee shop where two women were sitting in the window eating something that looked good, a kind of pastry. Painted on the window was a picture of whatever they were eating, plus a cup of steaming coffee. We decided to go in.

The coffee shop had an original black-and-chrome Art Deco corner bar. The waiter was a young man with an open and pleasant face and we all pointed to the pastry the women were now polishing off at the table by the window. We learned that it was called *čevapi* and that coffee was *kava*. The *čevapi* turned out to be a freshly baked circular pocket of bread filled with buttery grilled onions and four highly spiced sausages. It was seriously good, seriously greasy, and I couldn't finish mine. The *kava* was as thick as warm molasses and came in a long-handled brass jug on a tray with a little cup already one fifth filled with sugar and a miniature spoon. The *čevapi* was the only food on the menu and I respected that.

By noon, our last teammate—Ruut Schouten, a Dutch police officer— had arrived and we drove in a convoy of five vehicles to the U.S. Army base to join our military escort to Vlasenica. The drive to the base, Tuzla Main, took about half an hour along a pretty country lane; then we approached a set of sandbag blockades staggered in front of a guarded gate. After being cleared by the soldiers, we turned up a dirt track between two woods, keeping to the ten-kilometer-per-hour speed limit.

Our military escort was waiting near the PX. Actually coming alongside the Humvees made our convoy of Land Rovers seem tiny. The military told us who would travel between the Humvees, which would also lead the way and bring up the rear, gunners in position with loaded weapons. We were to drive close together at all times, try not to allow nonconvoy vehicles to break us up, and keep our headlights on unless we had a problem such as a flat tire. There would be no passing and no speeding. As I memorized these commandments, I felt a bit nervous. We were about to drive into territory where the people who committed the crimes we would be uncovering were still at large.

When we arrived safely in Vlasenica, at the staggered sandbag walls we now recognized as the standard entrance to an army base, I felt relieved— even though the drive could have been a scenic European tour most of the way. Vegetation can obscure so many signs of war. I reminded myself to not relax too much, even as I watched the escort soldiers clear their weapons of the ammunition they had loaded for the drive by firing into a large container whose lid had a small opening for the barrels of the guns. We waved our thanks and drove past them into Camp Lisa, following the one-way dirt road around to our assigned parking area, where we left the cars in a very straight line, nose out for quick evacuation.

We soon learned that Camp Lisa was home to three thousand American Implementation Force (IFOR) soldiers. It consisted of a large cluster of camouflage tents, Humvees, tanks, satellite dishes, and temporary buildings known as containers, all joined by wooden deck walkways spread about a hill. There used to be other buildings on that hill, before the war, and their bombed-out shells had been turned into a laundry collection point and a PX. The soldiers stationed there could tell their families that they were in "RS," Republika Srpska, the part of Bosnia that was dispensed to the Bosnian Serb government in the Dayton Peace Accord. RS exists in both eastern and western Bosnia, but the eastern side—where Vlasenica is—bordered Serbia proper, and it appeared that NATO felt it held more danger for their troops: I heard that soldiers at Camp Lisa used to take showers wearing flak jackets and helmets. One of the first things I noticed was that they wore some form of combat gear even while eating, machine guns at their feet while they consumed stacks of pancakes. Up to one hundred of these soldiers would be protecting the ICTY forensic team on any given day.

The men on our team were given a huge tent with cots and no room dividers. We three women were given a blue container on the edge of an entire village of containers; Bill's container was somewhere in the village, as were those housing the men's bathrooms. There were only a few hundred women on the base but more than two thousand men, none of whom seemed to know where the women's bathroom was. We finally found it, tucked away in a distant part of the container village. We followed the deck walkways to the Chow Hall for dinner, which wasn't bad: salty chicken pot pie and peas. I noticed that Bill and Jose Pablo ate at a separate table from the rest of the team, along with Andrew Thomson, our project coordinator from Rwanda, and John Gerns, an American ICTY investigator.

After dinner, we met the deminers who would be clearing our site the next morning: Peter, a Norwegian; Jimmy, a Swede; and Moses and Stefan, both Mozambicans. They were from the nongovernmental organization Norwegian People's Aid (NPA) and would be using German shepherd dogs to detect mines. They gave us pamphlets describing the mines commonly found in this region of Bosnia. I was startled to see photographs of round *plastic* boxes, some camouflage-colored, some buried with only a little trigger sticking up, no taller than a blade of cut grass. I wasn't expecting antipersonnel mines, and I certainly wasn't expecting them to look so much like grass and dirt—so much like what we work in when locating graves.

Before going to Bosnia, I had seen photographs of mines found in the former Yugoslavia but they were all antitank mines: metal, about the circumference of a small hubcap and the bulk of a large telephone directory, some with thick antenna triggers sticking straight up out of the middle. They were staggered every few feet on a paved bridge, so that a car wouldn't be able to drive around them. They almost looked like a modern art installation. People were even walking past them. I must have imagined that all the mines in Bosnia would be large and obvious like this, but the NPA pamphlet was changing that perception, and fast.

I listened to the deminers closely as they gave us fundamental safety instructions: "Stay on tarmac and veer around deep potholes—especially potholes filled with water or debris." But our job takes us off the tarmac, almost by definition. I glanced at my teammates: how were we *ever* going to spot these tiny, tricky, man-made death boxes?

The deminers' pamphlets made a lasting impression: I've had several dreams in which I step on mines or realize I am in a minefield. Sometimes I am a soldier and sometimes I am myself, with teammates. The dreams have never reached the moment when the mines explode; I usually wake up as I tell the people I'm with in the dream that they should move away while I try to disengage myself from the mine. I learned eventually that this isn't the right way to go about things after you step on a mine, but the lesson came three years after the dreams began. I was in Kosovo, at the UN's Priština headquarters, listening to a lecture on ordnance found there since 1999. We were told that if we stepped on a mine with a lift-off trigger (as opposed to a pressure trigger), the best thing to do is stand absolutely still. Even if you have to stand still for two days, you are better off waiting for help than trying to disengage from the mine. This was known as the STOP system: *Stop* and warn (the people behind you); *Think* and assess (your situation); *Orient* (yourself on a map so you can radio for help with sector information); and *Plan* (your next move). This detailed education on mine awareness (followed by a spot-the-tripwire exercise in a yard overgrown with weeds) came on my *sixth* mission. The education was unnerving, because it brought home the reality of how difficult it is to see mines and tripwires even right in front of your feet. Plus it turned out that local communities often have their own warning signs (such as cattle skulls hung on trees). I wonder how many signs like this I missed in Bosnia.

Even though I didn't know STOP in Bosnia, I did follow the Norwegian People's Aid deminers' golden rule to stick to the tarmac, at least while driving. Of course, it's hard to see tripwires, especially if they're strung across the road several feet above the tarmac and you are driving at seventy kilometers per hour. Besides that situation, though, the golden rule is great. But what do you do when you are traveling in convoy, at speed, by military order, and your teammate is driving the Land Rover in front of you over the rain and mud-slicked roads in third gear—when he should be in second gear? What do you do when you see the rear end of his vehicle fishtailing in front of you, his wheels slipping into the ditches on either side of the road, because he is going too fast in too high a gear and so has none of the high-revolution control of a lower gear? What do you do when you realize that if his vehicle slides into the ditch and hits a mine large enough to destroy it, your vehicle—only a few feet behind, by military order—may be destroyed too?

This scenario unfolded several times on my second mission to Bosnia, in 1997. On sunny days, driving between Srebrenik and Brčko, we could see the mines on the side of the road, marked by little red flags placed by nonprofit demining teams making their way slowly around the country. The mines, mostly antipersonnel, sat like little turds in the meadows, the tall grass cut down around them so you could see where they were. Crime scene–style tape sometimes skirted the road; it had red and white stripes alternating with an image of a skull and crossbones beneath the word MINES! Whenever I watched the vehicle in front of me sliding toward a ditch, anger and fear leapfrogged through my body, leaving me hot, then cold. I would grasp my own steering wheel, wanting to slow down, to drop farther back, but fighting the urge, obeying the rule that our vehicles should never be far apart. Driving under these conditions requires intense mental concentration; you don't want to be angry on top of that. I knew then that I didn't truly care about the petty things some people did that made me cringe—I didn't care if they wanted to drive in convoy without their headlights on, or wanted to exhume bodies before completing their hepatitis vaccine series, or purposely and rudely mispronounced *"Do vidjena"* ("See you later") as "Dos vaginas" every time they left a Bosnian shop—but I *did* care if they took risks with my life.

But all of that was ahead of me when I woke up the first morning at Camp Lisa. It had been a night of mild interruptions, so constant that they had hardly any effect after a while: helicopter rotor noise, and people meeting and talking right outside our container door, which we had propped open for air. Although the team was eating breakfast before seven A.M., that wasn't early enough for Bill, who wanted to get the cars fueled up *before* seven. Naturally, he hadn't said a word of this to the drivers the previous night. My gas tank was already full, but this didn't save me from being rushed through breakfast only to sit waiting for an hour, watching the sun rise, while Bill and Andrew had a meeting with the military. I realized that our team was quickly becoming divided into "management" and "workers." I joked with Jose Pablo later that he was eating meals with the management, but he didn't deny that this separation was developing. I wondered how much of it was due to our living on a military base where even our movement plans were on a need-to-know basis for security reasons, and how much was due to having new team members. Whatever the reason, it didn't feel like the same old family gathering in Rwanda.

When Bill and Andrew emerged from their meeting, word passed from car to car that the military had been involved in a conflict the previous night. Apparently, the Serbian media had stated that IFOR was coming to arrest General Ratko Mladič, one of those indicted for the Srebenica massacres, so local "elements" had mobilized busloads of civilians to confront the American soldiers. The clash resulted in the death of one civilian and the animosity of many others (and was responsible for the noise and helicopters we had heard in the night). Now it was unclear whether we would even leave the base because the military was not inclined to give us an escort to Cerska, our site. We sat for another hour, watching soldiers walk back and forth in an intermittent but endless stream while the sun rose higher and gained in strength.

Finally, Bill returned and we were off, in convoy: two IFOR Humvees in front, then several of our cars, the deminers and their dogs, Jose Pablo, Cosme on the backhoe, and another set of Humvees bringing up the rear. This was our established convoy order from this point forward. We trailed out of camp, going very slowly because the backhoe's maximum speed was thirty kilometers per hour. When we approached the main road in Vlasenica, I was surprised to see a lot of reporters lined up to film and record our departure. They had plenty of photo opportunities because our convoy came to a halt while the military organized itself and some Bradley armored personnel carriers joined us from Camp Demi, a nearby American base. After a while, we got on our way, the backhoe loudly and laboriously setting the pace and the Bradleys' not able to go much faster, but certainly louder with their treads clacking against the tarmac.

THE ROAD TO CERSKA took us downhill, past woods, and into a valley of farmland and occasional houses in various states of completion. We went through a little town called Milici, then Nova Kasaba, and then we turned off the paved road onto a heavily rutted path that wound through a stream and next to meadows, finally reaching our site in a narrow valley. There was a steep slope to the left of the road, dropping down to the stream and some trees. Directly on the right of the road was a hill climbing sharply upward. These two slopes made the road so narrow that two vehicles could only just pull up next to each other. Some of the Humvees had driven down this road with us while others stayed at the mouth, by the main paved road. We were informed that other soldiers were already in the area, on the road beyond the site and in the bushes—soldiers we would never see except in an emergency—and there were helicopters on standby. We had to drive past our site to turn around (one by one, in something like a sixteen-point turn because the road was so narrow) and park in convoy order formation to facilitate speedy evacuation.

I remember clearly what it was like to stand at the Cerska site that day, July 7, 1996. There is a particular quality about a forensic team's first day at a pleasantly secluded location like that one. Often the place will look like a good spot for a picnic because it has sun and shade, a stream, and is quiet enough to allow one to hear the rustle of high leaves in the trees when a breeze comes through. Cerska is also on a curve of road that allows you to hear cars approach before their occupants can see you, whether you are down by the stream or higher up the hill. For the same reasons of strategic solitude, this sort of location is also a good place to murder people without witnesses. The problem of how to get the bodies into a grave is also mitigated here. If the victims are lined up along the edge of the slope leading down to the stream, their bodies will just fall down the slope, below the level of the road, and can be covered by dirt. After the growth of some vegetation, the place looks like a picnic spot again.

This appearance is challenged some months later, when vehicles drive up and stop at the spot. A forensic team alights and unpacks its equipment and the quiet valley is filled now with the sounds of shovels being piled against a tree trunk, of the heads of pickaxes being nailed onto their handles, and the chirping of a metal detector as it is passed over the road—a road that is also a repository for shell casings from the murder weapons all those months before. The rustling of leaves is now drowned out by the constant hum of a backhoe engine.

Within a few days, the forensic teams I've worked with manage to turn picnic spots into exhumation sites by emphasizing their crime-scene characteristics: marking bullet scars on trees with yellow string, surface remains with red flags, test trenches with fluorescent tape, and map orientations with plastic north arrows. So it is only on the first day that one can sense the incongruity of the place, because the balance of material is mostly normal, with little touches of evidence: seven mismatched shoes strewn about a place with no other signs of human occupation—almost a hint of a grave but still mostly picnic site. After the first day, the place offers up mostly evidence, with little touches of normalcy: as you bend over three skeletons, a butterfly passes your face in its erratic flight—almost picnic but mostly grave site.

Cerska was such a place. It was the demining team that broke the spell first, saying, "Well, good-bye," before walking over to the hillside with their German shepherds.

THE DEMINERS DIDN'T FIND any mines. They then made a safe path for us to walk through the vegetation to the stream, and another path to a spot we'd use as a toilet. The forensic team had a meeting to discuss our excavation strategy: our first goal, given that we had had a late start, was simply to photo-document the entire area and map and collect the projectiles (bullets and shell casings) on the road. There were hundreds of casings visibly embedded in the dirt road but nowhere else, which suggested that the gunmen stood along the road shooting toward the top of the slope. The hill that rose from the other side of the road appeared to have a cut out of it, made by the front bucket of a backhoe—this, we speculated, was the "borrow" area for the soil covering the bodies on the slope. During the day we made progress but we suffered (as in Kigali on the first day) from too much sun, the lack of a way to keep our plastic bottles of water cool (the water was actually hot), and the usual first-day inefficiency, compounded by the lack of proper equipment or the inability to find it among that brought down from Zagreb.

The most pressing problem was that the electronic mapping station was missing a part, which rendered it unusable. This meant that we had to map each projectile on the road by hand, using a triangulation method, and we had to develop mathematical equations to calculate the height of the slope. Becky powered through this quagmire, but a point that should have taken us less than a minute to map was taking up to five minutes. We drove back to Camp Lisa that night somewhat demoralized, very tired, and very hungry.

We were moving a bit faster the next day, though it didn't begin well: breakfast was an infuriating experience, as it seemed that even a hello was too much for some of the "management," who were barely communicating with the rest of us. I ate outside, on the porch of the Chow Hall, looking at the view of distant hills, enjoying the breeze and thinking of California. My mood improved during the drive to Cerska because it took just an hour now that we had left the backhoe at the site.

Our first activities at the site were related to the fact that those respon-

sible for the crimes were still at large: Ruut took the overall morning photographs to record any signs of tampering while the IFOR soldiers removed the concertina wire they had set up on the perimeter of the site
before we left it unguarded overnight. When a soldier we could barely see
in the bushes tried to pick up an improperly set flare, we saw a bright flash
and smoke, and then we heard him yelling something that sounded remarkably like "Fuck, *fuck,* FUCK!" Within two minutes, a helicopter had
arrived to evacuate him. I was conscious of two things: that I jumped at the
flare because I thought it might be a booby trap left for us by people who
wanted to stop the exhumation, and that I was astonished at how fast the
helicopter flew in.

Our goal for this second day was to map the rest of the projectiles on
the road, map projectiles on the grave slope as the metal detector identified
them, and then start the trench above the grave to determine the depth of
the first level of bodies. We accomplished these things quickly because the
NPA deminers offered to do manual labor for us, taking our backdirt as we
began to expose the top of the grave, parallel with and closest to the road.
Our hired labor and security from Sarajevo hadn't arrived the day before,
and we were still trying to find out why.

By the end of that second day, we had exposed human remains at the
top of the slope, so it was paramount that the site be guarded overnight,
but the Sarajevo security still had not arrived, and IFOR had made it clear
before the mission that it couldn't or wouldn't guard any grave sites. We
had to wait for the security. At 7:30 P.M., Bill and John sent the team back to
Lisa. Three Humvees remained with them, the soldiers sharing their Meals
Ready to Eat (MREs) as dusk fell on the site.

The rest of us had to drive painfully slowly behind a hay truck, but this
gave us a chance to see the towns more closely. Our convoy was the
evening entertainment for local folks and since it was later than usual, we
saw more people. The evening was balmy, so it was a perfect night to be
outside with a cool drink. We waved and received some friendly whistles in
return, which was interesting because as far as we knew, the few people left
living in those RS towns were openly supportive of Radovan Karadzič and
General Ratko Mladič—portrait posters of them were plastered on the

sides of some buildings, the captions exhorting NATO not to "touch" these alleged war criminals if they wanted peace.

It didn't take long to get into a daily excavation routine of exposing remains across the top of the grave and working our way down the slope. Although we rarely made it back to Camp Lisa in time for dinner, and we were *never* there when the laundry was open, we were making good progress. This was important because we finally learned that the lives of our Sarajevo security contingent had been threatened by locals near Cerska. As a result, the security personnel were not going to work for us at all. So Bill and John continued to sleep at the site, next to the grave, either in the equipment container or in a Land Rover. By doing this, they forced IFOR to protect the two of them, and thus, effectively, the grave.

However, the situation eventually posed problems. I already knew from our time in Rwanda that Bill slept only a few hours per night; this, combined with his concern for our speed, meant that as soon as there was daylight he started working in the grave on his trench. When the team arrived for the day, we had to work out both what he had done and what effect, if any, it had on whatever we were working on. Since he was already working when we arrived, Bill stopped calling the morning strategy meeting. Daily goals and logistics information were now only passed from person to person, if they were communicated at all.

Jose Pablo eventually began sleeping at the site in order to give Bill or John a chance to rest. The first evening I saw him after one of these stints, he was eating dinner alone in the Chow Hall. He looked angry. I asked, "Are you okay?" A whole minute passed in silence while he shoveled food into his mouth. Then he said, with his signature staccato delivery, "I didn't sleep at all last night." Trying not to smile, I asked, "Why not?" He put his fork down and looked at me before saying, "Have you ever tried to sleep in a Land Rover?" There is a slight curl to Jose Pablo's lips when he speaks that can make him look as though he finds some amusement in what he's saying, so I was already smiling, but even if he hadn't looked amused in a beleaguered way, I still would have laughed out loud. It was an opportunity too good to miss. "That's the price of being management," I told him.

Since the nonexistent security contingent would have doubled as labor, we were fortunate that the grave consisted of less than fifty centimeters of soil on top of the bodies. Even after the deminers' departure, we were able to efficiently use picks and shovels to loosen and remove the soil, throwing it to the bottom of the slope where we could drag it away at the end of the day. It soon became clear that although there were only one or two layers of bodies, they lay across the breadth of the slope. We decided that we would expose the whole top layer before exhuming any bodies, which, even at this early stage, appeared to be all men and boys. Working on a slope again, I was reminded of Kibuye; here was the same damp heat, the same flies that didn't discriminate between dead bodies and live ones. The memory was good, particularly as I had it while working on another grave. That's the place to have them. You don't want to be remembering the details of exhumation when you're sitting back at home, clean and safe. To recollect them there is to invite discomfort mixed with longing.

11.

I'M JUST A WORKER HERE

BACK AT CAMP LISA, I NOW FELT RELATIVELY COMFORTABLE: I
knew my way around and the soldiers were generally uninterested in our
activity, except for one who wanted to have deep conversations about our
shared Jewish heritage and the privilege I had of working with the dead—
exactly the sort of topic that is difficult to talk about when you *are* working
with the dead all day. In the evenings I would sit outside the women's container, enjoying the last of the light.

My moods fluctuated for the next two months: I could be demoralized
by my perception that our previously close-knit team had divided into a hi-
erarchy, but then on a daily basis I could be elevated beyond those feelings
by working with human remains. Nine hours of clearing earth from on top
of bodies and disengaging their limbs from one another for transfer to
body bags was uniquely mellowing and fulfilling for me. Every time I felt
irritated by what seemed unnecessary managerial secrecy, my work in the
graves reminded me of why I would tolerate being treated as "just a
worker." Unfortunately, on this mission I eventually learned just how many
units of pique and its attendant stress it might take to outweigh my desire
to do this work. On the other hand, the good thing about being piqued is

that it enables you to draw up a list of how you would like things to be done differently. I took note that summer in Bosnia and remembered what I'd learned when I became part of "management" myself a few years later, at the Tribunal morgue in Kosovo.

The good feelings I had at Cerska were aided by enjoying the company of my new teammates. Becky Saunders was a consummate archaeologist and just the sort of person we needed to direct the excavation because she never showed stress, could delegate, and was positive. As for Dorothy Gallagher, I called her the Indispensable, because she had gone from excavating the slope to taking on the busy role of doing all the anthropologists' paperwork (including filling out the field osteology forms), bag labeling and sealing, and bucket hauling for everyone still working on the slope. It was demanding work, requiring her to know in advance what people would need and to understand what she was seeing from above the slope. One day, Dorothy—who never took breaks—succumbed to heatstroke and had to be rushed back to Camp Lisa. Very little was accomplished without her that afternoon. I also really liked Ruut, who had a very dry—almost cruel—sense of humor. I was further inclined to like him because his accent reminded me of Pierre Heuts. Ruut and Jose Pablo had become close, and although Jose Pablo was essentially "management," he still had one foot in the workers' camp. Dorothy and I found a shared joy in teasing him about this.

These good interpersonal relationships and a general sense of team identity enabled efficiency: by the middle of July, we exhumed more than 150 bodies from the grave at Cerska. As we uncovered more bodies, it became difficult to stand or crouch on sections of the slope itself, either because there was no clear space between the bodies or because the slope was too steep. Once we had removed all the topsoil, our method was to exhume the bodies from the top of the slope first, because those bodies slightly overlaid all the bodies farther downslope. I was partnered with Jose Pablo at one end of the grave; we developed a system by which one of us crouched on the slope above the body we were going to exhume while the other crouched in the bucket of the backhoe, which Cosme was holding in midair against the slope. In the bucket, we had a labeled body bag ready to receive the body.

The trick of this system was to not drop any part of the body or any of its artifacts in the small gap between the bucket and the slope. In addition, the person on the slope had to avoid pitching forward while lifting the body, and the person in the bucket had to avoid straining his or her back muscles while leaning toward the slope to pull the body in. These difficulties reminded me of the struggle of the Rwandan soldiers to retrieve the bodies of the men they had shot in Lake Kivu: similar means to very different ends. Along with our efforts came the discovery that some of the people in the grave had been shot while their hands were tied behind their backs. It wasn't until we started to analyze the bodies at the morgue that we learned more about the circumstances of their deaths. There were many echoes of Stefan's phrase in Kibuye: "I mean, Jesus."

Meanwhile, international journalists arrived at the grave site every morning shortly after we did, and stayed almost all day. They congregated behind a perimeter line of crime scene tape close to the edge of the grave at which Jose and I were working. Every day, Bill gave them briefings or chatted with them, but he made it clear to the rest of the team that we were not to talk to the media. The instruction was intoned in such a way that we actually felt rather antagonistic toward the reporters, a stance I now regret, particularly as a journalist, David Rhode, had been responsible for finding some of the first evidence of massacres in the Srebrenica area. It was a find that came at some cost to his own safety, for he was detained for more than a week by the Bosnian Serb police. In a way, the journalists were standing sentry over one of their stories.

AFTER WE EXHUMED all the bodies from Cerska, the media preceded us to our next site, Nova Kasaba. They were already camped out by the road, satellite phones at the ready, when we arrived in convoy on July 22. We finally had some workers—Bosnian Serbs from out of town who were braving the wrath of local people to work for us. They arrived wearing their own coveralls but with no food or water. Some of them rode in our vehicles while others slotted into the convoy in their own car, which looked even smaller next to the Humvees than we did in our four-wheel drives.

Our convoy had another new addition, the Wolf. It was a long, multi-wheeled vehicle with a snouty nose and tiny rectangular portholes of thick glass high up on the sides. Its only door opened at the back, and the bottom was V-shaped with the point going down toward the ground, designed to deflect the force of the blast if you drove over a mine. Our particular Wolf had come from South Africa, where police had used it to drive through townships during the violence of apartheid days. Now it was painted UN white and had tags stuck on its sides that read "Physicians for Human Rights." We were going to use it to transport and secure equipment. The contradiction between the Wolf's past use and its current use was not lost on us. David offered to drive it and immediately lost half his weight in water from sweating so much in its bulletproof interior. But its bulk did provide shade and we began a tradition of eating lunch underneath it.

At Nova Kasaba, we were confronted with a large, grassy area between an abandoned building and a small river bordered by trees, so we had to determine which portion of the field to trench first. Fortunately, we were able to consult satellite images of the local topography, made in 1995, to identify areas where earth might have been moved during the war. In areas of conflict, disturbed earth on a scale visible from the air or a satellite can be an indication of a mass grave, but it is not always a sinister sign. At Nova Kasaba, however, these images had weight because they came in combination with the testimony of survivors.

We were soon clearing the vegetation from on top of the first probable grave, trenching it to determine the edges, and then digging some test pits in the other probable grave areas. We found two more graves, one quite near to the first and the other on the far side of some trees, accessible by walking out to the road.

At the edge of the field closest to the road, Bill created another "media line" with some crime scene tape. It seemed rather far from the site, compared with the setup at Cerska. Bill also had Cosme park the Wolf directly in the journalists' line of sight. I didn't know why he was making their lives more difficult, when he appeared to be on such good terms with them. However, they soon found a way around the restriction. I smiled to myself as I saw some photographers climb up into the second-story ruins of a nearby house, attach massive lenses to their cameras, and take up residence for the day. Seeing us make progress, they kept asking Bill to allow them to come closer. He finally agreed to give them a brief tour of one grave, but first he wanted that grave to be fully cleaned so that the clothing and bodies would be visible in the journalists' black-and-white photographs. Fernando and David had been working alone on this grave, so I joined them to help finish cleaning it and "pedestaling" the bodies so they were supported, but not surrounded, by earth.

Fernando and David work quietly, as do I, and the only thing we talked about as we cleaned was whether the men in the grave might have been made to climb into the hole while still alive. Some of them were on their knees, having fallen face forward when shot by a high-velocity weapon. Their hands were tied behind their backs. If they had been shot while on the edge of the grave and then fallen in or been thrown in, we would have expected the bodies to be more extended. The preservation of the men's remains was quite good because they were in a deeper grave; there were remnants of faces, and facial and head hair was present.

It was at times like these, when media or other visitors were coming to a site, that we had the rare opportunity to linger over the bodies and take in more fully the import of the grave. Detail-cleaning the bodies in the Nova Kasaba grave reminded me of cleaning the head of the woman with the pink plastic necklaces in the grave at Kibuye, the woman I'd bent over while Bill briefed Madeleine Albright. I would think about the Albright visit again, later in Kosovo, as I leaned over the body of a boy whose trouser pockets had spilled marbles onto the floor of his single grave while I waited for members of the UN Interim Administration Council to arrive for a site tour.

Cleaning the grave at Nova Kasaba afforded me another link to Rwanda: there, seeing similar trauma on opposite sides of the country made it seem as if bodies lurked on all the hills between. Now at Nova Kasaba, I sensed that ubiquity again: we were perhaps a fifteen-minute drive from Cerska, and the setting was very different—not a hill but a flat field, not an opportunistic grave but an excavated one, not down a tiny dirt track but just off a major road. Yet the bodies could have been the same: again, their hands had been tied behind their backs; again, they were all males; again, there was a range of ages; again, they were wearing civilian clothes. I knew there were thousands of men missing from Srebrenica—we had only uncovered about two hundred by then. Just as in Rwanda, I sensed them in other fields, up other dirt tracks, an entire community—albeit just males—of dead all around us.

I felt anger toward people who deem murder an acceptable political policy. I felt the last of my naïveté drain away as I uncovered more and more people shot while their hands were tied. And I felt two kinds of duty: one to the bodies—to identify them and allow them to incriminate their killers; the other to their relatives—to help return the remains to them.

WE CONTINUED WORKING at Nova Kasaba for about a week, during which tensions around us increased: first, at the site, IFOR located a Claymore antipersonnel mine in their parking area across the street from us. They were going to detonate it, so would we please get into our equipment container and sit tight? We gathered ourselves up and got into the container, except for John, who, I wrote in my journal, "is too cool for that and stands just outside the door smoking a cigarette, and Bill, who must always be cooler than John." Although we were expecting it, the detonation blast was huge, rocking the container and seeming to resonate out into all of Bosnia. We heard later from our favorite IFOR officer, Captain Boswell, that the blast frightened a horse, which was pulling a cart with an old man on it; the horse upended the cart, putting the old man in a ditch, and then bolted and jumped over a cow, which also began to charge around wildly. IFOR medics tended to the old man. The blast gave us a reality check concerning mines: a Claymore, designed to take out a football field's worth of people via a spray of metal projectiles, won't just maim you; it will kill you. Even John missed a puff on his cigarette. Just.

Then, in the middle of the night, our container village at Camp Lisa had to evacuate and we sat for hours in the gymnasium tent. We heard lots of helicopters and shouting before we were finally allowed to go back to bed at three in the morning. We found out the next day that a soldier a few doors up from ours had locked and loaded, meaning he had put live ammunition into his various guns, and then threatened to shoot his immediate superior. Later, he revised that threat to include anyone who came near him. He had just come in from several days of disarmament patrol and his superior had told him to wash his Humvee. This was a big job, he was already exhausted, and he lost control. He was eventually subdued and evacuated from Camp Lisa. The last we heard, he was sitting in a U.S. Army base in Germany, waiting to be court-martialed.

On top of these strains, the men on our team had now been living for a month in a sweltering tent with no privacy. They'd strung up towels between their cots, but that didn't help. When Jose Pablo was there, he burned insect repellent coils so large that you couldn't even see him within the plume of smoke, which drifted into all the neighboring cot areas. The men's tent became more crowded with the arrival of a new security contingent: six French mercenaries and their Alsatian, Ben. I described them to my parents as "very Van Dammage" (our family nickname for the action star Jean-Claude Van Damme) because some were tall and built like tanks. Others were small and well muscled and they all spoke just a little English. The UN had supplied them with two armored Land Rovers. I discovered the following year that although the vehicles could withstand bullets, the doors didn't have locks—*this* was classic UN.

Along with the security came the pathologists. This created a time crunch because the morgue, located outside Tuzla, was not ready. It was decided that Jose Pablo would travel to Tuzla with the pathologists and logisticians to help set up the morgue. Bill asked him who he'd like to take from the field to work with him, and Jose Pablo told me that when he replied, "I'd like to have Clea," Bill responded, "Well, you can't have her." Jose Pablo described this as Bill creating "an illusion of choice." At lunchtime under the Wolf, Bill told me that, of the anthropologists he had in the field, I'd be the first he'd send to the morgue to get it running as he wanted, but I was also the last person he wanted to send out of the field.

Becky then chimed in that she refused to suffer the double loss of Jose Pablo *and* me, so that day I wondered whether I was, perhaps, more than "just a worker."

The day after finishing the exhumation at Nova Kasaba and sending the bodies up to the morgue in the refrigerated container, we learned that the deminers would not be able to clear our next site quickly enough. John boasted that he could demine the site by driving over it in the Wolf. As I suspected, Physicians for Human Rights wouldn't hear of such behavior, even if it appealed to some people. So we spent a while at Camp Lisa doing make-work: cleaning the vehicles and equipment, getting spare tires repaired, and so on. I worked with Bill in his container, sorting the slides from the Kigali mission and writing the final Kigali report. It was odd to be working on this while on another mission. While Bill went to various high-level meetings, he left me with his audiotapes from the excavation at the Cerska grave; I was to transcribe his field notes and enter the case information into our database. The notes were fine until Bill got a cold, then they became mostly snorting, mucusy noises and strange descriptions of clothing. In between these were diarylike comments about being in the convoy at dusk when they transported the Cerska bodies up to the Tuzla morgue—watching the lights of the refrigerated truck in the night. I felt as though I was privy to Bill's innermost thoughts; if we ever had a chance to just relax and talk, I thought we would enjoy the conversation—as in Kibuye when we had exhumed the baby together.

Bill's container became a congregating spot for the team while we were stuck on the base and one evening he held a party of sorts for us, commending us on our progress with the exhumations. Later that night, Bill returned from a telephone call that informed him that demining wouldn't be complete for another *three* weeks, so he had decided that the field team would have a holiday on the Adriatic coast for three days. "Be ready at eight A.M.," he said, and sent us off to bed.

I WAS EXCITED the next morning because I looked forward to seeing more of the country than its scenes of crime. Even though Bill was driving, it felt good to be out on a trip and we were filled with the buoyancy that marked all proper downtime with Bill. Outside the grave his desire to try anything was charming, the restlessness that seemed to mark his waking hours was amusing, and when he slept—a kind of catatonic process that sometimes took him unawares during the day—I observed him with a great deal of fondness. Since the Kibuye mission, he had been avuncular toward me, at least when he wasn't being a teasing critic.

The only difficulty we had on this holiday had already become a running joke among the whole team: Bill's driving. He drove so fast there was no question that if his Land Rover had been equipped with a CarLog, it would have been beeping. Becky and I were in the backseat, with no seat belts, and at every one of the sharp curves in the mountain roads, we slid around the seat so much we were on top of each other for most of the ride, prompting Dorothy to joke that Becky and I were "*really* getting to know each other." It was one of the few times I laughed about Bill's driving.

We arrived at the coastal town of Split at nightfall, and ate excellent pizza at a small restaurant on a square by the water, with disco music and young people converging from all sides. There were several mishaps looking for a hotel, given that we had no map and few language skills to read the tourist signs. After driving the wrong way down one-way streets and cobbled roads, and doing lots of backing up and many ten-point turns, we finally found accommodation at a waterfront hotel. Dorothy and I shared a room; although our balcony overlooked an adjacent apartment building, we were so tired that we didn't care. The bathroom reminded me of the one in Kigali, with identical green tiles on floor, walls, and tub, giving the impression of a glossy grotto. This time I didn't inspect the grouting for blood splatter.

The next morning, Bill rushed us through breakfast because he had decided we should take the early ferry to the island of Brač. It was a clear and sunny day and we sat next to one another on the top deck, sunbathing fully clothed like the odd little family we were, the patriarch wearing his stinky gravedigging hat. During the ride, Bill somehow picked up two local girls who offered to show us "the best beaches in the Adriatic." On land, the girls directed us with competence to the town of Bol: we traversed the top of the dry, rocky island before descending a winding cliffside road to the spectacularly blue water.

At the Hotel Elaphusa, Becky, Dorothy, and I shared a hot room with a balcony, several floors up. We could just see the ocean past the pine trees, so we went in search of the beach. But by the time we climbed down the cliff to get there, all we had the energy to do was fall asleep. By our third and last morning on holiday, I was refreshed; up early and sitting on our hotel balcony in a nice breeze, listening to morning noises starting up: seagulls, breakfast preparation, only a few voices from below. I regretted that I hadn't been able to fully enjoy the beach: it was rocky and crowded, and it didn't feel like a beach, like being on the edge of a continent, because the neighboring island seemed so close. I also hadn't expected the beach to be topless; I didn't want to run into my male teammates, because I had already seen them, jaws dropping, stumbling on the rocks as they checked out the women—taking the pain with the pleasure, I supposed. I don't know whether I was more embarrassed or annoyed by their behavior.

The town of Bol, though, was one of the most picturesque places I'd ever been: old stone buildings fronting the water, dark green shuttered windows on houses with iron balconies; at night, when the shutters were open, I could see through the lace curtains to the whitewashed walls and varnished wood ceilings of rooms glowing in an inviting light, people out on their balconies having dinner with their dogs, enjoying the perfectly temperate air. One night, the moon had risen full, with Venus as its companion, and on the island across the way, I could make out the occasional pair of Durrell's "blond headlights"—the island surreal out there across the water, looming and dark with one small cluster of lights at the water's edge. I enjoyed seeing how, even at 10:30 at night, people in Bol walked on the stone promenade.

So on this last morning, I had a strong desire to take a walk by myself along the beach. I had come to realize that people on the team didn't do enough alone anymore: we not only lived with each other in the same rooms, but we ate together and relaxed together. I walked until I was a good distance away from the hotels, then climbed down the rocks to the water and took a photograph of myself using the timer, the Adriatic coast stretching behind me. At the time, I thought I looked independent, but when I saw the photograph again a few years ago, I found I just looked miserable.

BILL HAD PROMISED we would drive at a "reasonable" pace to Mostar and Sarajevo, staying in Sarajevo for one night perhaps, then head for Tuzla to see what the morgue situation was and how the demining was going. We didn't spend the night in Sarajevo in the end, just drove through Sniper Alley, past the Baščaršija (the cobbled-road Old Town), IFOR headquarters, and the old, shelled library. We met John there and ate dinner at a fish restaurant he knew by the river, near a bombed-out bridge. Then we drove straight on to Tuzla in the rain. I was in Bill's car, sitting behind him. It was pitch-dark out and we rarely passed any other vehicles: it was just our headlights picking out shelled tarmac and temporary army bridges. I started talking to Bill just to keep him awake, because everyone else in the car had fallen asleep. We ended up having a good conversation about his work, where he'd be next, these missions and what they needed to be successful. His driving even seemed to be less frenetic.

Once in Tuzla, we checked into the Bristol hotel, where Jose Pablo had been living, subletting a room from a Reuters journalist who was out of town. It was cozy and lived-in, with lots of electronic equipment around. The next day, Bill moved us into a house rented by PHR for the people already working at the morgue. There weren't actually any spare bedrooms, but since we only expected to be there while we waited for the next site to be demined, the men slept on settees in the dining room while the women slept on the floor of the living room upstairs. During the day, we worked on ancillary jobs at the morgue, trying not to get the team there dependent on the extra help. But then three things happened in quick succession. First, the demining was postponed indefinitely, so I was fully integrated into the morgue as an anthropologist, taking on casework. Second, the demining suddenly went ahead at the same moment Bill had to go to Scotland for two weeks. Thus the third thing: Jose Pablo took over the field team, and I was put in his spot at the morgue.

12.

THE MORGUE

THE MORGUE WAS ACTUALLY IN KALESIJA, A SHORT DRIVE FROM Tuzla. It was set up in a bombed ex–garment factory with shell splashes in the concrete outside and bullet holes in the exterior and interior of the building; there were fewer windows than window frames, but the damage allowed in a breeze, which whistled among the old abandoned accoutrements. There were also heavy-duty steam irons, hangers on an industrial-sized runner system, and a kitchen area. There was no running water, but Geoff had trucked in water and set up prefabricated showers and toilets in one large container outside the building. The old factory bathrooms were our makeshift changing rooms; there were no doors, so there was a lot of yelling of "Clear!" in the mornings as the men had to pass the women's doorway.

My first day at the morgue without Jose Pablo was one of those times when you just take a deep breath and walk into a maze of other people's emotions. In the time I'd been helping out at the morgue, I'd already gathered that the team had had little or no time off since they'd started work, three people had had some sort of breakdown involving crying and screaming, and one person had left the mission altogether. On one of my days as a temporary assistant, I was outside cleaning some bones when I heard a long, exasperated scream. I couldn't work out where it came from; later, I found out it was from inside the morgue, but I never learned who screamed or why. The stress was palpable. Bob Kirschner, our chief pathologist from Rwanda, who was also chief pathologist here, had raised his voice a number of times in the week I had been there, and *that* was unusual.

I didn't want to open up a can of worms by asking what had been going on. Apart from Peter "the Great Dane" Knudsen, the autopsy technician who had worked with us at Kibuye, and Juerena "JR" Hoffman, a Texan who had preceded me as a student of Walt Birkby's at the University of Arizona, I didn't know the morgue team. They were an international mix of Scottish, American, and Turkish pathologists, British and Swiss autopsy technicians, a Dutch photographer, and mostly American anthropologists. I just hoped things would improve soon; after all, the morgue protocol was straightforward and unvarying, day in and day out.

The bodies yet to be examined were in a refrigerated container, near a set of double doors that led into a hallway of the building. Autopsy technicians would carry into this hallway the day's first cases, all of which would have been next to one another in the grave. The cases were assigned to pathologists and brought in one at a time to the X-ray room, where the body bag was placed on a table. The bag would be unzipped and the contents X-rayed with a fluoroscope. The pathologist and autopsy technician would stand around the table wearing lead vests as the radiographer moved the lens of the fluoroscope over the body; the X-ray images appeared on a TV monitor hooked up to the fluoroscope. Watching the monitor, the pathologist was able to locate projectiles inside the body by using a probe, which, being radiopaque, would show up black on the screen, as would bullets, shrapnel, belt buckles, jewelry, and anything else metallic. Once the probe touched the object, the pathologist would document the location of the projectile, extract it from the body, and submit it to the evidence technician.

Once the body had been "fluoro'd," the body bag was carried across the hall to one of several autopsy stations in the warehouselike main room.

Here, the autopsy technicians removed the clothing, which was then taken outside to be washed with high-pressure hoses. After the clothing was removed and the evidence technician had collected any accompanying artifacts, the pathologist would begin the autopsy while the anthropologist examined and removed the bones of anthropological interest. These, along with the head and any bones that exhibited trauma, were taken outside to be washed and laid out on one of five Anthropology tables. Procedure tended to speed up here for the anthropologists and I described it in the back of my journal as follows:

> Take cranial pieces inside to dry under heat lamps in preparation for reconstruction [bone holds glue better if it's dry], then go back outside to lay out bones in anatomical position, with those exhibiting trauma on one side of the table and nontrauma on the other. Clean pubic symphyseal faces, rib tips, [and] clavicles and age all of these. Get one other anthropologist's reference on the aging and record the information in the Anthro log.
>
> Clean the femur, measure maximum length, and calculate stature estimate.
>
> Then begin cranial reconstruction while sitting indoors at the table with the heat lamp, trying not to burn fingers on the glue accelerant [called Hot Stuff] as it burns the skin, will melt through surgical gloves and will stick anything in its path to your fingers or your thigh, if it drips below the table. As soon as you've reconstructed the head, take a peek at the teeth and try to track down the accompanying path [pathologist].
>
> Take the path outside to the Anthro table and bring the reconstructed head back with you. Start by going over all postcranial trauma, discussing whether it's peri or post [perimortem or postmortem] and what caused it; then move on to cranial trauma. Finally, dictate the dental chart, with #1 being the upper right third molar in this system and #17 being the lower left third molar, indicating for the path whether each tooth is present, its state—sound carious (or as James Grieve, one of the pathologists, pronounces it in his Scottish brogue, "kerries" or "kerious"), amalgam, reconstruction, extraction—or whether it's missing postmortem or absent due to extraction.

Discuss with the path which items from the postcranial they'd like pho-
tographed, then take those elements along with the skull into the morgue to
the photography station and set up those photos along with your own three
Anthro photos of pubes, ribs, and clavicles. Place all elements on the green
background cloth [a surgical gown laid out flat] or the sandbox, in the stan-
dard orientations for the photographer; hold or place the ruler with the case
number next to each element. Also take a dental shot for the families or any
dentists [the success we had in Kigali showing video stills of the smile made
me hopeful for the identification possibilities from these photographs]. Pho-
tograph the head from all sides except base, then remove a premolar or
molar for DNA; bag them and deliver to Evidence station.

Bag the Anthro samples and head together and return all remains to
body bag, with clothing that has since been cleaned, dried, documented by
the pathologist, photographed, videotaped, and rebagged. Then carry the
body bag toward the second refrigerator for eventual load-up inside in piles
of thirty or so. Mark off on the Anthro sheet that all samples have been
taken and all things measured and move on to your next case.

As in Kigali, doing casework was the straightforward part of working in the
morgue. It was dealing with the live people that diminished one's sense of
perspective about the progress we were making. For example, although
morgue procedure was much improved by having an evidence technician
and a computer data-entry administrator, the difficulty remained that we
had only one extension cord to power the heat lamps. The cord was quite
precious because there was no power in the building and all electric equipment ran from the generator that Geoff brought for us. The heat lamps
dried the cranial bones that needed reconstruction and, since almost every
case had gunshot wounds to the head, almost every head had to be dried
under those lamps before the trauma could be observed, drawn, and photographed. But sometimes you went to the heat lamp table and found the
extension cord was gone. As an anthropologist, you're under significant
time pressure to complete your case and provide the head to your associated pathologist before he or she goes on to another case (or two), so you
go off looking for the power cord only to discover your associated patholo-

gist in a back room, using the cord to power her laptop. When you ask her for the cord, she says you can't have it because she's waiting for the head for her case. Hmm. She's waiting for the head, which will never dry and be reconstructed because she is using the cord that powers the lamp that will dry the head. Though this sounds trivial now, it was frustrating because it made you feel like you weren't all part of the same team.

LIFE OUTSIDE THE MORGUE wasn't much better. PHR rented a second house for the burgeoning morgue team but all meals were still consumed in "House 1," where I had moved into a bedroom with JR. A cook, Jadrenka, had been hired to prepare breakfast (usually sautéed eggplant, bread rolls, and fruit) and dinner and to launder our sheets. She was supposed to be paid by whoever ate the meals but no one was designated to collect this money. So on any given day Jadrenka might be going around the house, changing sheets while crying about not having been paid. And, at breakfast, there would only be enough food for those who had paid, even though the rest of the team were tucking into the meal regardless.

So JR and I started to collect meal money and keep lists of who was eating which meal. This helped, but early birds arrived to sit in our dining room by 6:30 A.M., and night owls stayed after dinner and into the wee hours. We, the actual occupants of House 1, had no privacy and found our accommodation treated like a hostel–hotel–party center. In addition, when Bill (who was actually being paid to do this work) blew into town from Scotland or Croatia or the field, he slept on our dining room settee instead of going to a hotel, so often you would be roped into logistics conversations at very odd hours, Bill always being on while the rest of us were exhausted.

Days off came rarely and unexpectedly, so you had little to look forward to. One time when I did manage a midafternoon nap, I was woken by automatic gunfire just outside the window. I rolled off the bed onto the floor and listened for signs as to the danger level. I could hear people shouting as if they were having fun, so I got on my knees and peered out the window to see what appeared to be a wedding party in the backyard across the way.

A man—the groom, perhaps—was shooting an AK-47 assault rifle toward the sky while the rest of the party clapped. After he was done shooting, children ran among the grass looking for something, I presume shell casings. It was hard to reconcile this happy scene with what I saw in my mind's eye when I was woken by the gunfire: the killing of the men in Lake Kivu, as usual. It took some time to relax after that.

The best days off were when a group of us would go over to the house rented by several of the NPA deminers. They lived on the outskirts of Tuzla in a place that could have doubled as an Italian or Swiss chalet, though bordered by tall cornfields on each side. They let us do laundry in their washing machine, took us to the pizzeria where they knew the locals by name and learned bits of Bosnian, and showed us how they trained their demining dogs on buried charges of TNT.

Meanwhile, back at PHR House 1, I had become one of the team drivers: I herded people up from the breakfast table and out to our rickety UN minivan with its gearshift on the steering column and squeaking foamless seats, did a head count, and then drove more or less hell-for-leather around potholes out to the morgue in Kalesija. At the end of the day, I drove my carload back home again before sundown. It didn't take long for me to start feeling responsible for people, especially as Bill and Bob both left the mission at the same time to attend to commitments in other parts of Europe. And because JR and I had been sorting out the team's meals, we somehow became the first people to brief the frequent newly arriving team members on life in Tuzla: when the water actually came out of the taps (from five A.M. to seven A.M. and again at four P.M., for an hour if you were lucky and you were home), where to use a phone to call home (the post office in town), and why it's easier to keep your UN ID tag tucked inside your shirt when you walk around town (it just is). The difficulty was that some other people on the team came to *expect* JR and me to do all of this, so even when I wanted to just lie down after work, some pathologist without a UN driver's license would come running upstairs to say, "We saw some of our people at the bus stop. You'd better get over there to pick them up!"

On August 11 I wrote in a letter to my family: "I've been better, but I've also been worse. Feel out of touch, homesick, and cynical about too many things." By the end of August, I was writing in my journal that I had lost track of who I used to be, because I could barely remember the things I used to like and even when I did remember them I couldn't remember why I liked them. I particularly missed one close friend, Michelle Chase, who I thought of as one of my "reflectors." I'd barely spoken to Michelle on the telephone in eight months. Even when I did make it to a phone box to call home, I would burst into tears just at the sound of my brother saying hello. I was unable to explain why.

Around this time, our project coordinator, Andrew Thomson, approached me and said, "You know, Clea, if you ever need some time off, just say the word and we can arrange for you to go to the Croatian coast for two or three days. We need you to be strong—you're part of our core team." I don't know whether he had heard that I had been feeling stressed, but I was too macho to admit anything; I just replied that I appreciated the consideration and drove back to the morgue.

I attributed my general fatigue to the problem of not having enough time alone. In my journal, I even tallied the number of hours I had been alone since arriving in Tuzla, because there were so few of them and most of them involved being in the loo. When I did have a moment to write a proper journal entry, I could barely find the "mind space" to write, because I was so occupied by team issues—mostly logistics. There was no time to be contemplative. I knew that, despite the importance of the work we were doing, a toll would be exacted by this life. I didn't know what kind of toll, or when it would happen, or how long I would last.

13

DOUBLE VISION

WHILE I HAD FOCUSED ON LACK OF TIME ALONE, I HADN'T AC-
counted for the unusual situation I was in: the previous month, I had exhumed bodies from a hillside and now I was handling those bodies daily in
a morgue just over thirty kilometers from the town where most of their internally displaced relatives were probably living. I had seen some of these
relatives on the local Bosnian television news: they called themselves the
Women of Srebrenica, and they were calling for investigation into the
whereabouts of their loved ones. They met in public places, holding signs
and photographs of their men, wailing and crying, and also voicing their
need to hold even just one bone if that was all that was left.

The Women of Srebrenica practically came into our living room too,
when Laurie Vollen called a meeting at House 1 with the morgue team.
Laurie's work on the antemortem database had progressed. She now had a
cache of computers and an international (though mostly Bosnian) staff,
who interviewed family members and entered data on missing persons.
Some also tracked down far-flung relatives. The latter were known as "trac-
ers," a term that, it seemed to me, emphasized the gravity of their under-
taking, especially in concert with their grim expressions as they drove away

from the office, maps open on the seat next to them. Laurie had also started talking to the Srebrenica women and had recognized that they possessed a particularly valuable capability for identification, more valuable than the photographs they had of their missing men: their memories of their own sewing.

You see, because the inhabitants of Srebrenica had lived under siege for several years, they didn't have access to new clothes, so the women had repaired the same garments, month after month. Thus, they could recognize their own stitches, could describe the type of mending they did and what material they used, and remembered exactly what part they had mended. In the morgue we found that where, say, head hair was no longer present on a body, a triangular fabric patch was still holding together the inside of a trouser pocket, the color of the thread still vibrant, a beacon illuminating the varied stitchwork that could identify the man whose trousers they were. With this evidence, in combination with the anthropological analysis of the body wearing the trousers, an identification might be made. As in Rwanda, clothing on its own could only be the basis of a presumptive identification (it is only worn on the body, not intrinsic to the body), but the particular conditions of war and deprivation in Srebrenica imbued the clothing with greater significance.

I think my acute awareness of the Women of Srebrenica triggered the double vision I had first experienced in Rwanda when I saw the priest's niece. I realized that the bodies belonged only temporarily to the Tribunal (as evidence of crimes against humanity), while they fundamentally belonged to surviving relatives. In Rwanda, the double vision made me want to give remains back to relatives, regardless of protocol about bodies as Tribunal evidence. I even wanted to give the relatives just a bit of clothing, because their loss seemed so complete and was palpable to me. Six months later, on August 20, that feeling of empathetic loss overwhelmed me.

I was at the morgue in Kalesija, preparing the outdoor anthropology stations for the first cases of the day. My teammate Mike Warren was washing the bones from James's case, CSK-10__, which I would be analyzing. Mike called me over to look at a bullet still lodged in the femur. My initial reaction was "Neat," because the bullet had entered the femur while tumbling, had flipped around, and now was lodged in the bone with its nose toward the entrance wound (obviously, there was no exit wound). I took the femur from Mike and kept looking at it. Then Mike brought over the first bucket of washed bones. While I was laying them on the table in anatomical position, I noticed that the iliac crest on the hip bone was not completely fused, indicating the person was under twenty-one years or so. Then I noticed that the humeral head and ischial tuberosity were just fusing, putting his age even lower, around sixteen to eighteen.

As I almost subconsciously noticed all this, an image came into my mind: I "saw" this young guy, there at Cerska, on the hillside where we had just been digging, and I "felt" the pain of the bullet entering his thigh just above the knee; I could sense his youth and the tragedy of it all and I thought of his family and what they were missing, and I thought of what one of the Women had said—how someone had told her they last saw her son getting on a bus with lots of other men and he was crying—and how that was the last she ever heard about him . . . and I lost an element of self-control. I felt so awful, so full of hurt and emotion, and mixed in with that was a knee-buckling sense of privilege that I was touching the bones of someone whose family was out there and wanted more than anything to have him back, no matter what condition he was in, and yet I was the only one holding him. I felt I was betraying him, or his mother; I couldn't work out which.

Holding myself together with great effort, I trotted inside the morgue, to look for Molly Ryan, a teammate who'd become a friend. She was entering data at her computer station, but took one look at me and walked me out of the morgue, around the back of the building, away from everyone. The local men Geoff had hired to wash the clothes from the bodies must have noticed my change in expression because they stopped working altogether. Molly held me and kept me walking, letting me talk but also telling me this was normal: I was processing our work as I should be. She told me how she herself had broken down just from entering the words "bullet, left maxilla," and "homicide" into the computer hundreds of times a day.

By the time we had circumnavigated the building, which took about seven minutes, I was prepared to go back to work, but all day I felt as though I were under water, struggling against a strong current, looking out at other people who were walking around unimpeded by the overwhelming force of the water. Kamble, our backhoe driver—a witty, multilingual Indian I became good friends with—had seen me with Molly and he had rushed up then, very concerned and wanting to know what was wrong, but Molly had kept him away until I was composed. Now he came up again and asked me what it had been. I just said that the young age of a particular body had taken me by surprise and that I felt bad for him and for everyone in the world. Kamble looked at me, his eyebrows raised in concern, and then he said, "You know, you really *feel* what you are doing. You are a real good girl. Really." But I didn't feel like a good girl. I felt sick, sick that I had had this happen—that while I was working, something slipped through whatever it is that allows me to work with dead bodies without feeling tragedy *as* I work.

ALTHOUGH MY LOSS of professional distance only lasted about ten minutes, the experience shocked me. I had become a forensic anthropologist for two reasons: one was that making bones talk was what I most wanted to do; the other was that the first time I was faced with a dead body for anthropological analysis, I felt many emotions, but not distress. When I analyze human remains I am interested, not repulsed. Trauma excites a curiosity in me about what instrument caused it; it does not frighten me. Even maggots—while not my favorite life form—on a dead body are meaningful to me despite my limited knowledge of forensic entomology. (This is the science of making the bugs "talk" about how much time has elapsed since death and about the body's location.) Not being upset by bones, bodies, and trauma is a basic requirement of the job. When working in the field, I am distressed by fruitless digging, but once we unearth human remains, I am energized and even happy. I had thought those positive feelings came naturally; I had not been aware of actively wrapping my mind in a cloak of distance before analyzing human remains or exhuming bodies from mass graves. I had sometimes been distressed after work by ruminating on issues of pain or fear or whatever marked someone's last moments before I met him or her as a dead body. But to have issues of life intrude on my thoughts so painfully while I was actually working worried me deeply.

The double vision that caused me to look at a skeleton as the missing relative of a person I might pass on the street was dangerous: it would challenge my stamina for the work we had to do, especially if it dropped in front of my eyes like a veil at any time. I knew my distress was peculiar to forensic anthropologists doing the volume of casework I was doing *and* exhuming at the scenes of the mass murders that resulted in the casework. It was the combination of these factors that led me to feel the bones were almost shouting at me, and it was the stress-based fatigue I was working under that made this shouting so painful.

Perhaps because I didn't want to think about the implications of that intrusion, I decided that I was simply tired; I didn't need to make massive generalizations about my capability for the job. I worked like an automaton in the morgue for the next couple of days, but I could feel myself reaching the breaking point in fatigue. Then Bill called the PHR house from Scotland for his usual check-in with me about which anthropologists to move from the field to the morgue. He seemed to know about the stress I was feeling: he said, "I need to get you out of there; how would you like to go to Vukovar on Tuesday?" Just thinking about the possibility invigorated me.

The last time Bill had asked me if I wanted to go to Croatia was when we were in Kibuye. The site was a mass grave in Ovčara, which the UN and PHR had attempted to investigate in 1992 and 1993 before being run out by local authorities. That site, now under heavy UN military protection, was ready to be investigated, and several of the team members from 1992 were on standby to fly out there now.

When Bill arrived back in Bosnia—the day we finished analyzing the bodies from Cerska—he saw me at the PHR house and said, "Why don't you take tomorrow off and we'll go to Vukovar on Wednesday?" I said, "Great," and went to bed, noticing that I had a massive stomachache but too tired to do anything about it, figuring I would sleep it off.

The next morning I woke up early—very early, especially for a day off when we could sleep in—and had to run to the bathroom in order to vomit. Fortunately, the water was running so I was able to clean up after myself (a good thing when one is vomiting all morning in a house with only one bathroom for six people). The bathroom was occupied for forty-five minutes straight at one point, causing me to scramble around to find something to vomit into without waking JR. By midmorning, I was feverish, clutching my stomach, suffering chills, aches, and cramps. JR, worried, wanted to get me driven to a hospital but apparently Bob had reiterated vehemently that the PHR cars were not for "personal use." He was still angry because most of the morgue team had piled into a van that morning to go to Sarajevo for their day off. Echoes of Kibuye, when Roxana did not get a helicopter ride to Kigali even though she had malaria.

So that day I just lay in bed, getting hotter and hotter. I felt as if I were burning up by seven P.M. Bill took my temperature with the back of his hand, and Bob "examined" me and decided there was no need for me to go to the hospital. If I insisted, Bob said, I could go, but he wouldn't take me, and Bill couldn't because he was going to dinner with some journalists. Fortunately, Jimmy, one of the Swedish NPA deminers, was there, with his own vehicle, and he and JR carried me down the stairs. The rest of the team was having dinner and someone called out, "She's not smiling! It's a first—she must really be sick!" Bob quickly said, in his best there's-nothing-to-see-here voice, "She's fine, she's fine, not sick at all," and stood in the doorway to block their view of us.

Jimmy tried to drive carefully to the Norwegian hospital but every pothole and railroad track bumped the car: my whole abdomen was in pain. After a short wait, I was seen by a Norwegian doctor, whose diagnosis was: It's a fever, could be flu, could be malaria; take the water supplement, don't worry about eating, and take three days to convalesce.

That sickness saved me. I spent two days in bed; people who cared about me visited—Jose Pablo, Dorothy, and Shuala Martin, who had briefly been in the morgue with us, even drove up from the field. When I felt well enough, I wrote in my journal. In those two days, I reaffirmed to myself that what I wanted more than anything else was to complete this mission.

When I felt stronger, I worked three days in the morgue before Bill and I left for Croatia. The day I resurfaced, the work was going slowly because we were moving on to the analysis of the Nova Kasaba bodies and the order of autopsies had to be decided. Once we had done that, we were ready to get into a routine again but then a film crew arrived from the American television news series *Nightline*. They filmed Bob conducting autopsies, which meant that we had to wait to bring out more bodies. It took a while. It had to, because Bob had none of the help he had in "reality"— no autopsy assistant removing clothing, no evidence technician bagging bullets, no anthropologist disarticulating the head. In between these staged situations, Bob kept going off to smooth his bits of hair.

On my last evening at the PHR house, Jadrenka was crying again. I presumed she was worried about how she would get paid on time now that Jose Pablo was also sending JR to the field, and despite our efforts neither Bill nor Bob even knew who Jadrenka was or how the payment system worked. The team then held a good-bye dinner for three of us who were leaving Tuzla. We ate at Bill's favorite restaurant and the evening was the highlight of the week. I remember talking with Geoff about how many good-bye dinners we'd had on different continents as other teammates left when we stayed on, and laughing about when I'd left Kigali and he'd said, "Since I'll be seeing you in a few days in Bosnia, does that mean I don't get a hug?" This evening wrapped up with toasts for those leaving.

My teammates used my toast to tell me how much better I had made their stay in Tuzla, how my smile could brighten the absolute worst day, and how I was the best driver on the team. The sentiments were silly but warm. Most important, my teammates made me feel I had made a difference in their lives on the mission. It was some time before I realized that I had become almost entirely focused on people management while simultaneously becoming much less aware of our forensic work and its potential impact on the community in which we were working. The mission I was about to embark on in Croatia would swiftly tip the pendulum the other way.

PART FOUR

—

CROATIA

August 30–September 30, 1996

*The town of Vukovar is in the region of Croatia known as east-
ern Slavonia, bordering the river Danube and Serbia. A seven-
month war ensued after Croatia declared its independence from
Yugoslavia, during which Vukovar sustained some of the heavi-
est bombardment. For three successive months, Yugoslav People's
Army forces shelled Vukovar from the Danube; the town's inhabitants hid in basements while some Croatian national guards-
men and irregulars defended the town. As in the area of Bosnia
around Srebrenica, the fighting over Vukovar and surrounds was
intense for territorial reasons: Serbia needed to control the territory of eastern Slavonia in order to pass through western Slavonia and reach the Posavina Corridor. Once the corridor was
under Serb control, the majority Serb population in the western
Krajina would be connected with "Mother Serbia," to the east.
These strategic, and therefore highly disputed, regions became
United Nations Protected Areas (UNPA) in 1992. A cease-fire
and the UNPAs contributed to relative calm in Croatia until
1995, when Croatian troops swept first through western Slavonia and then through the Krajina, forcing the migration of tens
of thousands of Croatian Serbs, who mostly fled east, toward
Serbia.*

14

SEEKERS OF THE LIVING

I WENT TO VUKOVAR BY CAR, IN A WHITE UN LAND CRUISER, my duffel bag slung in the back. Bill Haglund was driving and Clint Williamson, the Tribunal prosecutor for the case we would be working on, was in the passenger seat. For almost all of the drive up from Tuzla, Clint had been talking fluently about the siege of Vukovar and the genesis of the eastern Slavonian region. I sat in the back of the car feeling as though I were in an interactive history lesson. Clint spoke of the railroad crossing where the war in Croatia is agreed by most to have started (with the killing of several police officers) and then *ka-dunk, ka-dunk,* we crossed those very tracks ourselves. I scanned the broken tarmac of the road but couldn't see clear signs that a war had begun in just that spot. Nevertheless, my view of the region was sealed: I saw it as a place frozen in time.

When I looked out of the car windows that first afternoon, I thought that perception was confirmed: it was five years since Vukovar had surrendered to the Yugoslav People's Army (JNA), yet the Borovo boot factory still sat abandoned, bombed and bleak; every other house had been shelled to its foundation; the pink train station with its baroque architectural touches was still scorched, and the white walls of the massive Communist-

era apartment blocks still wore dark wounds from mortars. These buildings looked like a medieval castle that has sustained the cannonades of an
attacking army, except for the places where the mortars had laced the walls
in a multitude of little holes tripping across to a very big hole. Once you
looked closely, you saw that the big hole was the entire living room wall,
gone. Seeing the destruction through the car window that first afternoon, I
didn't think anyone could be living in those apartments or in the one- and
two-story houses that lined the streets, because beyond the large-scale destruction of shelling, they had also been peppered by bullets; their front
gates were rusty and the pavements crushed by tank treads.

But eventually I looked beyond the rusty gates and noticed signs of life:
sections of front yards planted in neat rows of cabbage, a few flowers with
no weeds visible among them, a large ginger-colored teddy bear hanging
by its ears on the clothesline to dry after being washed. People had to be living there, but in the back. And people were living in those strafed apartments, too. Clint pointed out the signs to me: I could just make out
clotheslines on some balconies, and plastic sheeting over gaping windows.
When we drove past at night, I couldn't see any people around the apartments and there were barely any lights visible: there was no electricity for
them, no heat, despite winter's advance. Why? Because many residents
were not from this town. They were refugees: Serbs, "cleansed" out of
northern Bosnia or the Krajina in Croatia, forced to leave behind their
dead, forced to live, one step up from squatting, in the apartments of the
Croats who themselves had been "cleansed" from this town. A huge real es-
tate swap, desired by none of them; they would all rather have had their
own houses, yards, gates, roofs.

Property and ownership—these are material realities that are important
to living people and to their descendants. When I later met up with Barbara
Davis, a close friend of my family's who was coincidentally living in Vukovar while working for the Organization for Security and Co-operation in
Europe, she told me a story that was all about the material effect of phe-
nomena like ethnic cleansing. Barbara was renting a house from an older
woman in town. One wall of the house was finished half in one kind of
brick and half in another, the latter joined by fresh-looking mortar. The

owner saw Barbara notice the recent home improvement and rushed to explain. She said that she had been able to finish the wall only by taking bricks from her neighbors' destroyed house—they were Croats, "cleansed" into who knows where, maybe a grave, maybe Zagreb, but anyway, they weren't coming back, it seemed, and so she was using their bricks. She was ashamed but also defiant.

This wasn't about politics or beliefs; it was about opportunism, about making a home for yourself when you're already a pensioner and the world is going crazy around you. At least the old woman had a house to fix; I wondered how her house was still standing after November 1991. Did she tell the victorious JNA troops that her house was Serb-owned? Did she talk to the people who shot mortars into her neighbors' house and set it on fire? Did she help her neighbors leave safely? What did she know and what did she think now?

Two years after this mission, when the UN turned the eastern Slavonian region over to Croatia, I wondered what would happen when the Croats who had been forced to leave—the old lady's neighbors—came back. Would they argue over the bricks? Would she apologize? Would there be no overt comment, just understanding between people who have lived through the same war? To destroy a house is symbolic, especially in places like Croatia and Bosnia, where many people build their houses themselves, enlisting the aid of relatives or neighbors with skills in bricklaying or concrete and returning the favors later. The houses are usually built over a period of years, one complete floor at a time, while the family saves the money to build the next floor. Most neighborhoods have a fair number of houses with completed first and second floors, but maybe only the outer walls and roof of the third. To destroy what people have spent decades building, maybe even a lifetime, with the help of neighbors, and then to leave the neighbor's house standing, is a particular type of cruelty. The moment of destruction is intended to demoralize the owners and their families by sending a clear message: we undo your house, we erase your mark on the land. Don't come back, because you haven't enough lifetime left to start again.

Where it wasn't enough to destroy people's houses, their lives were taken—even under the nose of the International Committee of the Red

Cross. The red cross on the roof of the Vukovar hospital had not spared it from being shelled despite the covenants of international law. I have seen footage from the day Vukovar fell: in front of the hospital, a Yugoslav army general brushed off the Red Cross staff who wanted to ensure that all those in the hospital were given safe transport. Meanwhile, off-camera at the back door of the hospital, his soldiers were loading almost three hundred patients and staff onto buses and taking them to the first of two holding areas. At the second holding area, people were beaten, repeatedly and in turn. Two men died from the injuries they received there. The rest were taken in smaller groups, by truck, down a dirt track that petered out at an agricultural rubbish pit on the edge of a field. One man escaped from the moving truck and ran for his life. Because of him, we know the story of that day up to the point when the trucks reached the rubbish pit. Forensic science told us the rest.

THE UN COMMISSION OF EXPERTS had asked Physicians for Human Rights to examine the Vukovar rubbish pit in 1992. A small team of archaeologists and anthropologists was led by Dr. Clyde Snow, the first forensic anthropologist to "go global," and the founder of the Argentine Forensic Anthropology Team. They found scars from bullets on the nearby trees, spent 7.62mm cartridges on the ground on one side of the pit, and three surface skeletons of young males who exhibited gunshot wounds to their heads. In their two trenches, dug in a cross shape, they found several bloated bodies. The pit was now officially a grave. But the forensic team was run off the site at gunpoint by local Serbian authorities. The only solution was for the UN to protect the grave from tampering until a forensic team could return in safety. Soldiers ended up guarding the grave for four years, as PHR attempted to send further teams and was repeatedly denied permission by local authorities. During that time, eastern Slavonia came under the auspices of the UN, as both Croatia and Serbia vied for control of its fertile agricultural land and strategic position on the trade-heavy Danube River.

Also during that time, some of the families of the people who were taken from the hospital organized themselves into a lobbying group: the Mothers of Vukovar. They were sure that their men were alive, in prisoner-of-war camps in Serbia, and that political pressure—not excavation of rubbish pits—was what was needed to bring them home. They actually demonstrated against the commencement of our investigation: they didn't want to be survivors of the dead, but seekers of the living.

There is no question that forensic anthropologists are not seekers of the living. I thought about that on my first day at the grave site. We didn't approach it with paramedics in tow. We had stretchers, but they were for carrying out body bags, not the wounded living. And we approached at high speed only because Bill always drove fast, not because we had to get to the site before those buried in the rubble ran out of oxygen.

I couldn't see the site when we reached the end of the track at the edge of the cornfield because the UN had enclosed it with a not particularly sturdy screen made of gray felt stretched over a wooden frame. It was tall enough to block the view of observers, and by the gate, an armored personnel carrier (APC) was parked next to a small bunker with sandbag walls. Captain Hassan, whose Jordanian regiment had been guarding the site for at least the previous year, met us there. He was militaristically handsome: tall, slim, with a clipped mustache on a very close-shaven face. His spoken English was better than that of his soldiers, and it improved by talking to us throughout the exhumation; he was unfailingly polite and almost house-proud about the condition of the site.

Inside the screen, I was stunned to see a work site that far outdid conditions in Rwanda and Bosnia: there was a gravel-covered courtyard, and three white containers joined by a raised boardwalk. Behind all this was a waist-high white fence connected to a massive white UN tent with a wooden plank floor that reminded me of a country dancehall. Out the back doors of this tent was an uneven bit of land, filled with detritus and surrounded by barbed wire: the grave. Yet another nondescript piece of earth, which held unknown horrors and which, in a matter of weeks, we would turn into a neat, cordoned-off, dirt-and-bodies-only grave site. I felt strange as I looked at it. But as Bill and I walked the surface, eyeing it, I began to fall into my role: picking up animal bones and being quizzed by Bill. (I learned to identify pig teeth—very crenulated molars, tall and narrow.) Bill bitched that the "fuckwit" deminers had altered the surface of the grave; we would "probably" have to move the tent, and we would "definitely" have to move the fence, and, hell, that barbed wire was probably on top of the grave, too. Clint was gracious about all this, willing to accommodate where necessary, and he made promises about telephones, fax machines, office furniture, and toilet paper, all due to arrive the next day.

Clint also told me that the Mothers of Vukovar had practically shouted them down when they announced the beginning of the exhumation: the women wanted proof of the connection between the relatives they saw taken away from the hospital *alive* and the grave at Ovčara. I was surprised by their stance, and a little perplexed. What does someone like me, whose goal is to give something of the dead back to their relatives, do when those relatives don't want anything back from us because to get it is to acknowledge that their loved ones are dead? As forensic anthropologists, we enter the picture after death, by definition. I had always felt comfortable with our position in the order of things; yet I felt disloyal to those mothers as we began opening the grave the next day, looking for the edges while gathering cartridges from fired bullets.

Our work at the site was clear-cut, however, so I just stuck my head down and got on with it. First, we had to continue what the forensic team had started in 1992. An excavation always begins with an inventory of what equipment one has and what one needs. In this case, we had body bags (both white British bags and the deluxe green American bags with carrying handles), rubber gloves, cloth gloves, soap, towels, paper towels, shovels, picks, trowels, paintbrushes, rain gear, mapping pins, sponges, Brillo pads, brooms, buckets, disinfectant. Our list of what we still needed was relatively short: chopsticks for detailed cleaning, colanders, dustpans, trash bags, whisk brooms.

On August 31, we started a test trench and initial mapping and photography under the lenses of a British film crew making a documentary with the permission of the Tribunal. Though we were a small team—only four, as Bill was splitting his time between this grave and Lazete, a site in Bosnia—we all knew each other well and commenced with the efficiency born of familiarity and joint purpose. Doug Scott and Ralph Hartley were back, and Becky Saunders had flown in from the States. Most important, Becky, Doug, and Ralph had all been part of the teams that had attempted to excavate the Ovčara site in 1992 and 1993 with Clyde Snow. Thanks to their recollections and documents from that time, we located the southern periphery of the grave by the next day. The soil wall told the story: there was an interruption of the surface grass mat, a change in soil color, and a change in the color, consistency, and smell of the floor of our test trench. Then Doug and Ralph read the soil wall on our cross trench and found the western edge of the original 1992 trench. Next, we found Item __, also known as Green Shirt Man: we knew from 1992 that he was on the eastern edge. These accomplishments allowed us to begin estimating the overall size of this top level grave by measuring its north-south dimension (over eight meters); the original test trench already provided the east-west dimension (about seven meters). Of course, it was impossible to know then how deep the grave would be.

Meanwhile, Clint made good on his promises on "the other side of the fence," which is how those of us working in the grave viewed the administrative area of the gravel courtyard and the several clean containers being used for offices. Phone and office equipment was installed and a key arrived for the "ablutions" container, the condition of which was in keeping with the secondhand nature of our equipment. Apparently, the UN planned to burn everything we used—including the $6,000 dancehall tent in which we ate lunch—because they believed no one would use them after they had been at a grave site. Thus the toilets were stinky, only one of the three had a seat, the showers looked like they'd seen some hard time, and I wondered who was going to clean these babies—the floors were already muddy from people walking in and out during the course of one day.

Within the fence we had our challenges, too. It rained about three times a day, and because the surface of the site was flat, drainage had to be created to send the water runoff into pits that we could later pump out. Also, each time it rained, we had to lay multiple tarps down to keep the surface soil dry, and lay them again before we left at night. It usually rained during the night, so that when we arrived in the morning, we would have to form a bucket brigade to get the water off the tarps before removing them and exposing our work. We became quite skilled at quick and effective tarp laying, overlapping all the edges strategically so that one tarp's runoff didn't simply trickle down a seam onto the soil underneath the neighboring tarp. Last, in clearing the northeast quadrant we were hampered by a combination of cheap, poorly designed shovels and earth that was severely compacted: not quite like concrete, but close.

As for lunch, our outdated German rations, which were stored in boxes in the dancehall tent, were mysteriously missing items (usually sweets) every morning; some of our drinking water vanished every night as well. Bill continued establishing his control over the site by putting up flagging in the middle of the gravel courtyard and telling Captain Hassan that his soldiers had to stay on the gate side of the flagging. This did not go down well. The next day, before Bill got to the site, the rest of us took the fallout, waiting outside for about half an hour as Clint and Captain Hassan had a battle of wills over Bill's flagging. The sky clouded over and we knew it would be freezing once we got to work. We ruminated on how we were being held up outside our own compound as people's commanders were called and fingers were waggled and the ground was kicked and shoulders were hunched, and the film crew wished they could tape it all.

IN THE SPACE OF A WEEK, the routine of driving to the site was already grinding in the reality of the last hours of the lives of the people whose bodies we were searching for. Every morning, we left our containers on the Belgian UN base in Erdut and drove, flanked by a military police escort, down the same route the victims were driven after they left the first holding area. We traveled down another paved road past the farm building where they were beaten, and finally turned off onto a dirt track that paralleled the track that had taken them to their grave. On the morning drive and again in the evening, I thought about the Mothers of Vukovar, their anger toward us, and the signs we were already uncovering that confirmed the site held bodies.

One morning, though it was freezing, the wind had driven away a cloud layer overnight. We woke up to our first truly sunny day in Erdut—sunny enough to lighten the spirit and penetrate the pores with a bit of warmth. On the way to the site we collected our clean clothes from the local women who did laundry out of their houses as a business. I drank in their dustless dirt courtyard with its chickens, walnut trees, dogs, and geraniums, savoring the lived-in normality of the scene. The young woman invited me in to get my bag and I was overwhelmed with longing for my mother as I smelled the warmth of fresh laundry and ironing.

That morning I decided to try harder to see more signs of life. I began developing favorite spots along both drives: particular houses with picturesque wood-paneled balconies; front gardens planted out in an array of pastel perennials interspersed with baby's breath or alyssum, looking like wedding bouquets laid down along both sides of the path; glimpses of the Danube behind houses in Dalj, the sunlight glinting off the water and almost blinding me as I looked down the two or three short streets that led to the water's edge. I remember a passing glimpse of a black cat with a white belly balanced precariously on the windowsill of a small cottage in the sun. Its front paws were splayed out to the side as it tried to lick its belly. And I noticed a very "She Who Walks by Herself" black kitty, strolling around the shelled neighborhood in Vukovar. It was on the street where we turned right at the bombed-out Caffe London, with its peeling pink paint and a version of Big Ben painted on it. It had obviously been a hopping place once.

ON SEPTEMBER 6, the film crew left (bequeathing us their sweets as a token of their appreciation), our Czech ICTY investigator, Vladimir Dzuro, was away for the day, Bill drove to Tuzla, and all of a sudden it was just me, Becky, Doug, and Ralph on-site. I was so excited to finally have space and quiet that I felt happy for the first time in months, happy to be working, happy to be with my coworkers. Ralph, Becky, and I got down on our hands and knees and truly cleaned the floor of the northeast quadrant with our trowels, then mapped it in; Ralph photographed it from above, sitting in the front bucket of the backhoe. With all this effort, we now had a good sense of the grave outline, so we were able to utilize the backhoe to remove the surface layer of the southeast quadrant. Kamble, the backhoe operator, was so skilled he could feel through the controls when the consistency of the soil changed from compacted to grave fill, making him an early warning system for when we were getting close to bodies. The whole southeast layer came off quickly, and as we were doing the final clearing with sideways swipes of the bucket, I espied a shoe poking up. A sock and toe bones were inside and a second shoe was poking up just north of it in a very convincing anatomical position.

We discussed the likelihood of this body being on the edge of the grave area. The grave was looking small so far, but perhaps it was deep. Both quadrants were open now and very manageable in terms of size, which meant the backhoe could stay off for a while as we approached the next level by hand with picks and shovels. The question now was whether it was time to move from the known to the unknown to find the actual edge of the grave. Once we had the edge, we would be able to dig around it to "pedestal" the entire grave and give us a body-free place to stand.

It was while looking at the surface of the grave at the end of that day that, despite the sense that we had betrayed the Mothers of Vukovar, I started to feel a resurgence of purpose. You have to envision standing on an area of flat brown earth like the front yard of a brand-new suburban house before the grass turf has been laid, except this patch of earth is clean because any debris has been scraped off with a trowel, by hand. And in the midst of this compacted plane are the toes of two shoes, pointing skyward. They are unmistakable, and if you touch them, the toe bones inside are equally unmistakable: the big toe phalange chunky like a baby carrot, the other phalanges more like small licorice pieces, held in anatomical position by a sock because the flesh of the foot has decomposed.

The shoes were a harbinger of more bodies, and for me they instilled a drive to uncover and exhume. Stand there on that bit of earth long enough, though, and take in your surroundings—a small wood hiding its life-giving stream, the sound of soldiers stamping their feet somewhere behind you as they struggle to keep warm while standing sentry, the smell of a little bonfire—and then look back at those shoes poking out of the earth. They are not just a harbinger, they are the mark of past sinister goings-on in this non-descript place. I felt I could put up with the rain, the cold, the insufficient food, and the dirty toilets. Indeed, I would have stayed there indefinitely to recover the bodies that lay beneath my feet.

Those shoes, in combination with our hypothesized grave edges, allowed us to start excavating in earnest. Within three days, we already knew we had at least two layers of bodies. In the northeast quadrant, Becky uncovered Blue-and-White Sweater Man with Turquoise-and-Black Sweater Man underneath, and I uncovered another boot. Over in the northwest quadrant were very smelly pants and tennis shoes: something was decomposing underneath them. We decided to start digging out our second test trench to use as a working area and also to start exposing some remains so that when Bill arrived, he would have at least one pedestaled skeleton to look at and to exhume if he wanted.

Meanwhile, Captain Hassan seemed to loosen up a bit. He invited us for a traditional Jordanian lunch, *mansaf:* chicken in yogurt sauce with rice, with the same sauce to drink. All chili-pepper-hot. We sat on the other side of the felt fence, in the captain's private container, which housed his desk and bed. I noticed that there were rather a lot of magazine pictures of Princess Diana taped to the wall.

He asked me, in a serious tone, "You know Lady Diana?"

"Well, not personally," I replied apologetically.

He gestured at her picture with his cup: "Lady Diana: very strong woman. Very clean. Prince Charles: bad man."

Back in the grave, our ever-smaller team—now just Doug, Ralph, and me, because Becky had had to return to the States—was still steaming along: we had three drainage situations that all worked beautifully; we had up-to-the-minute maps as well as photo and evidence logs; we had cleared the site of all loose rubbish and flagging, only keeping the "media line" up; and Kamble had put a lock on the storage room door while all the rations were moved to the second office container.

With Becky gone, Bill still in Bosnia, and several nonforensic people (Clint and the investigators) also trying to help us, grave-related questions were somehow being directed at me: Is this a bone? Is it human? Can you consult with me on this? Shall we take this area down? What about *this* area? Clea, the film crew is on the phone and wants to know if they should come back sooner—can you talk to them? What should we do about the tarps? Do we have any nails? Where should we put the backdirt? I loved answering these questions and being the one to make decisions. Of course, excavation-related decisions were made in concert with Doug and Ralph, the archaeologists, and we all deferred to one another's areas of expertise.

The three of us agreed that, to facilitate exhumation, soon we would have to stop thinking about the grave in terms of quadrants and would have to approach it as a whole, removing grave fill from either our north or east trench, or from both. I realized that we were getting closer to the core of the grave one day when I was in the office container, taking a phone call from Paulette from the film crew. While I was reassuring her that they weren't missing the "unveiling," just some initial exposure, I realized that my coverall really stank. I hadn't noticed the stench while in the grave and I inwardly apologized to Clint, who was sitting, clean, at the other end of the room. We were no longer just excavating grave fill and outlying skeletons; we were getting close to many more bodies, bodies that had defied skeletonization for five years.

15.

THE TRANSLATOR

THE INITIAL EXPOSURE OF BODIES WAS THE CUE FOR THE TWO Croatian (Croat and Croatian Serb) human rights observers to attend the exhumation. Clint asked me to give them a synopsis of our progress so far. I uncovered a skeleton we had fully excavated and pedestaled for Bill, and described the whole site. They asked me a few questions through our interpreter, Andrea. Was the skeleton one of those found in '92? (No, those were in plastic bags in the trench.) Did we think there were more bodies over this way or that way? (Yes or no, depending on where they pointed.) Did we think they'd all be bones? (No, definitely not, because the remains could be preserved by water.) The observers came to the site almost every day and would stay even during the lunch break, sometimes discussing points with each other. One of them, who had been standing behind me for some time as I scraped away at the soil while on my knees, said, "You are *really* working." He shook his head. "I think it is going to be difficult."

As we uncovered more human remains, the site received a regular flow of official visitors. They stood on a small wooden platform that abutted the grave so their shoes wouldn't become muddy or stinky; the platform also helped to contain them so they didn't walk around the crime scene. Clint would brief the visitors on the history of the site and the associated indictment, and they would look down at the grave and then at those of us working in it, as though we were exotic and slightly disgusting animals at the zoo. We would continue working, looking at them with our peripheral vision, trying to guess who they were or where they were from. Then the "zoo-sense" would shift when Clint would ask one of us to explain to the visitors what exactly they were seeing, and we left the "zoo" and became human beings again. Giving these "tours" made me feel that the forensic team was the most ordinary element of the grave, besides the bodies, while the visitors were the curiosity.

On September 13, it was cold and rainy and Doug was sick. We were just about to cover up the grave when we remembered that General Jacques Klein, the UN administrator of eastern Slavonia, was coming to visit, so we had to change into coveralls again and jump down into the grave. We removed the tarps even though it was drizzling—something we preferred not to do—and tried to create some drainage areas. We were sliding around in the mud when Klein and his entourage arrived in a train of cars and four-wheel-drive vehicles, spraying the gravel of our entry courtyard as they parked in formation. General Klein exuded an air of having just bought the place, as Wodehouse put it. He seemed larger than life—in part, no doubt, because he was standing above us on the observation platform—wearing a leather aviator jacket and a dark blue baseball cap, pulled down low and with all manner of military patches sewn on; he was smoking a cigar and keeping ash off his jacket. The people with him were all wearing suits or dresses appropriate for the office—not a wet day on a muddy wooden platform looking down at a mass grave.

Clint asked me to give the group a tour of the grave and then one of the entourage, an American man holding a clipboard, asked, "That's a pair of jeans there, right?" I said, "Yes, that's right." And then Clipboard Man said, "But there's nothing in that clothing, is there?" The body he was looking at was well fleshed. It was hard not to be sarcastic, but I refrained from saying, "What do you think this is, a mass Goodwill grave?" I just said, "Yes, sir, there is a body inside that clothing. All the clothing you see here has a body inside of it."

I was incredulous that he couldn't see a body. But as I watched him twisting his neck, trying to get the proper angle to see it, I realized that he actually couldn't see what I saw when I looked at the grave. It wasn't the angle. It wasn't the distance. It was that he couldn't *conceive* of it. I had to respect that.

One woman looked upset; another woman refused to come out of the tent. Then it started to rain harder, and those of us in the grave began working on the drainage some more. Suddenly General Klein barked: *"These people need a tent.* Get me a phone. I'm gonna get these people a tent." Half his entourage went scurrying off, either to get a phone or just to be seen to be doing something. Clint told us later that Klein whipped so many people into a frenzy that the phone in our office container started ringing off the hook with engineers trying to schedule immediate delivery of a tent. Then, on his way out through the dancehall tent, Klein caught sight of our outdated lunch rations and ordered soup and bread to be brought to us fresh every day.

I saw that some of the general's entourage were looking at me with pitying expressions as they took in my wet, muddy coveralls and my well-used trowel. The woman who had refused to come outside watched from behind the glass window in the door of the dancehall, behind all the others, and the tortured expression on her face horrified me; *she* was having no trouble seeing exactly what was in that clothing. As soon as they left, I asked Andrea who she was. One of General Klein's translators, Andrea told me, a Serb. She had told Andrea that up to this point she had believed what had been reported in the newspapers for years: that this grave did not exist.

This is the power of human remains, even before anthropology and pathology unlock their testimonies. When a government or military denies the murder of its own citizens, then to find even three bodies, let alone more than one hundred, is to lay waste to those claims, or at least undermine them. In a way, it is immaterial who is in the graves. The image alone can undo years of propaganda. The Serbian public's disbelief, for example, at the discovery of bodies brought from Kosovo in 1999 and buried behind their local police stations was overtaken by outrage.

Two days after Klein's visit, the soup started arriving. It would be brought

at exactly noon by two Belgian soldiers from the UN headquarters in Vukovar, a big tureen in the back of their jeep, along with bread and butter. They
had no idea how grateful we were for this soup: on a cold day, it was absolutely wonderful to have warm chicken broth with two carrot slices and a
huge chunk of bread spread thick with butter.

The tent arrived as well. It wasn't like any tent I'd ever seen. It was constructed on-site by about twenty Slovak engineers and their Australian
foreman, Bryan. All the Slovaks were wearing dark green, baggy trousers
with paper-bag waists and the requisite pale blue UN caps. They spent an
afternoon expertly manipulating massive metal rods into a frame for the
tent, which was going to rival the size of our dancehall. The next day,
the same team brought the fabric: thick canvas that had to be woven onto
the frame via an intricate pulley system that required the smallest of the
engineers to scramble onto the roof of the structure and guide the fabric
across the metal frame.

When the Slovaks were finished, it was as though the grave site was inside a tall fabric barn whose doors were open at each end, the openings
large enough to allow our backhoe to reach the edge of the grave to pull
away backdirt. With great effort, smaller flaps along the tent walls could be
lifted and clipped back to allow in more light. The finished product was extraordinary; we'd come a long way from Kibuye, where we had fashioned
cut tree branches into a simple frame over which we stretched multiple
thin tarps. The Ovčara tent was completed on a day that had started out
frostily cold, with no water in the bathroom at the base. Thanks to General
Klein, at least some of our difficulties were being surmounted.

Of course, with a tent we could keep working even in the rain, so with
the arrival of Melissa Connor (to overlap with Doug's impending departure), we began picking down the grave fill in earnest, treating the site as a
whole and working from the edges to the center, careful to leave one earth
walkway, which would allow access. We started encountering a lot of wet
soil, as though from an underground spring, but a fetid one: an underworld
spring. You would clear away some soil, and water would bubble up slowly.
If you kept scraping, a puddle would form. When the team compared
notes at the end of the day, everyone reported getting wet spots; we knew

from prior experience what that meant. I wrote in my journal: "There are bodies down there. . . ." Melissa described the wetness as "very Kibuye," an image we shared because we had all worked there.

Perhaps that was why Rwanda kept coming into my mind on this mission, even when I wasn't on-site. On my twenty-fourth birthday, I took the day off and walked around the little town of Erdut, just outside the gates of the base. Pigs were snuffling through the silty earth on the edges of the roads, but I didn't see any people. The houses were damaged, their yards claimed by tall weeds growing around debris both blown in by wind and blown off by device. The windows and doors were gone and I could see into abandoned front rooms and hallways, all strewn with clothes and dolls and bits of broken furniture. The houses reminded me of Ntarama church near Kigali. It was something about the preponderance of ordinary objects reduced to a matted scatter, dirt and dust undifferentiated from dried blood and smears of manure deposited by roving livestock.

Back in the grave, Rwanda was on my mind again as we uncovered more of the top layer of bodies: several bodies had trauma to their finger phalanges that suggested defense wounds and I thought about Banana Man, who was one of the few skeletons from Kibuye with cuts on his fingers, hands, and forearms. The Ovčara grave was also beginning to show its individuality.

In Europe, hospital staff wear white, open-backed clogs. Sometimes the soles are made of wood, sometimes of rubber, while the top of the shoe is almost always smooth leather or vinyl with regular, small holes punched throughout the material. I first wore such clogs in the ICTY mortuary in Kosovo in 2000. But the first time I ever saw them was in the grave at Ovčara. I was working in one corner when I uncovered the first pair. The feet of the person wearing them were still inside the clogs even though the body was lying on its side. Since such clogs are backless, this surprised me. Were they still on because the person wearing them had been made to lie down before being shot? This person was likely one of the last killed, because they were on top of all the other bodies. What did they see before they died?

As I excavated my corner, I found six pairs of shoes still on feet. All these people were lying on their sides. Some of the shoes were also medical staff clogs. Lying some distance from these people was a man wearing a cast on his left arm, which was flung over his head, crooked at the elbow; he lay on his back, and by his feet was an orangey-yellow rubber tube of narrow diameter. At first I thought the tube was a random artifact—it wasn't connected to the man with the cast—but as I continued excavating him, I found that the tube disappeared into the clothing of another body below Cast Man. It could have been connected to a catheter. Could have been something else.

Some of the bodies were wearing pajamas. One man had X ray films tucked down the back of his pink-and-white-striped terrycloth bathrobe. I couldn't believe it. Those X rays were like a message in a bottle to me. Seeing them was like a cross between hearing the dead woman's voice on the 911 tape back in Arizona and seeing the pink plastic necklace on the woman's body in Kibuye: the X rays were tucked—*hidden*—in the bathrobe. I didn't know whether they were his X rays, or whether he had brought them when he was being "evacuated" from the hospital because he thought he would need them at the next hospital. Or did he stick them in the back of his bathrobe because he suspected he would be beaten and they would give him some protection?

Thinking about that man as I write this makes me cry, but at the time it was as if he had left us a note. Did he suspect that he was going to die, and thus secrete the X rays to make him identifiable if his body was ever found, to help get his body back to his family? An object hidden in the back of someone's clothes carries a different emotional charge from the items people carry around with them all the time, like wallets, keys, or lipsticks.

Even before the bodies in the Ovčara grave were anthropologically analyzed and identified, the evidence emphatically indicated that these were at least some of the people from the hospital, some of the hundreds who had not been seen since November 18, 1991. Finding the bodies in the pit and then observing the subsequent accumulation of medical material was like watching several raindrops on a window merge into one large droplet whose weight drags it down the glass, leaving a trail you can trace with your finger.

As we revealed that trail, I felt confident about the right of the Tribunal to conduct the exhumation despite the objections by the Mothers of Vukovar. The more I saw of the bodies and the items in the grave, the more I saw our discoveries as evidence. These bodies, by their very presence, were dismantling years of the perpetrators' propaganda that the grave didn't exist, that the missing men were probably larking about in Italy, that a crime against humanity hadn't taken place five years earlier. I was invigorated by the knowledge that forensic analysis would enable the victims to incriminate their killers and write history as accurately as possible, but I could not forget that the Mothers of Vukovar didn't want anything we could give them precisely because we *were* forensic scientists. For them, for now, we were at the wrong end of science, criminal justice, and law enforcement.

16

VOICES OF THE DEAD

SEVERAL WEEKS INTO THE EXCAVATION, I WAS STILL BROODING over the Vukovar Mothers but the feeling of determination I had gained from exposing the remains drove me, even when Bill returned on short visits to the site and treated me with the same inconsistency that had made our interactions in Bosnia so difficult at times. One morning, he castigated me in front of the team for "allowing" ICTY investigators to dig in the grave. This was salt in an open wound, as I'd been trying to get them out of the grave for days but didn't feel I had the administrative clout, given that I'd never actually been put in charge. Yet that same evening, Bill was asking if I could come back to the mission after my cousin's wedding on October 12, saying jokingly, "I'm going to have to bring up . . . let's see, Patrick, Dorothy . . . Jose Pablo—and that's just to replace Clea!"

Bill had a lot of planning and management to do, since exhumations were under way in both Bosnia and Croatia. He could not be in both places at the same time, and I think he wanted to be. This probably explained his high-speed driving between Tuzla and Ovčara every other week, his Land Cruiser turning up covered in reeking pig shit after taking his own shortcuts.

I presumed that Bill's inability to be in two places at once was the source of his apparent frustration with me, whether it was manifested in dressing me down over the presence of nonscientists in the grave or in chewing me out for taking phone calls from the film crew, something I had done only at Clint's request. I was more concerned with mitigating the severity of the cold I had caught from Doug before he left, a cold I passed on to Ralph, who went to the bathroom one night with a toothbrush and a hairbrush instead of a toothbrush and some toothpaste, a cold also passed on to Bill, who said, on the tape of his field notes that I later transcribed: "Body number sixty-one is wearing a blue, uh . . . knit . . . sweater with horizontal stripes and a long-sleeved belt." Did he mean a long-sleeved shirt? Just a belt? Both? It needed cross-referencing with the paper field log.

My mind was also overwhelmingly occupied by trying to make sense of the grave. I had excavated a body that was lying in fetal position. Was this man made to get in the grave before being shot, as we had surmised at Nova Kasaba in Bosnia? Had he curled up after being shot, hugging his knees to his chest? A number of bodies were wearing green trousers and blue sweaters; I learned these items had been a donation to the Vukovar hospital. I uncovered a body with gauze wrapped around his head. Some parts of the bodies were skeletonized while other parts were fleshed; for example, the anterior iliac spine (the front of the hip) of one man was protruding from the grave, skeletonized, but his torso was fully fleshed and his shirt seemed to be rucked all the way up to his neck. Near him, I uncovered a head with dark brown hair. I expected to find his body lying horizontally across the top of the grave like the others. But it wasn't. I kept scraping in the soil with my trowel, expecting bone or saponified tissue but finding only the hips and feet of neighboring bodies. Eventually I was able to see that the dark-haired man's body disappeared *down* into the grave. He was effectively sitting or standing in the grave where everyone else on the surface layer was lying down. A bright turquoise mold was forming in little circles on his forehead.

This man has come back to me in both dreams and nightmares. Usually, his head is flattened, only a few inches thick. In one dream, I am trying to clean a wooden tabletop and don't realize at first that his head is embedded in it; I am just dragging the sponge back and forth over the waxy surface, pulling the dark strands of the hair on the crown of his head left and right, over and over. In one of the nightmares, I have to climb a tree to recover the body parts of someone who has blown himself up, and as I climb the tree his face is hanging on a branch just behind me and his eyes are following my movements.

Those dreams didn't come until after I left the mission. While I was there, decent sleep was ensured by the day in–day out routine: the escorted drive every day (when I would look up from reading Misha Glenny's *The Fall of Yugoslavia* at just the right moment to see my favorite gates and gardens, or an old man happily cutting his front lawn with an implement the size of a butter knife, his shoulder muscle and wrist doing the work, like the men who kept the lawns of the Kibuye Guest House clipped short by using just a machete); the long day at the site, trying to understand the evidence, while also bearing up against the bitterly cold wind. If you weren't already exhausted, the late, heavy supper of salami or sausages with applesauce finished you off. I would find just enough time to tap in a journal entry before falling asleep at the computer before ten P.M.

The grave was still close to the size we had predicted it would be at the beginning of the month, but we now had more than fifty people exposed on top of it. Since we removed almost all the fill from on top of the bodies, we were able to pedestal the grave by digging even deeper the trench we had encircling the grave, so the top layer of bodies was at about waist height in most places. The grave and our trench were so deep now that Kamble cut stairs into the dirt walls of the site so we could get down safely. Those two shoes I described as just breaking the surface of the earth back when we were still looking for the grave edges were still there, but now they were just one pair of many on a heap of bodies that jutted above the ground like the top of a soufflé. Now that we were effectively underground and under the massive Slovak-built tent, the feeling of being in a zoo grew stronger. At any given time, there were the human rights observers, the film crew, and official visitors—mostly international police and people from the European Community Monitoring Mission (ECMM)—standing around two edges of the grave, their heads tilted, trying to make sense of what they were seeing.

What they were seeing was an effort by those of us in the hole to clean the entire surface of the grave so it could be photo-documented prior to exhumation, mainly for use at the trials of the indictees. We knew the importance of the cleaning step from Bosnia, but having Ralph there as archaeologist and photographer ensured that it was given priority: he knew that in a photograph dirty bodies just look like dirt. So we were scraping the clothing clean of dirt to reveal the color of clothes or hair. Some of the team was working around the edges, and some of us, like Melissa and I, were working from the walkway or cap of earth we left in the center of the grave. We had to be in a sitting or crouching position, leaning forward and pulling earth from in front of us back and up, into our waiting buckets. It was hard work and we used to trade off scraping and running buckets of backdirt down the walkway for each other. Because of this system, the bodies in the center of the grave couldn't be reached after we had pulled the earth and walkway back beneath our feet. They would only be accessible once bodies closer to the edge had been removed.

Melissa and I spent several days just pulling handfuls of soil out of deep gullies between bodies. One day we worked as ominous clouds built up above our tent, which was buffeted by the wind in a rhythm to which I hummed "Corazón" from a Silvio Rodriguez cassette Jose Pablo had given me in Bosnia. Melissa and I were making progress picking, shoveling, and emptying buckets. I felt sorry for Evangeline, the Filipina ICTY investigator, who had been relegated to cleaning around the edges of the grave— one of the least mobile jobs and thus the most horrible on a cold day. I took in the quiet, the rustling of the trees in the wind, the autumn leaves blowing into the tent, plus Evangeline making noises of cold and pain before she finally left to get some coffee. It was then that I found that she had been sending all her bits of backdirt into my now inaccessible dips and gullies among the bodies. I kept my peace, didn't voice my disappointment about the effect it might have on the photograph, and the effort of holding this in almost moved me to tears. To keep my temper, I reminded myself of how, when Evangeline accidentally opened the door of our storage container that morning while I was changing into my coveralls, she had said, "Oh, I'm sorry, my dear," and it had been so nice to be called that. Her tone was motherly; she meant well.

ON THE MORNING OF SEPTEMBER 20, I had an experience that was like stepping into a book. Clyde Snow, who would be heading up the analysis and identification of the bodies, had arrived at the site for a short visit at about the same moment that Judge Louise Arbour, the chief prosecutor of the Tribunal, arrived with a surprisingly small entourage for her own tour. Bill had already been drawn into an old-pals reunion with Clyde, so Clint had asked me to give Judge Arbour "an anthropologist's view" of the grave. But just as I began, Bill took over, so I was free to observe. Clyde, one of my professional heroes, was being reintroduced to the site by Eric Stover (whom I had been pleased to meet a week earlier), who had chronicled Clyde's work in *Witnesses from the Grave*, the book that had sealed my interest in human-rights-related forensics. I watched the two of them, thinking, "It's Clyde Snow. It's really him! And that's Eric Stover next to him! And Luis Fondebrider [founding member of the Argentine team] is right behind me, swinging a pick, offering me a swig of water and wearing a woolen hat like one my brother wore when we were kids! This is really too much." I couldn't stop smiling; it was like I had been dropped into one of the later chapters of *Witnesses*.

Then Eric called out to ask me about something, and I replied no, and then Clyde said, "Clea [he said my name!], what about scalp hair? Have you found any of that? Because that's a question on the antemortem database form." So I walked over and showed him a head with plenty of hair; he asked about beard hair, too, and I told him that we'd found it in Bosnia but not here so far. And then he said, "I don't think we've ever met," as he put out his hand, which I shook, saying, "I'm Clea, it's a pleasure to meet you," and he replied, "I'm Clyde Snow," and I said, "Well, I know who *you* are!" The three of us continued to talk and theorize about the site and he invited us all to eat dinner with him in Zagreb when we left, but I found myself just trying to take him in, to really look at him. Clyde Snow had been an idol of mine for six years. His capabilities as a forensic anthropologist, his willingness to use his talents far from home, and his determination to make the Argentine team self-sufficient had all inspired me and now here he was in front of me, tall, crumply, and smoking a pipe. I barely saw him again that day because the film crew spent the afternoon interviewing him, along with Eric and Bill. This project was at times thwarted by the noise of the backhoe or by the Jordanian soldiers singing on the other side of the felt screen, standing on top of their APC as usual.

As for Judge Arbour, she did more than just visit the site that day, she descended into the grave—some of her entourage looked slightly aghast at this—and asked intelligent and sober questions. She treated the area with respect and seemed to regard it as more than just a grave—as also a place that held answers she was sorry to see, despite the necessity of unearthing them. In turn, I accorded her great respect and was thrilled when she held my arm to steady herself as she stepped into our drainage trench. Four years later, when Judge Arbour came to Los Angeles to speak to a civic group, I was able to meet her in my "civilian" clothes. I was the last person in line to have a photograph taken with her; most of those ahead were local businesspeople and philanthropists. When it was my turn, I trembled a bit as I told her that I was the person whose arm she held when she stepped into the Ovčara grave. I presented her with a team photograph from that site and she took it with great surprise and pleasure, asking whether I knew Clint Williamson, her deputy for the site. I introduced her to my parents and she said to them, "Your daughter is very brave."

Judge Arbour was tough and uncompromising during her tenure with ICTY, and she also recognized the importance and potential of forensic investigation. In Los Angeles, she gave an eloquent and educational talk about the future of international justice. I listened with tears in my eyes because I was so proud that I had been part of Judge Arbour's team, and because of something inexplicable to do with that cold, dirty day on another continent, standing atop a mound out of which the remains of more than 260 people were eventually pulled.

THE NEXT DAY, before we started working, Bill held a meeting that was one of the best we'd had with him because it was held in the dancehall tent instead of in the car, trying to listen to him over the wind, as in Rwanda, or in the grave, as in Bosnia—an experience that I described in my journal as taking place "in the presence of only a few of us, who invariably have to pay court to him, following as he jumps around the grave, talking low." In the tent Bill told us what a great job we'd been doing and said he appreciated how well organized everything was. We just needed to make it go faster. To that end, he had brought Fernando Moscoso, David Del Pino, and Patrick Myers up from Bosnia to help. Four of the French mercenaries would follow in the next few days as we approached the start of full-time exhumations. While we held this meeting, the photographer Gilles Peress walked down the remaining cap of earth and took photographs of the bodies in the grave. Dressed from head to toe in black, he looked strangely clean.

Within a week, our reinforcements had arrived from Bosnia and we began exhuming the bodies. Because we had ideal conditions (a grave on a flat surface, already pedestaled, with trenches running around three of its four sides), we were able to implement our usual procedures with maximum efficiency. One team had each numbered body photographed, electronically mapped, and logged on paper, and hands or hand bones were wrapped in a plastic bag secured to the body's clothing, before a second team came in with a numbered body bag to exhume the body, holding other bodies out of the way if necessary. The filled body bag was put onto a stretcher and handed, with great difficulty, up and out of the trench—this became much easier when Kamble built a ramp at the southern end of the grave—and then the stretcher was carried out to the refrigerated container just past the white fence.

The first day with new team members was rather hectic as our styles merged and Bill forgot that he'd been the one to insist that hands be bagged in advance. He kept yelling, "Where's this guy's hand? Where's this guy's damned hand?" and we would have to say, "It's in the bag attached to his belt," every time. Then the film crew was right in the trench, interjecting

questions to Bill ("But how does this make you *feel?*") and Bill would be exhuming and answering and waxing philosophical all at once. But even by
the end of the first day of exhumation, Bill was already saying how much
faster body removal was progressing than he had expected. I noticed that
Patrick, David, and Fernando were all wearing the same midnight-blue
sweater so I asked them why and Patrick said, "Oh, Bill likes us this way."
Thus they came to be called Bill's Boys and Bill's Body Removal Service.

As much as I liked those guys, however, the first thing I noticed when
they came in as a "crack team" was that the condition of the site deteriorated rapidly. Our trench was suddenly polluted with used surgical gloves,
the paper packaging from fresh surgical gloves, and used flagging. On top
of this, at the end of the day I was finding buckets, shovels, and paintbrushes all over the grave, caked in gray muck, and dirty trowels stuck in
the walls of the trench to harden overnight into uselessness. One evening I
mentioned to Bill that some cleanup was in order; he called out across the
site, "Hey, everyone, you have to put rubber gloves *here,* not in the backdirt," and he collected the gloves, but everyone ignored all the other material lying around. Melissa, Ralph, and I would clean up the whole place
after everyone else had left to change out of their coveralls. We would
scrape and stack the tools by type (long-handled shovels, short-handled
shovels, separated into pointed-tip and straight-edge, picks, trowels), clean
and stack all the buckets, gather and fold all the plastic bags for collecting
hand bones, gather all the paper bags for cradling heads, line up the two
stretchers, and lean the wheelbarrows against the wall so debris couldn't
collect in them overnight.

We did all this not just to make a point; the exhumation could not pro-
ceed quickly the next day unless all the equipment was in its proper place
when people needed it; trowels wouldn't be lost in the backdirt and no one
on the team would be injured by stepping on the business end of a long-
handled implement. Moreover, keeping equipment clean is the only way to
make it last, and when you're working in an underfunded situation, you
would be advised to take the long view.

When I found myself infuriated because the storage container where
we changed clothes had become a stinking, mud-caked hole *despite* our sign

reading "Socks Only," I knew that I had become possessive about the grave, the bodies in it, and all of us who had been working there for weeks. But then I was reminded of the bigger picture. When I helped to lift a body and found broken crutches underneath him, when Luis pointed out the wallet in the inner pocket of another body's suit jacket, which lay like a shroud of threads over him, I knew that within days the identifications of these men would be confirmed. The Mothers of Vukovar would soon be able to know the truth.

17.

THE MOTHERS

BILL MADE THE STORMING OF THE GRAVE SOMEWHAT EASIER BY
frequently joking about my departure on September 30, which was now
imminent. "We'll pull an all-nighter on the twenty-ninth and then drive to
Zagreb airport at about four in the morning," he declared. Me: "Yeah, I
won't need a shower or anything." Bill: "No, just lots of open seats around
you on the flight, but since we can't guarantee that, you're going to have to
stay here."

The night before I left the mission, Bill insisted that the entire team go
to the Lady M, a restaurant in Vinkovci that he, Clint, and I had stopped at
when we drove up from Bosnia in August. We all went, even the French
mercenaries and the film crew. It was a good night, highlighted by an exu-
berant discussion about how we would feel if it took decades to arrest and
try the indictees for our sites, as has happened in the cases of some accused
World War II war criminals.

By the time we left the next afternoon, after a morning of exhumations
and computer data entry on the logs, almost seventy bodies had been exhumed. That was the entire top layer of bodies and the beginning of the
next layer. Ralph was also leaving, and we said good-bye to the team as well

as to the Jordanians, who gave a bit of a salute, the French, who gave me many kisses on both cheeks (Gerard, a paratrooper who had never learned to write, promised to write to me, and he did), the Belgians, who waved, the film crew, who gave me their business cards, Luis, who told me, "Relax, don' worry, enjoy Zagreb," David, who said, "I think you are leaving in good company"—he apparently thought he was in for a long, tiring ex-humation—and Vladimir, who asked me to smile just one more time, hav-ing given me fifty pfennigs for every time I smiled during the past couple of weeks.

We drove off with Bill, at speed as usual, his belongings—a roll of toilet paper, a flashlight, pens, a grave tie—flying off the dashboard. I watched out the window until we got through the part of the highway with the tall hedgelike trees because after that, you make the turn onto the Brother-hood and Unity Highway and then I knew I could relax: Ralph would take over the driving. I took stock of my aches and pains. I had Trowel Thumb, Gravedigger's Back, Left Knuckle Callus, Inner Thigh Pick Bruise, and Right Index Finger Trowel Callus. Bill, sitting in the back with me after Ralph took the wheel, started to read a Peter Maas book but fell asleep. The sun began to set and it was lovely being on a paved road that didn't have potholes, or horses and carts to weave around, or young boys and grand-mothers leading cows or pigs to avoid, or wild dogs to run under the car, and to be sharing the road with other decent cars, not fake cars made out of a cart rigged up to some kind of lawnmower engine. Of course, I miss those things now as I write this, but at the time, I had had enough of the veering unpredictability of it all.

Bill resumed driving once we got close to Zagreb. We immediately got lost because we were passing the road signs too fast to translate them. It was dark but there were streetlights! After making an illegal U-turn through a pedestrian crossing and almost going through a hedge, Bill rec-ognized the street McDonald's was on and screeched into its parking lot. We went inside, very dirty compared with all the stylish Croatian young-sters, and ordered hamburgers and fries. Then we checked into the Hotel Dubrovnik, where I became giddy trying to look at the bathtub and the television and the view into the cobbled square simultaneously. I could see

old-fashioned trams, covered carts selling pancakes, and couples promenading arm-in-arm.

That night, the contrast between the view out of the hotel window and
the view from our minivan for the past month put the latter in full relief.
We had only driven several hours down the highway but it seemed we'd entered another world. I was remembering all that had become so familiar,
like the old woman I saw every evening sitting on her front porch with an
empty stool next to her, sometimes sitting on the stool because she had a
visitor, and always accompanied by her little dog. I remembered the less familiar things as well, like the day UN vehicles were stoned in Vukovar, forcing our military police escort to take us home on a different route: we
passed a statue whose concrete base had been spray-painted with a green
plus sign and a reversed "C" in each quadrant: a Serbian nationalist symbol,
four Cyrillic letter "S"s around a cross, standing for *"Samo Sloga Srbina
Spasava"* ("Only Unity Saves the Serbs"). And I thought about the grave,
now relinquished to others, and about Clyde Snow waiting for the bodies
to arrive in Zagreb so he could start analyzing them. I thought about how
some of the men in the grave were wearing two pairs of trousers, like the
bodies in Rwanda. Rwanda, where my life of missions started. It was only
ten months since I had been in Kibuye but I felt I had been doing this work
for much, much longer. And yet I could remember the two pairs of
trousers or underwear on the bodies in the Kibuye grave as if it were yesterday. I still can.

THE TEAM AT OVČARA eventually exhumed more than two hundred
and fifty bodies from the grave. Clyde received them all in Zagreb, logging
them in as they were carried out of the refrigerated container. Autopsies
and anthropological analysis continued side by side with the analysis of the
evidence and comparison with the antemortem database of the people
missing from the Vukovar hospital. What with people's wallets and X rays
still on their bodies, presumptive identifications were made quickly and
were backed up just as quickly by anthropological data on each body's age,
sex, height, hair color, and anomalies. There are thousands of people miss-

ing from Vukovar, but these bodies were definitely those of the people taken from the hospital, the ones described by the witness who jumped off the back of the moving truck. Soon it was time to inform the Mothers of Vukovar. I was told that many of them wouldn't accept anthropological identifications, didn't care that the body matched their relative down to the number of teeth missing from years before or a healed fracture, on top of being the right age, height, and sex. What those women did respond to were the artifacts—again, items forensic scientists consider only presumptive identifiers. One woman believed when she saw the front-door key to her old apartment, found in the pocket of the trousers worn by the man anthropologically identified as her husband. Eventually, the Mothers of Vukovar came full circle, as almost all the bodies were positively identified. Public funerals were held for weeks and some were televised. To see footage of them made me cry. We had revised these women's—and everyone's—memories of the past and thus were affecting the future.

PART FIVE

—

KOSOVO

April 2–June 3, 2000, and July 3–July 23, 2000

After Serbian president Slobodan Milošević stripped the province of Kosovo of its autonomy in 1989, Kosovar Albanians were subjected to systematic oppression. In particular, teachers, police, professors, doctors, and miners were sacked and replaced by Kosovar Serbs; others had their houses burned, and yet others were killed. In 1999, President Milošević rejected the ultimatum brought by the United States and its European allies to remove Yugoslav National Army troops from Kosovo and return autonomy to the province. Within a month, NATO began bombing Serbia and Kosovo; this eventually ended the mass expulsion of almost 2 million Kosovar Albanians orchestrated by Kosovar Serb police and the Yugoslav National Army. When the Kosovar Albanian refugees returned from neighboring Albania and Macedonia, almost 100,000 Kosovar Serbs were either forced to leave the province or fled in fear of reprisals; indeed, more than a thousand were killed. Several thousand Kosovar Albanians were also missing. In late 1999 and 2000, international forensic investigators were sent to Kosovo in connection with the indictment ICTY had brought against President Milošević for crimes against humanity and war crimes.

18

"WHAT'S ICK-TEE?"

FIVE HOURS INTO THE FLIGHT TO ZURICH, I PULLED OUT AN article from my bag. Its subject was my final destination: Kosovo. The article was two years old, dateline Racak. It quoted residents of that town asking for international forensic scientists to autopsy the bodies of people killed there recently. They wanted to prove that the people had been murdered, not killed in combat as the local police claimed. The edges of the article were dog-eared from my handling. First, I had just loved it because now I knew that the potential of forensic science had entered the consciousness of people who were being oppressed; so aware were they of its importance that they requested forensic investigation into the dead before requesting humanitarian aid for the living. Then I had used the article when I lectured to students while working on my master's degree in anthropology. At some point, I had to put the article in a protective plastic sleeve. I would hold it in the air in front of a hundred students, refer them to that morning's newscast about Kosovar refugees flooding Albania's borders, and say, "Here is a province where whole neighborhoods are burning, more than seven hundred thousand people are on the move, others are being killed, and what are they asking for? Not peacekeepers. Not military observers. Forensic scientists."

This consciousness of forensics wasn't significant to me for its own sake alone. It felt personal. The Racak request was the antidote to the funk I had been put in by a different article published just a few months before it. That one had also been about forensics, but the dateline was Democratic Republic of Congo. That was General Laurent Kabila's new name for Zaire after he ousted President Mobutu. During the takeover, many civilians were killed or went missing, among them 250,000 refugees from Rwanda who had fled as that genocide came to an end in 1994. Since then, they had been living in camps in the eastern portion of Congo. Now reports were surfacing that they had been killed by Kabila's troops and buried in mass graves. The United Nations sent the Argentine Forensic Team to Congo to investigate the allegations but when the team arrived, Kabila stalled them for weeks in Kinshasa (in the west) while reports trickled back from the east that troops were exhuming the graves and burning the bodies over well-tended pyres.

I had put down that article with the realization that a dogma I'd been carrying around since reading *Witnesses from the Grave* when I was eighteen had just been proven wrong. Back then, I had naively—or perhaps optimistically—decided that forensic anthropology and its related sciences, when applied to the investigation of international human rights violations, would lead to the eradication of state-sponsored murder of civilians. Despots of the world would stop using murder as the shortcut to the success of their political agendas. Instead, the article from Congo told me that perpetrators continued to murder civilians. Only now, they attempted to hide evidence from investigation—*forensic* investigation.

Losing a core belief about how the world works would have been hard enough without having to make other adjustments as well. I had returned to graduate school on the heels of two missions to Bosnia in 1997: a PHR project for the International Commission for Missing Persons, to Sarajevo; and another ICTY forensic mission, to Brčko. Within days of returning to the United States, I had gone to my first class at the University of Nebraska–Lincoln wearing field clothes and feeling surly and out of place, just waiting for someone to ask me something so I could say, "I don't even have a pen," and then yell out, "Why are we sitting here discussing the intricacies of matrilocality and its effect on gender identity when there are people dying all over the world *RIGHT NOW*?" But I soon discovered that three of my professors were both erudite and very much of this world. I relaxed and gave the university the legitimacy it deserved, recognizing that things like free-choice subject papers would allow me to research topics like precolonial Rwanda, or to take my newfound comprehension of the effects of, say, sex ratio imbalances on Eskimo populations and apply it to postconflict groups like the Women of Srebrenica.

Paradoxically, being away from the field while focusing on it intellectually drew me closer to my work for PHR and the tribunals. The more I read about the context of the events that led up to those graves, and the more I used academic tools to help understand those events, the more the bodies and our analyses of them took on emotional potency. Some days my nerves would tingle because I would wake up from a dream about being in the field, then go to class, where I would learn some concept that made me think, "That totally applies to Rwanda." Then, driving home, I would hear a special report on the radio about one of the indictees from Vukovar being arrested and sent to the Tribunal in The Hague. So when I read about Congo, I actually became physically ill. And then when I read the requests of the Racak inhabitants, I felt they were talking directly to me. That article was the first thing I put in my hand luggage when I packed for Kosovo.

AT ZURICH AIRPORT, a clutch of Zimbabwean deminers strode past a group of European tourists. I knew the deminers were likely bound for Kosovo via Macedonia, since Kosovo's airports hadn't been reopened yet, so I followed them to their gate and sure enough, there was Jose Pablo Baraybar.

The flight to Skopje took us over country that initially looked Swiss, full of Alpine ranges, then like Austria with lush, rolling pasture and farmland, and finally like inland California's low, rolling, yellowed hills. But instead of

California oaks there was rust-red scrub. As we approached the airport, I saw more farmland and lots of the red-tile-roofed houses with unfinished upper floors common in Greece, Bosnia, and Croatia. From the air, Skopje was like the bottom of a ladle, with edges curving up gracefully. Beyond, in the distance, was Kosovo, with its sharp, snowcapped peaks looking painted on the sky.

Skopje airport reminded me of Zagreb's: a small, angled-roof building to which the plane just pulls up and stairs are brought over. There's something great about walking out of the back door of a plane onto open-air stairs. Like being in Africa, maybe. Inside the airport, we were met by two ICTY administrators, an affable American named Phil and a young Dutch woman, Madelon Schara. I had exchanged many faxes and e-mails about plane tickets and mission dates with Madelon over the years and it was interesting to finally meet her; her well-dressed prettiness seemed incongruous with the mission setting at first, but I eventually learned that she was adaptable and efficient. A straggly blond guy was behind us in line for a visa and Madelon asked him, "Are you with ICTY?" He looked confused and asked, "What's Ick-tee?" Madelon quickly replied, "Never mind," and turned away from him. It was a James Bond sort of response, and I liked that.

A lot of baggage hadn't arrived, including that of Justine Michael, a scene-of-crime officer (SOCO) with the Australian federal police who was the only other woman to arrive on our plane. Her bags hadn't made it past Singapore, so I offered her the extras I'd packed into my hand luggage— everything from clothes to toiletries—in case such a predicament had befallen me. We were driven to the ICTY office, which happened to be the former Yugoslav embassy: a big white three-story house with a wide view of Skopje. It was in a suburban neighborhood of gated houses and rosebushes, all looking down to the city with its blocky high-rise apartments, one expensive hotel, and a river running through it all. In the office, photographs were taken for our temporary identity papers and we signed a variety of documents before being driven to the Hotel Tasino Cesmice.

I shared a room with Justine, who was bubbly with relief that I had a hair dryer. As she tried to get a satellite connection through her high-end laptop, I tried to stop my secondhand circa 1990 laptop from suddenly turning off, as was its wont. I felt incognito. I'd been on five missions before this one, but only Jose Pablo knew it. Although some aspects of our arrival had been familiar, others were new; being met at the airport with such formality (name checked off on a list) and then immediately taken to sign papers seemed to bode well. Perhaps ICTY had upgraded its handling of the forensic missions since we had started them four years earlier. Maybe we would even be provided with scalpel blades that fit our scalpel handles.

The next morning, four more archaeologists and another SOCO arrived, and several drivers were on hand to take us to Kosovo. Justine and I got in a vehicle with our driver, Blerim, who was from Priština. We convoyed up and drove out of Skopje's center, which was characterized by flatness and a profusion of NGO Land Cruisers and therefore of car exhaust, until we reached the border with Kosovo, partway up the mountains but on a plateau within a valley. The wait at the border was about twenty minutes—negligible compared with the wait at the Sava to cross on the ferry from Croatia to Republika Srpska. The queue was made up of civilian cars, KFOR (the NATO Kosovo force) convoys carrying tanks, and some pedestrians. The border guard booth was so high off the ground that the officer inside couldn't see us, nor could we see him. Blerim just held all our passports out the window as high as he could for a whole minute and finally a hand appeared. The guard didn't even look down or stamp the passports, just took our visas from Macedonia. That was it.

We continued on a good road through the plateau for a while, the snowcapped peaks to our left in the great distance, and some houses in the middle distance. The first houses and buildings we passed were being rebuilt. Roof tiles, bricks, and lumber were everywhere, reminding me of towns around Vinkovci, near Vukovar, where the government had been handing out roof tiles to all who would move back and rebuild. As the valley widened, fields stretched out on either side of us for miles. Many were tilled as though ready for imminent planting; I saw three men tilling with a tractor in dark, rich brown soil. On the road, which got worse as we continued, we were surrounded by long convoys of KFOR Humvees carrying

American soldiers, and this reminded me strongly of being in Bosnia. The land was different, though—great valleys or flats with mountains in the distance, in contrast to Bosnia's ubiquity of mountains.

Blerim told me that Priština had only about 250,000 inhabitants but I found it looked bigger because it was built upward. I thought of the film *Blade Runner,* because of the tall buildings on narrow streets and the sense the city gave of being fully inhabited, even congested, with vehicles and people wearing black. Underground passageways and satellite dishes hinted at a futuristic double life known only to locals. Half the congestion was NGO traffic: Pharmacists Without Borders, World Food Programme, Al-Haramain, Caritas, Catholic Relief Services. Like Kigali before the UN pulled out. At the UN headquarters we tried to pick up our ICTY identity cards. It was here that I saw that ICTY might not be as efficient as I had hoped.

At first, we couldn't even get into the ICTY office because the guard wouldn't admit us without IDs. We explained that we were there to get the IDs. He didn't like that, so we tried a new tack: "We're with Blerim." But the guard was skeptical, didn't seem to know Blerim or trust him. It was worse than being held up outside of the Ovčara compound by our Jordanian guard unit. We were at a stalemate until an ICTY employee happened to pass through the hallway, recognized us as the forensic team, and invited us in. The guard was surly—"Fine, whatever"—as he waved us through the metal detector.

We spent the next hour filling out paperwork in a freezing conference room. Our field coordinator, an Irishman named Eamon Smyth, entered the room, explained what we'd be doing for the next few days (looking for places to live in Prizren, receiving mine awareness training), and gave us a briefing packet. Yes, a briefing packet. This prompted me to write in my journal, "Everything *appears* more organized than on prior missions, but it's really just added bureaucracy and they still aren't really telling us anything about the sites." Sure enough, Jose Pablo—ICTY's chief anthropologist—came to the conference room several *hours* later to say that he knew nothing and we should just remain ready for instructions in the next couple of days. In the meantime we would be driven to Prizren, the southwestern town where we would be living.

Blerim drove on the road that goes by Kosovo Polje, the out-of-commission airport, and the town of Mališevo. There was evidence of damage to houses in and around Mališevo but also the signs of rebuilding. Though burned out, the houses were now inhabited again, a satellite dish tilted just so on every soot-blackened third-story balcony. More signs of human occupation included a pile of sheepskins; a roadside Kosovo Liberation Army (KLA) graveyard with bright wreaths, flags, and a street lamp to keep it lit; a number of fresh, marked graves in fields; lots of vegetable plots covered by plastic; and vineyards before the descent into the town of Orahovac.

In Orahovac, Blerim stopped in front of a tall gate and honked the horn. A guard opened the gate and Blerim parked in front of a low linear building, the ICTY morgue. I walked around it in wonder, comparing it with the makeshift morgues of prior missions. Inside the newly remodeled building were a reception room, an area for families to view clothing, evidence rooms, multiple bathrooms, a lead-lined X-ray room, electricity and water, and—get this—autopsy tables with table-mounted sinks and fume hoods. I was in shock. My teammates couldn't appreciate this, I felt: for one thing, none of them were pathologists or anthropologists who would be using this equipment, and for another, they couldn't know how far we had come from the inflatable tent in Rwanda or the windowless, electricity- and water-free Bosnian morgue from 1996. Then I wondered what use this specially constructed building would have after ICTY left, as this was supposed to be the last season in which the group would send forensic scientists to Kosovo. Would local forensic teams use it when they created missing persons commissions, as had happened in Bosnia?

There, Ewa Klonowski, a Polish anthropologist I had met in the Kalesija morgue in 1996, asked Becky Saunders and me to conduct PHR workshops on exhumation techniques for law enforcement throughout Bosnia-Herzegovina in 1997. Next, the International Commission for Missing Persons asked PHR to assess the equipment needs of the new local teams. Ewa and I conducted that study by interviewing mortuary staff, mayors, and hospital pathologists; we made the report, and $250,000 was eventually meted out to the teams. In keeping with her spirit of spritelike determination, Ewa has never stopped volunteering her time for the Bosnian teams. But it was early days here in Kosovo and I told myself not to ask too many questions.

Blerim, workhorse that he was, loaded us back into the van to continue on to Prizren. By now, most of us were starving or had full bladders but we were forced to endure our discomfort as we encountered stretches of road so shelled out that, despite Blerim's best efforts, we crawled. Drivers in front of us had to slow nearly to a halt as they eased their low-bodied sedans into potholes so big the cars almost disappeared from view before revving up out the other side. The closer we got to Prizren the worse the road became and cars, horses, carts, and vans going in both directions were weaving slowly over any part of the road (save the grassy verge) that would allow them something like forward progress. The dust kicked up by all the traffic created a permanent fog backlit by the restaurants on the outskirts of the town. Eamonn had said earlier that Prizren was the most beautiful city in Kosovo. I knew to wait until morning to make that judgment.

We were booked into the Hotel Prizreni, where I roomed with Justine again. Our room was cold and the beds sagged, but it was better than being outside in the rain that had started. Also, water actually came out of the tap, had pressure, and was hot, and the lights worked. I fell thankfully into bed under a thin salmon-colored blanket whose insulating quality was reduced by an abundance of cigarette holes. Before going to sleep, I pondered in my journal whether the forensic team was now being treated like UN employees and thus more like difficult children, shooed from place to place, or whether it just seemed that way to me.

IN DAYLIGHT, PRIZREN DID REVEAL itself as a beautiful city, with a rock-wall-lined river winding through it. The old town was on the far side, reached by ancient stone footbridges. We wouldn't have time to take in its beauty quite yet, as we were on our way back to UNHQ Priština, where we met Nancy Barrett, the coordinator of the Transcultural Psychosocial Organization (TPO). TPO was a team of local and international medical doctors, medical students, and psychologists who would be in the field collecting antemortem data for presumptive identifications of bodies both in advance of us and as we worked. Barrett explained that they would be supporting families at the sites, as well as supporting us. I didn't know whether she meant psychosocially or administratively; either could be helpful. The most important aspect of the current setup, she went on to say, was that the TPO workers were a part of our team. She was totally positive (without being abrasively upbeat), totally NGO, and I could just see her in about three weeks' time, frustrated because most of the people she would deal with at ICTY would not share her let's-hold-hands attitude. Her several colleagues introduced themselves: Amor was the field coordinator, and Benny had worked with PHR the previous year collecting testimonies from displaced Kosovar Albanians who'd managed to flee to Albania. Then Barrett asked Jose Pablo to introduce his team. He did a bit of a Bill, mumbling our names but not saying what we did, leaving TPO in the dark about who we were. However, Barrett determinedly pressed on, inviting us to share their refreshments and have a meet-and-greet.

Benny, Amor, Luigi (Luigi had studied cultural anthropology), and I talked about what to do when families want to see remains. They had found that relatives respond variously, so TPO tries to assess what each person can handle. We also talked about how the forensic personnel may find that they have their own emotions to deal with. In telling them about the priest's niece in Kibuye, and how I had wanted to do more for her, I had to blink back tears; now I wondered how I was going to cope with having families graveside while we worked, as Jose Pablo had told me was likely.

After refreshments, we were given the most detailed instruction I'd had yet on mine awareness and avoidance. It was locally specific, so we saw slides of the markers most commonly used in Kosovo to notify people of mines: bottles sitting on twigs, piles of rocks, felled branches, crossed twigs, paths going wildly out of their way, cow skulls strung up between trees. The slide show was followed by a field trip to the UN Mine Awareness program, where we were shown examples of types of mines recovered so far. Then we were taken to an abandoned yard between two buildings with the carcass of a military jeep sitting in it and told to look for twenty-five signs of mines or ordnance. We missed most of them—not just the tripwire we were standing on but also the star-shaped triggers in the tops of the antipersonnel mines nestled in the short grass. The soldier instructing us indicated a spot on the ground with his telescoping pointer; I couldn't see anything until he pushed a few little weeds aside, and there was the trigger. I have rarely seen such a small object look so menacing. When we went back to Prizren, I noticed that an abandoned house I'd walked past several times bore markers of a sort we'd just learned about: green upside-down "V"s spray-painted around the front door.

The last of the scheduled activities before the teams began their work was a talk by James Mills, the ICTY welfare officer. This was the first mission I'd been part of where ICTY had brought in a counselor of sorts; I was looking forward to hearing him and seeing others' reaction to him. Eamonn introduced James thus: "I think what this man has to say is of the utmost importance, so I ask you, even if you don't think you need to hear it, please, just keep your opinions to yourself so those who want to hear him can do so." James began by explaining all the physiological aspects of stress: increased blood pressure, for instance, and the unconscious clenching of muscles. He described "critical incident stress" and the fight-or-flight reaction. Naturally, I thought about the night of the lake shooting in Rwanda: my hands shaking even hours later, my loss of appetite, the way I had held my hand over my heart and my sense of increased hearing capacity. Other symptoms had persisted after that night, and I tensed up each time I heard a speedboat. I also remembered the relief—the incredible relief—at finally being able to leave that place.

My recollections clearly connected with what James taught us about the difference between short-term and sustained stress and how one adapts until the adaptation can no longer be maintained and is replaced by exhaustion. He cited the examples of local Kosovars who worked as translators for the UN in Mitrovica (northern Kosovo). One woman couldn't even look at a man whom she had seen being beaten; another was having terrifying dreams about the night she had heard her neighbors being beaten: the noise came through the wall. Meanwhile, in The Hague, the people—some of them from Kosovo—sorting through photographs and compiling witness interviews were themselves suffering from post-traumatic stress. James said he believed that a period of time off would allow them to continue working over the long run, instead of losing their jobs.

James also said he'd counseled a "high-ranking, career UN person who shall remain nameless," who worked in Rwanda. This man had been handed an infant by a woman who told him it was her last surviving child. "Please take my baby," she begged, "I can't bear to see any more of my children die." At that moment, the infant died in the man's arms. Since then, the man had experienced feelings of guilt and impotence, as well as bouts of weeping and nightmares. He was given a debriefing and took six months in New York on leave; I imagine he must still be recovering.

I had heard about debriefings but never learned exactly what they were. James defined a debriefing as a psychological, educational, and cognitive process designed not to make you forget disturbing events but to place them somewhere so that you can move on. Our team was told that we would all have a "redeployment debriefing" with James before we left the mission, in order to prepare us to adjust to our normal lives. (Yet, somehow, I was never debriefed. I was really looking forward to it, too.)

James urged us to pay attention to our well-being—physical, spiritual, and intellectual. He reminded us that peer support was crucial: we should look out for those around us who might be on the brink of exhaustion and invite them out to coffee to talk. I figured the physical was doable—I was already picturing evening promenades along the river in Prizren—but wondered about the spiritual and intellectual, the very realms that are difficult to explore while in the field. Would this mission be different? I warmed to my colleagues, because their response to James was respectful, by and large. I had barely spoken to most of them; I wondered who might become a friend, beyond Justine.

My enthusiasm was checked rather smartly when James asked whether anyone had comments or questions. One person, an American, raised his hand, so James asked him, "Do you have a question?" The team member responded with a long silence and then said, "Yeah. How do you use the phones around here?" James responded evenly, "Well, you pick up the handset, wait for a dial tone, then dial. It helps to have a phone card, which you can get at the post office." I think we were all embarrassed by our teammate's rudeness. I didn't want James to think that we were all ignorant of important issues related to stress or emotion, but I also didn't feel like exposing myself to ridicule, as I had in Kibuye. Thankfully, Tom Grange and Aldo Bolaños leaped into the breach.

Tom, an ex-cop from the States, nearly brought me to tears by saying that he'd been on both sides of a war: "In 1968, we thought we were helping and we weren't, and now I want to help people who can't help themselves." Aldo, a Peruvian archaeologist I'd worked with at Brčko, asked about a dream he had had in Bosnia the previous year: he was running from some soldiers who caught up with him. He got down on his knees and begged, "Please don't shoot me," but they shot him in the head. James replied that Aldo must have identified with a body he had seen in a grave, and that Aldo's brain was just trying to deal with that while he was sleeping. I was grateful to Aldo, not just from a personal standpoint but because it showed that even he, one of our most experienced archaeologists and a pretty macho guy, could suffer emotionally from the work. I was surprised that he had had his nightmare while in the field. Most of mine had occurred once I had flown home, except for the dreams I had at the Kibuye Guest House, of legs in the bed with me.

However, in Kosovo I had my first complete, in-mission dream—one that wasn't a nightmare: I was at the ICTY morgue in Orahovac, taking the next body to be autopsied out of the refrigerated container. The body was that of an adult male, fully clothed and very cold. I put the body on the autopsy table and was preparing my tools, about to remove the clothing, when the body started to blink its eyes open and closed. I started, then stared at him: he wasn't dead, he was just frozen, and he was now thawing out on the table. I kept looking at his face, a little frightened. Then he opened his eyes all the way and said to me, slowly and thickly, "Thank you." I was incredulous but then remembered that his family was outside, waiting for the results of the autopsy, so I picked him up again and carried him outside in my arms to where the family was standing in a huddle. I walked up to them and they just looked at me, confused. The body meant nothing to them. I wanted to call the man by his name but I couldn't pronounce it because it had so many X's in it, so I just blurted, "He's alive. He's alive!" And he smiled at them weakly but reassuringly and after a moment, realization hit the family and they started screaming and crying and trying to hug him. They hurriedly took him from my arms, and I just backed away—they were complete without me—feeling deeply emotional and strangely proud.

19.

THE GRANDFATHER

BY THE TIME OF MY DREAM ABOUT THE MAN WHO WOKE UP, A
month had passed and I was working in the morgue. I had started out in
the field—work that, although I was an old hand, had new aspects. On previous missions, we had dealt with large clandestine graves. But witness
statements in Kosovo described postmortem interference with bodies,
which meant remains had been scattered by alleged perpetrators or had
been hidden in preexisting cemeteries. In other cases, families who had fled
Kosovo had returned to find lying in the street the decomposing bodies of
people they believed were their relatives, so they had buried the bodies in
cemeteries. It was estimated that the remains of several thousand people
were in these various states of interment throughout Kosovo. The forensic
teams would have to fan out from our home base in Prizren across the
province to accomplish our mandate, so Jose Pablo divided us into several
field teams, each with a leader and a security warden.

My first team leader was "Wollie" Wolmarans, a South African police
officer. Our routine was to meet in the parking lot of the Lion Restaurant
on the main road out of Prizren; from there, all the teams would either
drive in convoy to sites or split off to separate sites, one team to a car. Our

drives were usually long and started early, and I used the time to learn Albanian, having heard my landlady's daughter, Fllanza, gently remind a teammate who had greeted her with *"Dobar dan"* that, although everyone in Kosovo can speak Serbian, Kosovar Albanians now speak only Albanian. Naturally, I had learned some Albanian specifically to communicate with the locals who would be working with us as laborers—like *"Prit, ju lutem"* ("Wait, please"), which I learned from our interpreter, Azven—but Fllanza had also taught me hello and good night (*tung* and *noten e mire*). During these drives, I noticed that the land looked benign, as if nothing bad had happened here, but the buildings told a different story. Envision a row of houses, each standing intact but with empty gaping windows, while above the top lintel of each house are dark smudges of soot. The soot is so evocative; I sensed what it must be like to see all the houses burning at once, flames licking up out of the windows.

The first time we drove through the town of Djakova, I felt I saw the burning at its most systematic. We had gone there to pick up deminers and security forces from the Italian KFOR base, but even before we reached the town, we could see large-scale destruction of some of the bigger buildings, which were partially collapsed. Once in the town, I could see evidence of destruction at a more individual level: single shops along the road had imploded, their contents a heap of rubble within the jagged walls of the buildings. As we passed through the old town I could see businesses along the main road being rebuilt in varnished wood, while just one street behind them, everything had been obliterated, leaving mountains of rubble and architectural skeletons. Many houses on the other side of town had blue tarps patching their roofs, or had roofs made only of tarps. As in Croatia, people were living there, in the back.

Our drive that day ended in the countryside near a river in the heart of the Serbian military activity zone, where we were to do a preliminary investigation of sites. First, we encountered a trouser cuff and skeletonized lower leg sticking straight up toward the sky from under rocks. A cranium with a gunshot wound was visible nearby, in the same rock cluster. Elsewhere, in a group of bucolic fields surrounding a single house on a hill, several big army vehicles and demining soldiers were waiting for us to park our convoy. The deminers had sprayed fluorescent pink paint onto small rocks, marking the boundary beyond which the ground hadn't been demined. Here, we dug through earth mounds but found only layers of dead grass, then compact gravel beneath. The fields themselves were well shorn by sheep and the shepherds appeared to enjoy having us around for a few days. Their large and friendly dogs visited us and the shepherds played their flutes sporadically throughout the day, often making me feel as if I was in the Iran of *People of the Wind,* my parents' documentary about nomadic shepherds. Several military helicopters passing overhead seemed discordant.

During those early spring days in the first two weeks of the mission, the weather was extraordinary: light clouds, sunny but not hot, with a breeze that picked up in strength as the day went on. We remarked more than a few times that Kosovo was truly beautiful. From where we worked, we had a clear view of the mountains beyond which lay Albania; at our feet were fighting positions dug into the earth that would have allowed snipers easy shots at Kosovar Albanians fleeing to those mountains in 1999.

Soon, the forensic teams had moved from these rural sites to cemeteries, where we exhumed both marked and unmarked graves. We noticed that some graves had a cup next to them, upturned on a wooden post marker. It was a custom that these cups stayed upturned until a year had passed since burial.

If a family had marked the grave of the person they believed to be their relative, ICTY asked permission to carry out the exhumation. The families often agreed to the exhumation and were present while we worked. Having them so close by was not as difficult as I had expected. It was as though there was no space left for vocal communication. And, as with the woman who recognized her brother's jacket at Kibuye church, I couldn't think of anything to say.

AT THE FIRST CEMETERY, we encountered burial accoutrements, for which we established a system that we went on to use for all such sites. Once a grave of evidentiary value to ICTY was identified, our local hired workers would set aside any wreaths from the grave, then remove the mound of backdirt, usually first exposing a layer of plastic. Under the plastic was often a *drraza,* a row of thick wood planks lying at an angle, like a lean-to, keeping the soil from resting on the coffin lid. Once the *drraza* was exposed, the workers would step out of the grave to allow archaeologists to expose the edges of the soil around the *drraza* for a clean photograph taken by the SOCO. Then the archaeologists would remove the *drraza,* generally revealing a coffin sitting in some depth of water—ground water that would have turned black from the decomposition of the body. A bucket brigade would remove the water before the coffin was photo-documented; next the coffin lid would be removed and the contents photo-documented. At this point, anthropologists would join the archaeologists to exhume the body, which was often wrapped in plastic or cloth. The SOCO would lay a numbered and labeled body bag on the edge of the grave and more archaeologists would help maneuver the body into the bag. This entire package would be lifted into a second clean, labeled body bag. The forensic team members would then climb out of the grave and carry the body bag on a stretcher to the waiting refrigerated truck while the workers were left to replace the *drraza* and dirt in the grave and lay the wreaths back on top.

The first time I worked at a cemetery site, I found this system odd and rather clinical because it involved so many people, each with a small job. I was used to having a section of a mass grave and dealing with several bodies over a period of days. During our lunch break it was raining and I sat with "Elvis," one of the local workers who was around my age and with whom I'd become friendly. His demeanor had been happy during work on the noncemetery sites; now Elvis seemed miserable. Wrinkling his nose and gesturing at the refrigerated truck, he asked me, "How does this make you feel?" I replied that it was different for me because I had chosen the work; I had traveled there to do it. He asked not to have any contact with the bodies, and I said of course he didn't have to and that I was sorry if he had been asked to do more than deal with dirt. We squatted under a tree, wet and quiet, and I looked at the family members and spectators standing in little knots in the cemetery.

After lunch, I worked on a second grave with Claudia Bisso, an Argentine archaeologist. We were in a corner of the cemetery near some hedges, accompanied by two workers; our interpreter, Dreni; and a man in his forties, dressed nicely, smoking in the background and occasionally spitting: the brother of the man whose body was presumed to be in the grave. The workers fully exposed the *drraza,* but Claudia and I helped from time to time because it was hard going: the soil was waterlogged and therefore heavy. Also, this grave was deep, so it took a lot of muscle to lift the backdirt on a shovel blade past the height of one's shoulders and hurl it onto the ground. After Claudia and I cleaned up the *drraza* and had it photo-documented, we lowered ourselves in again and removed the boards, exposing the coffin. Aidan, a British archaeology assistant, arrived at the moment when we discovered that the coffin lid had been nailed down. We would have to pry it off; we gave this unpleasant job to Aidan. The thumping of the pick against the coffin was horrible, as was the sound of splitting wood as he worked the lid off. I felt bad for the brother and looked at him, but his face was impassive. Serious, but impassive.

Once the lid of the coffin was removed, we could see that it held a body wrapped in plastic and awash in maggots and old pupa casings, reddish-brown in color. As with the other cemetery bodies, it was difficult to find a place to stand once the lid was off because the body took up all the space in the coffin, and in turn the coffin took up all the space in the hole. Claudia and I spanned the width of the hole by laying down a few boards and stood on those while getting the body out from underneath. Aidan, Claudia, and I were then able to lever the body out and double-bag it. While I was away in graduate school, I had forgotten how heavy and awkward dead bodies are, but the memory came back quickly. I was really stinking by then, and wet from the rain. As the workers began shoveling the dirt back into the grave, the brother smoked his last cigarette and walked away. It was a miserable day for working, but the exhumation in the corner was satisfying because we worked together on one body from start to finish. This was what I was used to and preferred.

Still, it wasn't long before I was familiar with my team and had adapted to the new system. I was glad to be in the field again and I looked forward to every new day. Then Jose Pablo reorganized us, and Derick Schoemann, a South African explosives expert, became my team leader. One of his responsibilities was to complete daily computerized site reports and photograph logs, along with adding to our database new presumptive identification information that TPO had gathered from possible relatives. Derick had delegated this responsibility to someone who was dedicated but not quick, so I made suggestions about how to speed up the process—by copying and pasting multiple items instead of retyping the same numbers over and over in several data fields, for instance. Derick had overheard me, and asked me to take over that day's report generating. That was fine with me, because it could be done within a few hours in the evening and wouldn't interfere with my daily excavation duties. The next morning, I discovered that I was wrong.

All the teams had moved to a new site, a place where witness information indicated that bodies had been buried without coffins, and Derick was so concerned that the site reports be completed before the day was finished that he told me not to dig or suit up at all. Instead, I was to just generate reports as the day progressed. I had to restrain myself from pointing out that he would probably encounter "loose" skeletons, which could only be properly lifted by an anthropologist, and that I was the only anthropologist on his team. Indeed, of the five team members, I was the only one with experience of more than one ICTY mission. And just because I knew how to use a few macros on the computer he wanted me in street clothes, next to the grave (or worse, just next to the cars), chained to a laptop. I was furious and embarrassed and incapable of expressing any of this in a diplomatic way. So I simply did the reports. When there were no data coming out of the grave, I sat on the edge and advised the people exhuming (one of whom had never even seen bodies before) on how to best bag a head without disarticulating it from the neck vertebrae and the importance of examining the soil under the body for loose teeth or artifacts. I was like a surgeon's scrub nurse, handing them the small bags needed for finger bones before they had even asked for them.

Derick was effusive in his praise of my speedy computer work, so I figured if I had to be a secretary, I was going to be a damned good one. Because Justine was SOCO for her team, she had to do site reports every evening. So we would sit together at the dining room table; she would have a stiff drink and I would have a peach juice. When we were finished, we would go into the living room and type in our personal journals. This wasn't my first tour as team scribe. It had happened in Kibuye toward the end of the mission, when it was discovered that the pathologists hadn't entered most of the autopsy reports into the computer. That work took several days, but at least it wasn't during the exhumation or analysis. And in Bosnia, Dorothy and I ended up creating databases for the morgue because we knew a bit of Excel. But that was years, missions ago. This felt different.

At the next site, a cemetery in a wooded area behind a small village, Derick was assigned three graves to open on the first day. Although I was to be scribe again, I donned a Tyvek protective suit to show my readiness to dig. The graves were on a low hill, a lovely spot with sunlight filtering down between the tall trees and a growing breeze blowing brown leaves down onto us along with the occasional blossom. To my pleasure, Derick sent me to exhume the third grave. I walked with two workers on a woodland path over to the far side of the cemetery, where we knew which grave to exhume because the grandfather of the person presumed to be in the grave had arrived. He told us that he had buried the body. His grandson had been shot in the legs, and, unable to run away, had then been shot in the back. The grandfather asked to stay and watch the exhumation, and he did.

Barney Kelly, an Irish police officer who was one of my housemates, took an overall photograph and then the workers removed the soil, exposing the *drraza* almost immediately. The workers were doing a beautiful job of squaring off edges and clearing away more backdirt, allowing us to use the ground right at the edge of the grave to lay down the body bag. I was impressed by how quickly they had adjusted to our particular needs. Barney photographed the *drraza* while Dave Green, a British SOCO, talked to the grandfather through an interpreter. Then I got in the grave alone and began removing the planks.

There was lots of water in the grave, a good fifteen or twenty centimeters. I knew the body would be wrapped in a sheet (the grandfather had told us) but I wasn't expecting it to be shoeless. Poking out of the water were two fleshed, slightly bloated feet. As I removed the rest of the planks, I could see that a sheetlike material was indeed covering the body from the ankles to the head (the face was, mercifully, covered). He was on his back, with his hands folded across his middle. The water was high, at his midline, so I informed Barney that I was going to bucket out some water before he took a photograph. I put one of the planks down next to the body to give me something solid to stand on but my feet were still underwater while I carried out a bucket brigade with one of the workers. We worked without talking for about five minutes, accompanied by the sound of the wind and the sound of the water being poured out onto the nearby ground. The grandfather and the TPO guy smoked and talked quietly. As we worked, the leaves were falling into the grave and covering the body's head.

When we were ready to lift out the body, the old man took a good long look at his grandson. I caught his eye as he turned away and he just shook his head. I pursed my lips. I wanted to say *"Me falni,"* ("I'm sorry"), and I would have said it if we'd been alone, but there were too many people around and the moment passed. I still regret my silence, because I wanted him to know that we weren't emotionless scientists who just exhumed bodies by rote, that we were capable of recognizing that this body was his grandson, and yet I was painfully aware that *me falni* wasn't enough. Just as in Kibuye with the woman who recognized her brother's jacket, what could I say? There I am, on the one hand in a deeply personal situation with someone because I am involved with his or her dead relative, and yet on the other hand we are strangers. So I say nothing because it is only my actions that can help.

As we lifted the grandson's body, its arms bent up inside the sheet, so that the hands tore a hole in it. Through the hole, I could see dead maggots and pupa sacs lying on his shirt: confirmation that he had lain on the surface some time before being buried. Derick worried that I might not have the brute strength to lift the body, but between us we managed and were even able to drain a fair amount of water out of the body bag by tilting the body on an angle over the edge of the grave. We then double-bagged it and the workers took it away on a stretcher; the grandfather watched it go past and then followed slowly.

My teammates at the other graves were finishing, so we were able to pack up the trucks quickly. Pleased that we had finished before Aldo's team down the road, Derick gave me a broad, dimpled smile and said, "You are much more useful in the grave than on the computer, Clea!" Relief swept over me, and indeed Derick never kept me out of the graves again.

Our teams drove out of the town in convoy with the bodies strapped into a pickup in front of us, a silver tarp cinched down tight over them. I watched the back of the truck on the long drive back to the morgue, thinking of the grandfather and his willingness to let us "borrow" his grandson. I was finally part of a reconciliation between the needs of the families as "owners" of the contents of the graves and the Tribunal as keepers of evidence. This was so different from the days when the Mothers of Vukovar protested forensic investigation into the grave at Ovčara, and although the circumstances were different, I wondered if the evolution in the Mothers' stance had helped create acceptance of forensic exhumations in Kosovo.

I also couldn't help but think of Suada, my landlady in the town where we lived while exhuming mass graves in nearby Brčko in 1997. That was the first mission for which the team was brought together by the UN without the aid of PHR. The difference was that fewer team members had an interest in human rights, and the new project administrators in The Hague did not appear to understand the reality of the forensic team's work—an understanding that had been crucial to the success of PHR-organized missions. The UN administrators had suggested that if any people we rented houses from asked why we were there, we could say we were building a road. But anyone doing our laundry would sniff out the truth. It didn't even take that much with Suada.

The day Becky Saunders, Ute Hofmeister, and I met Suada, we spoke in the fragmentary Bosnian I had picked up from my translator, Mirzet, on the ICMP job a few months earlier. After we drank some tea, Suada got up from her chair and motioned us over to a cabinet, whose door she opened. On the inside of the door was a piece of paper with a man's portrait on it, his birth and death dates printed at the bottom. She tapped the paper several times and said, "Brčko." We gleaned that the man was her brother. Suada knew full well why we were there. She knew, even though our Tribunal ID tags were hidden in our shirts and our license plates were marked as UN, not ICTY. She knew even though we hadn't started digging.

I didn't know if Suada's brother was even in a grave, but I felt I should have been looking for him, Suada's brother, not just working for the Tribunal. And although I knew that Suada's insistence on cleaning the mud off our (nonwork) boots every night despite our protests was an instance of her typical Balkan cleanliness, I wondered too if she was somehow trying to get closer to the grave. When I lay in bed in Suada's house, I often thought, "There has to be a better way," just as I had when the priest's niece viewed his remains in Kibuye. It was the old "double vision" in which I felt the graves and bodies belonged to relatives while the grave as crime scene came second, or was a parallel necessity. Now that, in Kosovo, we had "borrowed" the grandfather's grandson, that vision was beginning to coalesce.

20

THE BOY WITH THE MARBLES

NOT ALL THE DEAD IN KOSOVO HAD BEEN BURIED BY THEIR REL-atives. Some were buried by perpetrators during the region's "cleansing," others by cemetery staff after the conflict when bodies were collected from the surrounding neighborhoods by sanitation workers. As a result, we couldn't be sure of their identities. We spent more than a week at one cemetery where we were slated to exhume more than one hundred bodies. All the subteams worked at the site, so we were a very long convoy: three pickup trucks, a minivan, a reefer (refrigerated truck), and six four-wheel drives. Now that the end of April was approaching, the weather was becoming hot and humid, the clouds burning off by eleven in the morning.

Of the graves that had headstones or markers, most of the death dates were in May 1999 and most of the birth dates made the decedents younger than I: the years 1974 and 1976 were well represented. The composition of my team had changed: though Derick was still our team leader and Barney was still our photographer, Justine was now our SOCO, and two anthropologists, Carmen and Angel, had joined us. Carmen is a wonderful Peruvian woman, whom I knew from Bosnia in 1997, while Angel was joining us from Colombia. The portion of the cemetery we were to investigate consisted of a relatively barren clearing with only one tree and lots of fresh graves. Derick assigned me to a grave with Elvis. Carmen and Angel were on a grave next to mine, while Aidan was working farther away.

It was immediately clear that the forensic teams had been lulled into a relaxed approach to excavation because of the earlier ubiquity of *drrazas*: the boards had given us an immediate indication of how wide and how long to make the opening so that we could remove the coffin lid and thereby exhume the body. At this cemetery, none of the graves we exhumed on our first morning had a *drraza,* and without the boards to mark a grave's edges, we had to approach the excavation by determining the whole matrix of the grave before digging lower. Even so, the opening might have to be widened later as we actually uncovered the body; for instance, the torso might lie directly beneath the grave mound but the left leg might disappear into the wall of the grave, so we would have to widen that section from the surface downward. As is usual in cemeteries, the graves were packed in close to each other, so the mounds of earth on neighboring graves made it impossible to approach our graves from the side or to dig a wide opening at the top.

Unfortunately, all our morning excavations required expansion of the hole after we had already exposed skeletal remains because we continually underestimated the scope of the digging. There were no blankets or wrappings of any sort, much less coffins, so the whole process required more time and Derick was at his wit's end. He would stand above our graves making predictions that at this rate it would take us three weeks to exhume 150 graves. He would pace from grave to grave, asking whether we were ready for photographs yet, but I told him we'd learned on previous missions that "dirty bodies just look like dirt."

As for the bodies themselves, the first few that I exhumed were skeletonized men, wearing clothes but no shoes. One man's head was massively fractured, with soft tissue and pupa casings inside the cranium—this was another person who had lain on the surface before being buried. Another body was skeletonized from the waist down, but the upper body was saponified, with live maggots in the thorax. His right arm, his right cheek, and the right side of his jaw were fractured in many places. I remember the pungency of his brain matter and how it mingled with the heated humidity in the air when I bent over him. At that point, Aidan, too, was working below the surface of the ground and when I lifted my head to get mildly fresher air, I would catch his eye and we would smile at each other. Even though the work was backbreaking, we were glad to be doing it and glad to be working on our own graves.

When I took a moment to stand up and survey the graveyard one day, I thought we were quite a sight: a large group of people, most in blue Tyvek suits, and ten graves open at any time. The KFOR soldiers guarding us were respectful, keeping their distance and only coming in for a look when we all took lunch. Interestingly, at this site the interpreters and TPO people were a distraction: because the remains were unidentified, there were no families on hand, so they had little to do. They sat nearby talking with each other in an animated and jovial fashion that produced a constant buzz. Usually I find that laughter and chatter unconnected to the work at hand highlight the seriousness of what I am doing. I become more grim, feeling like I'm in a parallel world. I preferred the times when just Aidan and I came back to our graves before others returned from lunch, or when the day grew too hot for people to keep up the chatter. The monotony for the TPO people and interpreters was rarely broken at this site: because so many bodies were skeletonized, there were long intervals when the activity was hidden from view because the forensic folks were crouched in the graves, exhuming one bone at a time.

We were filthy and exhausted by evening, especially because it was a constant battle to keep the equipment cleaned, organized, and packed into the trucks carefully so that it would all fit. We also had to gather the rubbish left by our own team. Some days the gatherers were just me, Aidan, and Sam Brown, a newly arrived British anthropology assistant. My earliest memories of Sam center on her lips clamped around a cigarette to keep it away from the flammable Tyvek suiting as she wrangled it into our too-small trash bags. Others just stepped out of their suits and into a vehicle, done with the day's work, apparently oblivious to their suit being picked up by the wind to land on a headstone a few meters away. That so few of us were picking up the rubbish was indicative of how much the subteams had become separate instead of identifying as one group that was wholly responsible for its actions. Our dwindling supplies exacerbated the separation; we were down to about the last five body bags, for instance, and the logistics people didn't know when the next shipment would arrive, so the teams competed for the best of whatever equipment remained.

In the midst of our work at the large cemetery site, we received our first VIP visit. I expected the occasion to mirror those in Rwanda and Bosnia, where the VIPs simply helicoptered in and paused at the site before helicoptering out, but this visit was different. First, when we arrived at the cemetery in the morning, we found that KFOR had cordoned off areas with signs that read PRESS ONLY, and soldiers directed us where to park. We all changed into our blue coveralls, divvied up tools, and fought over the few remaining body bags. We were told to use plastic sheeting and only to deplete our limited supply of bags when the VIPs were there. Luckily, the Dutch KFOR battalion had donated fifteen body bags, so we had a temporary reprieve.

My team had a new area to work in, without a tree in sight. Our graves were marked with dark green tape; Justine was busy numbering them. As before, each of the five of us on Derick's team had his or her own grave. This time, in our morning session, we encountered relatively fancy coffins. My first one had a narrow top section that splayed out wide where the lid met the base container. The coffin was made of a dark cherrylike wood and there was black-painted metal scrollwork around the lid.

Our usual workers had the day off; I had a new helper I'd never worked with before, and we got off to a rough start. I would show him the width needed for the initial opening by putting my shovel at the edge I wanted the earth dug out to, and he would put his shovel in closer, as if to say, "Here would be fine, though." I ended up doing about a third of the digging myself because I couldn't force him to do it. Unfortunately, the only Albanian I'd learned was polite Albanian—you know, "Dig here, please," rather than "Dig here, dammit!," which would have been more useful with this guy. However, as the day got hotter and hazier, he decided to work in partnership with me and we ended up being efficient.

Eventually Jose Pablo arrived and called lunch, which I ate with my housemates at a good distance from the site and under a tree, with a view of the eminently watchable KFOR soldiers. And as had become usual with these cemetery sites, lunch felt like a picnic because the old parts of cemeteries are shaded by abundant trees, well cared for, and calming.

After lunch, I started working on my next grave and things became interesting. Again, there was neither *drraza* nor coffin, neither sheet nor blanket wrapping, just soil on top of a body lying on its back. The body was clothed in two hooded sweatshirts, a jacket, and tracksuit pants. The many layers of clothes reminded me first of the Kibuye bodies and then of the Vukovar hospital bodies. The clothing here was also notable because the weather was so hot. I was wearing only a T-shirt and shorts under my coverall and I was sweating so much my eyes stung every time I looked up to hand my worker a bucket filled with backdirt. But the person in the grave had probably been killed in early spring; snow would still have been visible on the mountains, as it had been when I arrived in Kosovo at the beginning of April. A cloudy turquoise marble had turned up in the soil above the body. I laid it aside in an evidence bag.

As I cleared the last of the soil away from the body's right shin, the bottom of the bone just above the ankle fell from its position. "Shit!" I thought, presuming I'd dislodged a fractured piece of bone. Then I picked it up and immediately saw that it wasn't a bone fragment loose from trauma; in fact, it was an intact distal epiphyseal cap of the tibia. It had not even begun to fuse with the rest of the tibia, and the superior surface of the epiphysis was billowy with youth. The skeleton was that of a young person. But I wasn't thinking about children.

Out of habit when faced with youthful bone, I glanced at the matching point on the other leg, peeling the trouser leg back a bit. The line of fusion was clear: dark, open, ominous. Quickly, I leaned over to examine the skull, which I had exposed but not yet detail-cleaned. I carefully cleared the soil away from the teeth. Yes: mandibular canine and second mandibular molar erupting, second maxillary molar still in the crypt. This person was probably between twelve and fifteen years old when his life ended.

With renewed vigor despite the afternoon heat, I cleared all the dirt until I had just the body lying on the floor of the grave. I could tell that items were lodged in the dirt-caked right hip pocket of the tracksuit pants. I didn't have to expose much more to see that they were marbles. Lots of them. A good handful. Suddenly I was thinking about children. About how I'd noticed young kids playing what I thought of as the "old-fashioned" game of marbles while the forensic teams had played soccer with the older children from our neighborhood a few weeks earlier. I had watched these little kids when I left the soccer field for a break (we'd been run ragged). Two little boys flicked their marbles in grass so long they could barely track the progress. It was great to see children playing a game outdoors, a game that didn't involve a television and that was perhaps passed on from parent to kid, from kid to kid. I was thinking about children, boys especially. About how they can be so different from young girls, who sometimes stalk their adulthood, wanting to wear training bras even when they have only the hint of breasts, or wanting to wear makeup before their parents will allow it. Boys can be slower in this race, perhaps surreptitiously checking their reflections in mirrors, looking for the first signs of mustache hair but otherwise trying to get away with juvenile behavior for as long as possible. The boy in my grave had a pocket full of marbles, and that told me more about his life than almost anything else could.

The marbles didn't necessarily have evidentiary value for the Tribunal, given that the skeleton with its trauma would tell the story that he was both a child and a noncombatant. But in the grave with him, I saw beyond the forensic facts to the boy he might have been. Derick had given me time to clean this boy's body and clothing because Bernard Kouchner, one of the founders of Médecins Sans Frontières (Doctors Without Borders) and the then head of the UN Interim Administration Mission in Kosovo (UNMIK), was due to visit the site at three o'clock that afternoon and Jose Pablo had decided that this grave was going to be a part of the official tour. I spent the rest of the afternoon with the boy and his marbles.

While I worked, I thought about General Klein's visit to the Ovčara grave and how Clipboard Man couldn't see the bodies right in front of him. Thus, I cleaned this boy's clothing well and gave his teeth particular attention; their whiteness contrasted well with the bones and clothing and they were recognizable, allowing the viewers to orient themselves, given that they would be seeing the body from an awkward angle. When I next looked up, I noticed that more KFOR soldiers had arrived, half concealed behind headstones and stationed every twenty paces or so, their hands on their guns. Finally, after four o'clock, a cloud of dust rising in the distance from a convoy of vehicles announced the imminent arrival of VIPs. Jose Pablo had already reminded all of us to be on our best behavior, to wear our blue suits zipped all the way up (despite the risk of heatstroke), and to keep working while he conducted the tour.

I focused studiously on the body and didn't look up. I heard Jose Pablo approaching, followed by about twenty pairs of well-shod feet at my eye level. I pulled the little bit of dirt I had just loosened away from the head of the boy, put it in the bucket, and then backed up toward the foot of the grave so the visitors could see what Jose Pablo was explaining: "Here you can see the condition of some of the remains, skeletonized, and this is a young teenager." I looked up and saw the group crowded around Jose Pablo, their heads blocking the glare of afternoon sunlight behind them. Sweat was running into my eyebrows and onto my lips, and my hair was sticking to my forehead. As I tried to shrug it away I made eye contact with a man tilting his head to listen to Jose Pablo. He was the person to whom Jose Pablo was directing all of his commentary. I was surprised that he wasn't looking at the body in the grave. And then he smiled at me, a sort of appreciative and apologetic smile, with very warm eyes. So I smiled back, but with a subdued smile-grimace. I found out later that he was Bernard Kouchner.

After Barney had photo-documented the body, some of the group lingered behind and watched as we prepared a body bag. Then the VIPs were on their way out and the journalists with them were running to keep up. I was sorry to see them go, somehow: it was nice to see people from the outside world.

When we finally carried the boy's body on the stretcher to the freezer truck, I was reminded of how much I value this part of the process. I used to think that this feeling originated in 1996, when we carried everything up that hill in Kibuye to the church or scrambled up the slope at Cerska, but I actually felt equally proprietorial back in Arizona each time we drove to the Human Identification Lab from the medical examiner's office with an unidentified person's bones in the trunk. Locking those bones in the trunk of our university vehicle or putting a body bag into the reefer for transport to the Tribunal morgue feels like the only quasi-ceremonial step that marks an Unidentified's formal entry onto the path of becoming an Identified.

21

THE SWEDE AT THE MORGUE

A FEW DAYS AFTER KOUCHNER'S VISIT, JOSE PABLO MOVED ME from the field to the morgue. He had to leave soon to testify at The Hague, and while he was away, my primary duties would be to perform the odontograms and to supervise the anthropology assistants on their first ICTY mission.

Jose Pablo and I had gone to Skopje to meet Patrick, an odontologist from England who had flown in for the weekend to train us in using the International System of numbering to fill out odontograms. An odontogram is a symbolic and written description of a person's teeth and orthodontia. In the forensic setting, a comparison of a postmortem odontogram with antemortem dental records should enable any dentist to determine whether the decedent was one of his patients. In Kosovo, ICTY odontograms would also be copied for the Victim Recovery and Identification Commission (VRIC), an international organization that would communicate with possible families of victims exhumed by ICTY. If either dentists or dental records weren't available, families might provide information with which to compare the odontograms.

Patrick trained us to notate all the odontological characteristics we already recognized, such as crowns, fillings, and bridges. But, more important, he familiarized us with the Interpol odontogram form in which the mouth is divided into quadrants of upper and lower, left and right. The system was slightly different from the one I had learned at Arizona so it took some time to switch my brain into the new perspective. In addition, Patrick taught us all the detailed and proper names for the architecture of bridges and dentures and how to recognize more modern synthetic materials used to bond and fill teeth. Fortunately, he had made a notebook for us with foundational information, exemplar odontograms, and photographs of clinical cases with their subtle features listed on a separate page. Patrick trained us for most of a day on the patio of the Hotel Tasino Cesmice and quizzed us on everything he'd taught us. Last, he gave us the notebook and wished us luck, apologizing that he couldn't be there for the whole mission.

As we drove back to Kosovo, Jose Pablo and Eric Baccard, our French chief pathologist, told me that besides receiving copies of the odontograms, VRIC would also get special summaries of the identifying information gleaned from ICTY autopsy and anthropology findings. It was hoped that this would improve VRIC's ability to get bodies returned to families without further physical examination.

The first difficult thing about working in the morgue was remembering to pack my lunch separately from my housemates who were still going to the field. But, naturally, things got harder. Working in a managerial role and preparing odontograms for all our cases pulled me out to another level from which I could see the bigger picture of our work. Instead of focusing on just a few cases a day, I had to be familiar with them all. Now I perceived a constant flow of people from this town or that town. I could picture their graves, too, having worked at most of the exhumation sites so far. I was also dealing more closely with many more live people than usual. I was a repository for staff requests and gripes, responsible for the needs of people who were sick or having breakdowns; I served as a tour guide for various external visitors and was continually evaluating people for progress reports to Jose Pablo. Had I simply been another anthropologist in the morgue, I would not have been privy to most of this, and I certainly would have been insulated from seeing our cases as an immense number of murdered people, because I would have been buried in detail work.

Casework presents a puzzle or a challenge that I, as an anthropologist, approach with professional relish; it requires the practitioner to be both active and cerebral. The activity always starts in the same way: as soon as a body has been brought out from X Ray and photo-documented and the clothes removed, you must examine it with clipboard in hand and check off the presence or absence of bones as you palpate it; when necessary, you must expose and extract the bones of anthropological and pathological significance; you must reconstruct bones fractured by trauma; you must discuss this trauma with the pathologist. Even if the case is upsetting, these mandatory steps ensure that you keep getting the job done. Then, on the cerebral side, when you have completed those steps, you must analyze the data you collected from the bones so you can estimate age, sex, and stature, and you must look at the trauma you have reconstructed and determine what caused it.

When you have completed a case and turned in your paperwork, you may still be thinking about it. But before that thinking takes you to a place where you realize that this case was just like the one you had before and maybe just like one from Kigali, before you notice that the case file says that your last case was the husband of the old woman being analyzed at the next table, and before you think about that or *feel* the sadness, you are assigned your next case and the pathologist is in a hurry and wants to get it done before lunch. *Snap!* You are saved from thinking and feeling until later, maybe much later, after you have left the mission and you find yourself crying into your pillow twelve thousand kilometers away, a world away, with your hands that touched and your mind that remembers and that elderly husband and wife are still dead, and you know the finality of that and you are left thinking and feeling indefinitely. *That* is what the demands of casework helps to insulate you from in a Tribunal morgue. I lost that insulation within two weeks of beginning work as Jose Pablo's deputy.

I spent most of my time in the morgue acutely aware of the interrelationship of the bodies to each other. They were family groups, as we knew from the TPO presumptive identification forms; if we had had such data in Kibuye we would have been faced with this same reality at the church: families fled together and were killed together, the survivors like the gliding, regal girl living today by chance or luck, or because their would-be killers were using machetes instead of bullets. Despite this contextualization, I felt I was keeping myself together admirably until my composure was thwarted by the living. One particular Swede was almost my downfall.

The Swedish government had donated to ICTY the services of two archaeologists and one anthropologist. They arrived while I was deputy chief, so I familiarized the anthropologist, a mature and intelligent woman, with the morgue and our anthropology protocols on her first day. I assigned her to put a relatively clean skeleton (that is, one with very little tissue present) into anatomical position. She began the case, and I left her to it. Some minutes later, one of the autopsy technicians told me I'd better check on her. She had left the room. On my way outside to look for her, I glanced at the skeleton she had been working on and saw that it was almost completely laid out, even the difficult-to-place smaller hand bones in perfect anatomical position.

I found her just past the doors, on the porch, sitting down, deflated and drained of color. She barely met my eyes. Waving her hand toward the morgue, she said, "I have never seen anything like that before. It's just a child. . . . How . . . Why . . . ?" Her voice trailed off; she put her head down and her shoulders shook. "I know, I know," I responded, squatting down to rub her shoulder, wanting to cry, too, because she was only saying what I would say if overcome. And yet I was angry with her—so angry. Why had the Swedish government sent an anthropologist who'd never seen "fresh" bodies to a forensic mission in a country where the victims had been dead for less than two years? Why was she there if she couldn't take this? Why was she there if she was going to force me to contemplate—during the working day—the bleak and harsh reality of these dead? I had to go back inside and keep up my end of things for another month. Why was she on my personnel list if she couldn't do the work? As I rubbed her shoulder, I was thinking, "Don't do this to me. Don't start me crying, because I might never stop." I didn't have casework to insulate myself; I'd be like that line from Paul Simon's "Graceland," with a window to my heart so that everyone would see it blown apart.

The Swede never came back to the morgue. She wasn't even there long enough for me to learn her name and I was sorry, my anger long gone. She was a good person, experienced in her specialist area of burned and fragmentary bone (albeit medieval, I learned), and I needed someone with her mature sensitivity working with me.

I WASN'T ENTIRELY spared tears during my time as deputy chief, but that wasn't on account of the bodies; it was the result of a good old-fashioned ass-chewing by our chief pathologist. That came later, though. In the early days we had to get the morgue up and running despite the logistical obstacles in our path, namely that the morgue was not fully functional when we needed to start cases.

The building itself was fine, because a Dutch engineering battalion had remodeled it to ICTY's specifications. However, the Dutch battalion couldn't do anything about our lack of equipment. Although the stainless-steel autopsy tables with their table-mounted sinks were in position and most of the X-ray and pathology equipment had arrived, the anthropologists and evidence technicians lacked crucial items: we had no glue for reconstructing bony trauma, no osteometric board to measure long bones for stature estimations, no pots in which to boil down bones with flesh still attached so we could do either age estimations or trauma analysis—indeed, we had no heating elements to boil the water, even if we had had the pots! As for the evidence technicians, they had no bags for clothing and no bags with sealer for securing evidence. If we had started work in these conditions, the pathologists would have been able to complete all but a few lines of their reports; but the anthropologists and evidence technicians would have been left with a backlog of bodies that would later have to be retrieved from the reefer for analysis and relogged.

But Eric, the chief pathologist, was feeling that same pressure for results that seemed to drive the team leaders in the field. Apparently The Hague used "productivity rates" from the morgues in Bosnia to estimate what they thought our Kosovo morgue should produce, ignoring the fact that these bodies were in a completely different state of preservation. But since Eric wanted to start, we negotiated to begin with a case that was not a complete body and wouldn't require equipment we either didn't have or couldn't fashion out of surplus materials (Eric actually bought some items we needed in the local shops with his own money).

Our first case was a body part (legs only) so that we weren't hampered by our inability to reconstruct cranial trauma. The case was brought out with some pomp and wheeled into the fluoroscopy room where it would be X-rayed. It was assigned to John McCarthy, a cheery British pathologist, and then a second case was brought out of the reefer for Eric. When it came out of fluoroscopy, Jose Pablo (who was there this day) told me that it had a prosthesis. Picturing a prosthetic limb, I thought, "No big deal, plus it'll be good for identification purposes." But it was a *dental* prosthesis—a full denture set, to be exact. "Shit!" is what I then thought, as I pulled out Patrick's odontology notebook and attempted to organize the appropriate forms in various trays and find an electrical outlet to plug in our light boards for reading X-rays.

Before I could get the anthropology area fully organized, John began the first autopsy, with both technicians and all four anthropology assistants in attendance. I managed to get Angel on top of the skeletal inventory, and then I was able to assign some people to work with Eric on the second case. That body was still well fleshed, with a loss of bone around the top of the head and forehead so great that it was all caved in, a big, pale, pinky-gray misshapen unhappiness. Carl Hogan, the ICTY logistics coordinator, stuck his head in from outside at the window and immediately asked why we weren't using the expensive fume hoods he had had installed. We had tried but they didn't work. Typical. A third case was brought out and assigned to John, but both autopsy technicians were still trying to get the clothes off the massive body Eric was working on, so I went to assist John as a technician for the third one. We started by removing the two layers of socks from the mummified feet. This was slow going for me, because it takes some talent to undress a body, and I don't really have that talent. A dead body is very uncooperative. While we were doing this, I peeked into his mouth: another prosthesis—*two* partial dentures! I informed Jose Pablo, who muttered, "We'd better start the first odontogram." So I assigned Angel to take over for me with John, told Sam to clean the head, and went off to the anthropology area with Jose Pablo.

To say that the first odontogram was a nightmare is only a slight exaggeration. We had to look up every single symbol we had to use: sound, antemortem loss, antemortem loss replaced by an artificial tooth (that is, a denture), clasp (the strut holding the denture onto the support teeth) "ss" (stainless steel), crown (silver alloy), postmortem loss—practically every symbol in Patrick's notebook. Then there was the problem of a denture having been repaired: if you counted the tooth numbers back from the central incisors on the denture, then by the time you got to a real tooth socket, the tooth number was one higher than it should have been. This took some getting used to, as did the backward nature of the Interpol odontogram we had to use, and Jose Pablo's apparent dyslexia didn't help matters. We began having slightly hysterical outbursts of laughter as we realized that this would be a learning curve so steep we were going to need seat belts. I enjoyed calling Jose Pablo's confident-sounding bluff as we looked at a tooth: "It's a full jacket with a post," he would say. Me, a beat later: "No, it's not." Jose Pablo: "Okay, it's not." Nervous titters and a rebending of heads over the skull.

The first odontogram took about an hour with both of us working on it. On the one hand, it was like diving in at the deep end to begin one's odontogram career because it involved a repaired denture, but on the other hand, it didn't take many of the more complex cases to make us more confident; soon we were finishing odontograms either before or at the same time as the case was completed. I even enjoyed them and, after Jose Pablo left, I trained two anthropology assistants in the method, but that first day, we felt under siege. Thinking about Jose Pablo leaving for The Hague soon caused mild panic. While we worked on the second odontogram he kept saying, "I think I'll leave early . . . tomorrow, actually," eliciting another fit of very nervous laughter from me.

We finally cleaned up at about nine P.M. We had managed to do three autopsies. But even cleanup at the end of the day was slow because we lacked some of the necessary equipment; we pushed the cleanser around the floor with a ragtag bunch of half-eaten sponges because we didn't have mops and the floor wasn't graded steeply enough toward its few drains. I wondered what anyone would think if they looked into the Tribunal morgue to see seven people in oversized blue Tyvek suits and white clogs using brooms to push water around the floor, amid state-of-the-art autopsy tables with fume hoods that didn't work. It was very cold in the morgue by then, and still raining outside, but we had come through a difficult situation together, improvising and staying upbeat to see how much we could accomplish. I felt close to everyone on the team that evening.

When I got home to my House of Four (whose other occupants had had the day off because of the rain and had been relaxing all day) I collapsed into bed only to have difficulty sleeping because I was thinking about all the things we had to do differently—move tables, move the whiteboard, get more chairs, get trays for our documents—and questions for Jose Pablo: Which of the two long-bone analysis forms are we using? What was the final decision about dealing with commingled remains? Whose responsibility is the clothing description? I finally made some notes on a piece of paper, in the dark.

By the end of the next day, the morgue had developed a normal routine but the anthropologists and evidence technicians still faced fundamental equipment problems that the pathologists didn't, so Eric was pushing for more casework to be done. Tom Grange, who was the evidence chief, Eric, and I met every morning to discuss our respective situations. Tom felt we had to either go very slowly or stop. I feared that if we got too far ahead, we would never have the time to go back to the incomplete cases; during other Tribunal missions I'd worked on, the pace never slowed enough to allow us to do things like rebag evidence. I think Eric understood the issues—after all, if we hurried, his early cases would also be left open until the rest of us could finish them—but the reality of the situation finally dawned on him when a head from one of his cases was boiled down and an assistant tried to reconstruct its trauma with masking tape. Not only did the tape obscure the cranial fracture patterns, but also its adhesive properties were reduced by the moist remnants of tissue, so chunks of fragmented skull kept falling off and hitting the table with a *thunk* while Eric tried to maintain a polite inspection of the assistant's well-meant handiwork. It was then that he was moved to fax The Hague with our complaints.

Within days, more equipment arrived: mops, gloves, coveralls, scrubs, a table, glue, and a glue accelerant with a different name but otherwise just like the Hot Stuff we'd used in Bosnia, at the Kalesija morgue. I was beginning to think about Kalesija a lot, remembering what I perceived to be the good old days when all we had was a scribbled body list from the field and we just handled the cases as they came out of the reefer. Here in the Kosovo morgue, I was already groaning inwardly at the number of forms we had to fill in when we'd completed something: X-rayed the body— check! Done the anthropology assessment—check! Gone to the loo— check! I remembered the autopsy tent at Kibuye, how wonderful it was to work outdoors. In Kosovo we were constrained by light, electricity, and ventilation. When I first used the glue accelerant indoors, I thought its fumes were going to bowl me over. At least at Kalesija the ventilation had been good, perhaps because all the windows had been blown out.

Jose Pablo left on schedule at the end of the first week; over the weekend, two anthropologists arrived. They were to take over anthropology casework while I continued with the odontograms, since neither of them had used the Interpol form. I had first met Shuala Martin in Bosnia in 1996. Cheryl Kazmarcyk, a Canadian doctoral student, was someone I had been looking forward to meeting: she had a reputation as a mature, experienced team player. Shuala and Cheryl were good friends from working together in the Bosnia morgue and Jose Pablo warned me that they might attempt to present a united front on any issues of lab protocol that differed from what they were familiar with from Bosnia. They did do this, perhaps unwittingly, but their first week's worth of cases were almost exclusively juveniles; just aging so many children from both bone and dental development took a group effort, especially because the odontograms had to be adjusted by hand to record deciduous (juvenile) teeth. As I looked at one skeleton, of a child between eight and twelve, the quality of the bone stood out to me. I hadn't seen this much juvenile bone since Rwanda, and I had forgotten how soft it seems: all unfused ends, pelvis still in three parts, and all those unworn teeth. I found it interesting and then surprised myself by finding it sad; the kid had been shot in the back of the head, the bullet exiting through the face.

That week, I dreamed vividly of trying to age bones and taking mandibles to be X-rayed. When I woke, or half woke, I was angry with myself that I had brought cases home. I told myself irritably that this was the time to sleep, not work. The dreams were like having the days continue all night.

WITH THE ARRIVAL OF Shuala and Cheryl, I entered into my role of deputy chief most fully because I was able to close the cases I had started as an anthropologist. But my responsibilities grew into areas I hadn't expected. Between assigned tasks, I sat in meeting after meeting, desuiting and resuiting five times a day between the Red and Black (morgue and administration) areas; receiving the unannounced visits of the British forensic team who wanted our anthropology standards or the KFOR soldiers who just wanted a peek at the morgue; assuaging the wrath of the Polish pathologist who wanted his next case *now* and who thought we had too much bureaucracy (we did); reassuring the Sri Lankan pathologist that I was on top of his travel arrangements (he was always saying, "I don't want to get stranded here," and laughing nervously); going to our stores for toilet paper and tables; consulting on the anthropologists' subadult cases; and both cursing and thanking Jose Pablo for having not given me more warning that I was going to be doing all this.

It was then that I started to get a broader view of our work. Although I was only dealing with teeth and with details the anthropologists wanted to bring to my attention, I became more aware of how many women we were seeing, and how many teenagers or youngsters, and of the kinds of evidence or artifacts associated with them. When I saw the first incendiary tracer bullet dislodged from the head of an old toothless guy and the familiar 7.62mm bullets dug out of the knee and shoulder of a twenty-two-year-old—a twenty-two-year-old I had exhumed the previous month from the grave his family had buried him in after finding his body in Orahovac, just down the way from our morgue—I felt things coming full circle. Bodies were returning to where they'd been found and I was charting the teeth of people I had taken out of the ground. I knew this detailed information because I could read our field notes on the database. I now had the full picture. I knew that the twenty-two-year-old was last seen being taken away from B—— to Orahovac and that he was carrying his wife's jewelry in a purse. We had the purse, its pockets turned inside out and empty. And we had the man, his shoulder turned green from the oxidization of the distorted copper-plated jacket of the bullet lodged deeper in the flesh.

Some of the bodies were fully fleshed—preserved by water inside their coffins or blankets—so once all our equipment arrived we were able to do almost complete autopsies, with organs being removed and fully examined. Brains were recognizable. Since I wasn't examining them closely, the bodies looked like dead people instead of cases. As I was finishing the odontogram for one case, I could turn and glance at a new case to see what state the teeth were in, and instead of just focusing on the teeth, I would see an old man's face, his stubble still looking just three days old. Or I would notice a woman curled into fetal position, still wearing her jewelry and carrying a baby's pacifier. This wasn't a good way to go through the day; I knew that from Bosnia. I needed to focus on the work, but something in me had changed since my missions in 1996 and 1997. I was now more interested in how the bodies represented what had happened in Kosovo, both in their trauma and in their accompanying artifacts. It interested me that they were wearing many layers of clothes, like those in Rwanda, because they knew they would have to be on the move but didn't know for how long. I was also seeing an extreme range of ages: some of the oldest pubic symphyseal phases I'd ever seen—almost off the Suchey-Brooks scale, in the eighties or nineties—and then the very young; the number of children bringing back Rwanda again.

The artifacts themselves were affecting me differently. When the first case with 7.62mm ammunition in it came out, everyone called, "Clea, come and see this!" I gave it only a glance, because I had seen more of that ammunition in 1996 and 1997 than I cared to remember. The professional thrill of finding bullets was gone. It was all just sad: violent and horrible and painful. My new teammates had little concept of how long the pathologists at Kalesija spent just probing for projectiles under the fluoroscope before we could even begin the autopsy. There could be fifteen bullets in the body and then the technician would tip the body bag up and another fifteen would fall out, with a few shell casings to boot.

I continued to miss the days when our morgue was a tent or a bombed-out building, when we didn't have to take our coveralls off completely in order to eat lunch. I felt that back then we had been a closer team; in Kosovo, I felt like a staff member, bounded by propriety and in-boxes and clipboards made out of cardboard with our names on them. Our white nurses' clogs (like the ones in the grave in Vukovar) even had to have our initials on them so they didn't get worn by someone else after being left on the shoe rack. And even though we now had more anthropologists and almost all of the necessary equipment, we had new problems. In my daily phone calls from Jose Pablo I tried not tell him that the morgue sometimes caused me great stress, but I always said, "Hurry back." The newest problem was a fundamental one, related to the assignment of cases to pathologists. The system for assigning the order of autopsies was that any body in the refrigerated container could be autopsied as soon as the field team leader had signed it over to the Evidence unit and turned in the databased field log; this could only be done when the site was completely excavated. This ensured that the chain of custody was maintained for legal purposes. We in the morgue would know when the bodies were available because an overview sheet for one of them would be in a particular tray in the Evidence room. If there wasn't an overview sheet, the body couldn't be autopsied, because the evidence associated with it hadn't been officially logged. To make sure that all went according to plan, Eric was supposed to assign the cases to his pathologists. Some mornings, however, Eric was in meetings or on the telephone with The Hague or otherwise attending to his myriad responsibilities as chief pathologist. One day one of his pathologists eventually became too frustrated to wait for Eric before starting a case. So, not knowing about the overview sheet, he sent an autopsy technician to the reefer to select the nearest body and take it to be X-rayed. At about this time, I walked in and saw that this pathologist had a case from a site different from the one we had been working on. Just when I was about to find out what was happening, someone from Evidence came charging into the autopsy suite, yelling that that case hadn't been logged into Evidence yet and Evidence must always be consulted first. The pathologist became angry and Eric was nowhere to be found so I tried to mollify both the guy from Evidence and the pathologist by getting him another case. I then went looking for Eric to ask him to keep his pathologists in line so they didn't just grab the nearest body bag.

A few days later, the same pathologist had begun his first case of the day and the same person from Evidence came charging in, waving a sheet of paper, and I thought, "Oh no, not again." It turned out that the body actually *was* ready to be autopsied, but the pathologist again hadn't followed proper notification procedure. I was a bit irritated with the pathologist, because the episode derailed the guy from Evidence for about an hour as he let off steam about being bypassed. Eric walked in and yet another meeting was immediately convened between the guy from Evidence, the evidence chief, and me to reorganize case selection. The pathologist, meanwhile, stood outside the door saying, "Can I start this case or do I need another one?" Eric was apparently oblivious to the tension in the room and told his pathologist to continue. He did so, with the speed born of impatience, and then the water for the morgue cut out. Ha! I couldn't believe the timing: the pathologist had tried to jump-start the system and he had learned that although this looked like a normal morgue, it was a UN morgue. Don't try to bypass the system—it will thwart you! The entire morgue was shut down for several hours, but the interval gave us time to streamline ourselves. And once the autopsy assignments were resolved, I actually began to enjoy the whole deputy chief thing.

22.

SPIRITUAL SUSTENANCE

THE MORGUE WAS SOON RUNNING EFFICIENTLY AND I BEGAN TO prepare for my departure by training two of the anthropology assistants on odontograms. Filling out the odontograms was a full-time occupation because the bodies had more dental work than we had expected. The assistants first studied Patrick's notebook, then did odontograms with me, and finally charted odontograms on rotation by themselves with me checking their work. One of the people I trained was Sam Brown, the British anthropology assistant, who had been brought in from the field. She had exhibited a particular aptitude for evaluating dentition, able to see even synthetic fillings (that is, tooth-colored fillings) at first glance while the other assistant had no trouble with gold fillings or bridges but missed synthetic fillings with regularity. In addition, Sam's finished odontograms were clear and legible—this was particularly important, as they would be copied and used by VRIC to positively identify bodies—while the other assistant produced odontograms marked by crossings-out of mistakes and stained with fluids from the bodies. Also, Sam appeared more willing in general to deal with the abundant mess of tissue and brain matter that often accompanied the job.

The morgue still needed another person fluent in odontograms, to cover when one was sick, but when Sam was on her odontogram rotation, I would look out across the room at the people in the Anthropology section and feel that the ship was running smoothly, all hands on deck: Shuala dispatching her cases so quickly she had time for a cigarette break between them; Cheryl providing an almost maternal presence as she guided assistants in some of the finer points of assessing age from ribs; Sam handling three concurrent odontograms that I knew would need only a cursory check from me. All the in-boxes were clear by the end of the day, our productivity was in a range that allowed Eric to relax, and my phone calls from Jose Pablo turned into a chance for him to tell me how hellish his life was, rather than the other way around.

Outside the morgue, life was already as routine as it could get. As the team had burgeoned and rented more houses around Prizren, the members knew each other less and less well. So a weekly team get-together was established at a tiny local place called the Best Bar whose candlelit interior was designed like a grotto. People who had brought their guitars played, and others danced and talked. Various team members were also issued walkie-talkie radios to improve logistics once we were all at our separate houses; people quite enjoyed this new form of communication ("India Echo 3-3, this is India Echo 3-5. Wotcha doing right now? Over." "India Echo 3-5. Watching TV. What*choo* doing? Over"), while Security struggled to keep it under control ("Break, break. India Mike Base to all India Echoes. This is *not* a telephone. I repeat: this is *not* a telephone"). Justine, Sam, and I also made forays to various restaurants in the Old Town; unfortunately, the ones most scenically placed with terraces leading to the river never seemed to have any food. One of them advertised "beefsteak, ramsteak, *čevap*," and another meat dish. The waiter first went down the list: "We have A, we don't have B, we don't have C, but we have D," and then he started again from the bottom: "We don't have D, we have B, we have C, but we don't have A," thereby canceling out his first list and reminding me of the Kibuye Guest House.

Every other weekend I looked forward to dancing to stereo music on the roof of the UNMIK headquarters. Our security wardens, IPTF (the UN

International Police Training Force), NGO staff, and local ladies of the night all mingled their different dance styles while Everything but the Girl's "Missing" washed over us. I also loved being on the UNMIK roof, party or no, because it had seating from the indoor restaurant. It was especially pleasant in the early evening because we could see Prizren from up above the dust and honking horns, high enough for an ever-present breeze that could blow the foam off the top of your cappuccino. Up there, I felt far enough away from our work to actually talk about it. One night I even told Sam about the Canadian documentary that showed the Rwandan father and daughter who had not found their wife and mother's clothing at the Kibuye Clothing Day. We were at the right elevation for looking out into the distance and that, and Sam's understanding silence, was enough to stop me from crying; I told her more every free evening we spent together. We'd sit under the canopy of an Old Town coffee bar, half the time sipping peach nectar by candlelight because power outages had rendered the cappuccino machines useless; but had made the streets quiet, lit by the dancing cigarette ends of the promenading Prizren youth, girls arm-in-arm giggling softly as they brushed past the boys at the cafés, in a summer evening ritual I've seen everywhere I've lived.

So when Jose Pablo asked if I would return to Kosovo for another mission as his deputy when he had to go back to The Hague in July, I said yes because of all that soul-warming conversation with Sam, a good working life among a wonderful team finally flush with equipment and well organized, and the knowledge that both Sam and Justine would be staying on for at least another month.

Any worries I had about taking on more work without the psychological insulation afforded by casework were displaced by two events. One was that VRIC returned the first bodies we had exhumed and analyzed to the families and community representatives. That gave me a feeling of relief and accomplishment. The other event was also related to identification: I did the odontogram for a case of Eric's where the man had retained two deciduous canines but we could also see his adult canines in the alveolus (tooth socket). The baby canines were small and yellowed and I felt they would help his friends and relatives identify him. I thought back to Kigali, when we had made video stills for the family who said they'd recognize their relative's unusual teeth anywhere. So I arranged with our photographer, Alain Wittmann, to have a special digital image taken of the facial teeth, as one would see in a smile, to be given to VRIC for identification purposes along with the usual paperwork.

Sam and Justine saw me off in Skopje when I left the mission, the same day Jose Pablo returned from The Hague. I gave him a memo on morgue improvements and told him that I felt strongly that we were doing a good thing and encouraged him to keep his own spirits up. I was looking forward to returning.

DURING MY MONTH AT HOME, I was occupied mainly by finding gifts for our landlord's family, plus sleeveless work shirts for Justine, lightweight work pants for Jose Pablo, and a mini Swiss Army knife for my housemate Derek Congram; for Sam, I asked my dentist to donate old toothbrushes and used dental probes for the odontograms.

It was on the flight back to Skopje, gifts in tow, that I remembered the hollowness I had felt at the beginning of my time in the morgue. I remembered walking over to check on the mouth of one of Eric's cases. The body was quite fresh and as Eric turned it over onto its back, the shoulders were lifted up, the head tilted forward, and it was just like turning over a sleeping person, another old man. My tolerance for autopsies I wasn't working on had been lower than I remembered it ever being: if I glanced at a table and saw a severed head with the scalp askew, I felt a bit sickened; when I prepared teeth for odontograms, I was sometimes disgusted at having to clean clumps of head hair from between them, an action that was repeated about ten times a day, every day. I felt I had changed since 1996. Then I remembered further back, to my time in the medical examiner's office in Arizona in 1994. Then, the autopsies being conducted at the tables next to our cases had also tested my endurance. The smell of fresh blood was much less tolerable than that of a decomposing body, and the just-sleeping appearance of the long-lashed teenager who'd shot himself under the chin earlier that day disturbed me for much longer than the fact that the bones of our nearby skeletal case had been gnawed by animals.

I wondered if my feelings of unease in Kosovo had arisen because I found myself in an unfamiliar fieldwork setting, followed by an unfamiliar morgue. I decided that it had to be because of my new role: I couldn't be truly absorbed in my cases anymore. Had I made a mistake in saying yes to another mission? It was too late to change my mind, so I had to think positively. I remembered back to May, when Eric had an edentulous (toothless) case, which wouldn't require an odontogram. I walked over to have a look at it anyway. As I reached the table, Eric showed me a massive fracture that surrounded the base of the skull. "I can't really explain it," he commented. I peered at it. I couldn't explain it, either. It was missing too much bone around the probable impact point, so there weren't enough edges to determine the nature of the implement that caused it. Then I rotated the head and looked at the frontal bone—the forehead—where I saw a shallow fracture. I said, "Oh, but this is interesting blunt force trauma here," figuring Eric had already noted it. But he seemed surprised. I showed him the rectangular defect with curved corners on the forehead—typical blunt force trauma that had not pushed all the way through the bone. I gave him a dental probe from my odontology stash; he ran it several times over the depressed lip of the defect and suddenly exclaimed, "Clea, you are amazing!" This wasn't his usual silly "Ah, you are so beautiful" tone; it was genuine. He said that it looked to him to be the mark of a rifle butt. I grabbed my special fine-toothed brush for teeth and cleaned the depression up some more, and there it was, plain as day, right on the forehead. Eric said admiringly, "You are a really good anthropologist!" and called over Alain to show him where to detail-photograph the butt mark, telling all the technicians how wonderful I was and making everyone get into a silly mood and shake my hand and slap me on the back for something that was not really extraordinary. Despite Eric's penchant for ardent drivel outside the morgue (he called me the Negreta of Rome when he saw me with a towel wrapped around my head, and the Black Mermaid once, much to my amusement), he behaved like a professional when we worked and I respected him as a forensic pathologist. This memory helped me banish my worries as I landed in Skopje again.

But the day I got back to Kosovo, it was clear that in the few weeks I had been gone, circumstances for the morgue and field teams had become strained. At the usual convoy departure point at the Lion Restaurant, Aldo, who was still a field team leader, stormed up to me, spluttering with anger over some personnel issue; his neck veins were popping out. His voice was drowned out by my dawning realization that something had changed, and that I was going to get the heat for whatever it was. Aldo yelling at me? We went back years.

Then, in the morgue a few days later, Eamonn, the field coordinator, approached me to say that a reporter from *Newsweek* would be arriving. Eamonn said he was to have complete access, as decided by ICTY; could I give him an initial tour of the morgue? The reporter was brought through and I started to tell him about our work, first standing by the doors and ex-plaining the general process. Then I took him over to meet Eric. Before I could explain why he was there, Eric let loose: "Who is this man? Why was I not consulted? I must be consulted before people are brought in. How dare you bring someone in to where we are conducting cases! This will not be tolerated. *I* am the chief pathologist." Unable to interrupt him, I simply stood there, feeling my neck and cheeks burn as he tore verbal strips off me in front of the reporter. The force of his invective was so strong that I was sure my hair had blown back from my forehead. When Eric was done, I couldn't trust myself to speak because indignant tears were already starting to tickle my eyes. While I pursed my lips, the reporter jumped in and tried to explain that it wasn't my fault, that Eamonn had asked me to bring him in and that he was there with the blessing of The Hague. This was the worst thing he could have said, poor fellow, because it *really* incensed Eric. He turned on his heel, motioning us to follow him into the Clean Area so he could attempt to tear a strip off Eamonn and call The Hague.

Eric steamed down the hall without looking back, so I peeled off into the women's changing room, trotted into the last bathroom stall, and started to cry before remembering that I didn't want Eric, or anyone else, to see my eyes red-rimmed. And anyway, what did the grilling matter? I agreed with him that random people shouldn't be allowed to just walk into the morgue; what bothered me was that Eric thought I was any less protective of our work than he was. I couldn't believe he thought I'd bring in a reporter of my own accord. I stood in the stall until I was under control, checking myself in the mirror.

Eammon sent for me before the day was out and apologized for what had happened, saying simply that it had nothing to do with me and that he'd take me out to dinner. As I lay in bed that night, I wondered if it was worth it to be "management" under these circumstances. I was willing to get into mass graves and work for three months under tough conditions for little pay, but *this* crap?

23.

THE OLD MAN'S THIRD BULLET

I FELT WARY OF ERIC AFTER THAT INCIDENT, EVEN THOUGH I WAS drawn to the manner in which he worked. He had been a general practitioner and when he worked on well-fleshed cases it seemed to me that he retained that approach. I don't know if he was aware of his stance: quiet, probing, his interest acute and unshakable. On top of this he seemed to touch the bodies with compassion. I marveled at how Eric dealt with some of the most miserable cases and yet remained isolated from them, like a GP who has just told his patient she indeed has a rare cancer but who is then able to treat his next case—a stubbed toe—with the same care.

Eric's style was most apparent during a particular case on this second mission. I was working as an anthropologist again because the morgue's productivity had fallen behind that of the field team. The pathologists were all new since May, as were most of the rest of the morgue personnel. I was pleased that Luis Fondebrider, one of my Argentine heroes, whom I had met at the Vukovar grave, was working with us on this day because the field teams had slowed down. We were working with Marek, a Polish pathologist, and Miguel, a rather stunning blue-eyed Argentine anthropologist working that day as an autopsy technician.

Marek's afternoon case was an older man, fleshed except for his head and right hand, and lying on his back on the table, left hand across his middle, mouth open a little. We had over eight X-ray prints showing locations of bullets and shotgun pellets in his clavicle, femora, pelvis, and so on. One pellet was visible right in the center of the forehead, near the brow ridge. Marek immediately dug for this with a probe, pushing the pellet farther into the head. Miguel stopped him from digging further, inspected the defect, and said, "You made the hole bigger." It was a quiet reproach. He continued, "We'll get the clothes off before we look for more metal." Marek backed off and Miguel stepped in. He lifted the left arm up and back, rotating the shoulder to first peel off the sleeve of the blazer, then the cardigan, shirt, and undershirt. Luis and I completed our initial inventory of bones by walking around the table, then stood at the foot of the table to wait for Marek to finish with the body before we accessed our samples.

Marek became impatient at having only one person taking off clothes, so he started removing the sleeves on the right side of the body. This was the side with the decomposing and skeletonizing hand. As Marek dragged off each sleeve, I watched the hand disappear into the material, then reemerge as the sleeve was removed. Each time, I was amazed to see the decomposing fingers still dangling by a thread, bouncing from the agitation. I was held by a morbid fascination, aware that a finger could disappear into the sleeve and I would then have to dig it out before the clothing was given to the evidence technicians, yet I wanted to see if the fingers could hang on. As soon as Miguel finished with the left side, he quickly stepped around to the right and took over from Marek, expertly finishing the job by manipulating the arm. Each manipulation of the body made the head roll from side to side, the neck extending but never breaking the flesh. Several layers of trousers were next to come off, then long underwear, while Luis and I removed the socks by digging out from within them the skeletonized foot bones and a lump of partially mummified sole.

Once the man was undressed, he seemed even older and more vulnerable. I was embarrassed for him, as I had been embarrassed for the woman in Arizona whose voice I later heard on the 911 tape. She had lain there with only her toenail polish on as two detectives, a pathologist, Walt, and I focused on her head injuries. Fortunately for us in Kosovo, Miguel was efficient and therefore fast, cutting open the old man's chest for immediate removal of a bullet from the left clavicle region. The next bullet was retrieved from the right side of the abdomen. We could see on the X rays that the third bullet was somewhere in the pelvis.

Marek was determined to find that third bullet but wasn't having much success when Eric walked over to the table. The challenge interested him and he joined in the search, first asking us anthropologists where we thought the bullet was, based on the X ray. Luis, Miguel, and I couldn't agree on its location because the X-ray image was so close up that it wasn't clear if the edge of bone we could see was ilium or ischium, two bones one wouldn't normally confuse because the former is flattish and flaring, with a crest, while the latter is chunky by comparison. Eric probed the iliac region first—nothing. So the body was turned onto its stomach to allow us to examine the posterior ischial region (the part of your bottom that you sit on). Eric had fully taken over the search for the bullet now and was slicing vertically every few centimeters through the tissue of the buttocks in a systematic fashion, even parting the flattened folds of the buttocks themselves and peering into the crevice. It was then that Eric seemed more like a GP than ever, because you could see that it was a necessary part of his job to look in private places, but only for a purpose and with compassion.

The exploration for the bullet continued under Eric's lead for about half an hour. As I stood there with Luis, I became overwhelmed with fatigue. The sadness came later. I went outside twice to stand in the sun on the porch where the Swedish anthropologist had sat in May and I closed my eyes, face upturned to the warmth.

Eric eventually took the body back to X-ray; there he found the bullet, and he came back into the autopsy suite with it sitting in a lump of flesh on a tray: it had been in the sacral region, not far from the ischium, but closer to the tailbone. Eric showed me how the bullet had tumbled, perhaps having hit something before entering the man's groin. Marek was then able to get on with his autopsy, and eventually Luis and I were able to remove our samples—the pubes and fourth left rib—to confirm the man's advanced age.

The case exhausted me because I had had to *watch* and therefore saw the body for what it was—not just a case, but probably somebody's grand-father.

That evening, back at the flat we were now sharing, I told Sam about the case and I couldn't stop crying. I felt so much emotion about what had actually happened to the people that came to us as cases—being shot in the back or in the face, being shot multiple times, being cut by something large and then burned—and then what we subsequently had to do to the bodies to make the medico-legal assignment of age or sex or cause of death. This was almost the same sentiment I had recorded in my journal back in Kibuye after I saw Bill tearing mandibles off juveniles in the grave so he could make preliminary age estimations. At that time, I had had a steamy anger, which now, in Kosovo, had condensed into tears, tears that didn't even emerge in sobs but leaked out of my eyes in a way I feared I couldn't control.

This was alarming, yet I was also rather relieved that the reality behind the work could still upset me as it had when I first started working on mis-sions. I was glad that my distress for the woman who recognized her brother's jacket in Kibuye was still inside me, hundreds of cases later. But it was only after leaving Kosovo that I realized that having someone to talk to—someone who wouldn't respond dismissively—was partly responsible for me letting go of my tears. Though I had become very close to Justine and had had dinner with other teammates, with Sam I felt an affinity both in our approach to the work and in our recognition that it was more im-portant to us than almost anything else. Here was a person for whom in-justice was even more infuriating than it was for me, someone who saw the forensic work for the Tribunal in its greater frame of providing both justice and a public service, and whose legal training gave her insights from which I also benefited. The time spent talking to Sam provided the spiritual and intellectual peer support that James Mills had told us was so necessary to keep our stress levels down.

No doubt my reduced stress was responsible for keeping me calm dur-ing an event that took place in my last week on this mission. In the midst of a very busy morning, João, the new Portuguese pathologist, walked into the morgue and said to me, "Eric needs an anthropologist outside." Always the charmer, he added: "He asked for a good anthropologist, so of course I ask you." I emerged into the sunlight in my scrubs and white plastic apron to see about forty coffins, lids off, lining the driveway and spilling onto the gravel verge. Each coffin was filled with a white body bag and a blue clothing bag. I had never seen the coffins in this state of readiness for return to families before, and they reminded me of a set of packed lunches at a children's camp, where someone has made sure every lunch box has one sandwich and one cookie, all the same so no one complains.

Eric was crouched in one of the VRIC reefers, poking through the contents of an open body bag. A blond American representative of the Organization for Security and Co-operation in Europe (OSCE), one of the VRIC partners, was standing near the reefer with a clipboard in her hand. I walked up and greeted them. The blond woman asked me at what age the distal femur fuses. I replied, "About seventeen to nineteen," and Eric held up the distal femur to show us that it was completely unfused. Eric then brought out the mandible in its own plastic bag to show me that the third molars were unerupted, although these teeth are notoriously unreliable for aging. We didn't need more than the femur to agree that the body was that of a youngster.

Then the VRIC team leader, another American, walked up with a clipboard on which he had the ICTY autopsy summary sheets as well as lists of bodies identified by families. He pointed at the body Eric was looking at: "This person's supposed to be thirteen."

I eyed his sheaf of papers with their curled edges and asked, "Well, what age range did we give you?"

"Ten to sixteen," he replied.

"Okay . . ." I said. "Thirteen is in that range." He just looked at me, so I continued, "Where is your concern?" It took some effort not to say, "So what's the problem?"

I couldn't believe his reply:

"Well, he's supposed to be thirteen, but he doesn't fit in the coffin."

It was my turn to just look at him.

So he continued. "I was told a thirteen-year-old would fit in the coffin, so I'm thinking he's not the guy."

It fascinated me that he and I had the same information and yet had drawn such different conclusions. The "problem" had nothing to do with the body and everything to do with the coffin. But then I was trying not to laugh because the man looked so upset and worried.

"Well," I said, "I can't tell you if he's thirteen, but I can tell you he's under seventeen. People are variable, you know."

He muttered something about this being the *second* body that didn't fit in a coffin and thanked me for coming out. I glanced at the blond woman and thought she looked apologetic. Eric was still interestedly poking through the body bag, having missed the import of the discussion: that someone from the Victim Recovery and Identification Commission was questioning the identities of certain individuals on the basis of whether or not they fit into the coffins provided.

At the time, I perceived the VRIC incident as a big problem, but the organization was actually functioning well: they had already returned one group of remains to the right families by the time I stood next to the reefer that day. This success was due to ICTY's cooperation—providing odontograms and special dental photographs as well as summary information from the autopsies and anthropological analyses. Looking back, I perceive that cooperation as ICTY's answer to my "double vision." Privately, I had had ideas about providing video links to grave sites so possible relatives could watch exhumations without compromising the crime scene. ICTY had managed something more simple and more personal: since you can't get around the need for bodies as evidence, let that process unfold as it must but then facilitate and speed up the identification and return of remains to families, and do this through a noninvestigative agency. In 2000, VRIC was that agency.

WHEN I LEFT KOSOVO AT THE END of July, I drove with several teammates down to Skopje on the mountain road that goes via Tetovo. As we went through the town of Brezovica, a young man driving a car on the other side of the road leaned forward and shouted at us, thrusting his hand out the window to give us—in our UN-marked vehicle—the three-fingered

Serbian nationalist salute. Just after that, we had to slow for the Russian KFOR roadblock he had just come through. The roadblock was in place to protect the inhabitants of Brezovica, one of the only Serb enclaves in southern Kosovo, from potential reprisals by Kosovar Albanians returning from refugee camps over the nearby Macedonian border.

Did the young man's gesture mean that he subscribed to the belief, disseminated by the Serbian media at the time, that Kosovar Albanians had *not* been persecuted and expelled as a population in 1998 and 1999? Did it mean that he thought the UN and NATO were in Kosovo for no reason, as part of a massive and expensive game? If he had known we weren't peacekeepers but forensic scientists, would his gesture have meant that he thought there was nothing for us to find, that we were leaving Kosovo because there wasn't any physical evidence of crimes against humanity? I wonder what he is thinking now, now that the evidence is out from Tribunal forensic findings. Did he finally believe in 2003, when Serbian exhumation teams unearthed the corpses of a thousand Kosovar Albanians buried in Belgrade's suburbs, police stations, and military barracks? If he knew what crimes had been committed in his name, would he still flash that three-fingered salute?

AFTER

A FEW MONTHS AFTER COMING HOME FROM THE KOSOVO MIS-
sion, I was invited to give a talk to University of California Extension students taking a course called "Inside the Crime Lab," taught by Barry Fisher,
the director of the Los Angeles County Sheriff's Crime Laboratory. As I reviewed my slides from former presentations, I thought about how I might
add details from Kosovo. There were the obvious developments in the Tribunal's approach to the forensic team, for example, but I wanted to go beyond that. I just wasn't sure how. I tend not to script things, so I didn't write
anything down and hoped that all would flow naturally once I was there.
My brother, Kimera, drove me over to the campus and we had dinner before walking up to the classroom.

The presentation took about an hour and a half, only interrupted occasionally by pertinent and curious questions from Barry's students. It was
during my concluding remarks after the Kosovo section that I became
more self-aware. I was noticing that when I was talking about Kosovo, I
was talking about Rwanda, and when I was talking about the dead, I was
also talking about the living, and when I was talking about me, I was talking about the people in that room. The connections and similarities—and
what was revealed by their differences—almost overwhelmed me.

I was realizing that ten years had passed since I read *Witnesses from the
Grave,* ten years since I had been inspired and motivated by the Argentines
and Clyde Snow. Inspired to "help reduce oppression by making the bones
talk." And here I was, telling the stories of the bones that had talked to me.
At this point, if I looked back on my life, I would see a curve I had been
rounding for a decade, a curve so steady and natural I had barely been
aware of it. Barry's class was receiving more than a firsthand account of

forensic work, because I had essentially been telling them about that curve: how it held both desire and disappointment, and not just inspiration but fulfillment as well.

I told the students that I'd had few expectations when I left for my first mission to Rwanda, but the one thing I did expect was that my working environment would be something like the one I had known in graduate school in Arizona. There, when Walt Birkby took us to pick up bodies from the medical examiner's office, we arrived and left by a back door that was well separated from the front door, where relatives of the dead might enter. On my way to Rwanda, I had expected that we would always have a "back door," separated from families and "living people with an interest" by crime scene tape or soldiers or the simple existence of rules concerning medico-legal evidence that has yet to be presented at trial. I had seen myself as a part of a crew of forensic scientists traveling to Rwanda to gather evidence, interpret it, hand it over to the Tribunal, and leave. All sterility, all separation. But it hadn't been like that.

Instead, living down the road from the crime scene, we were always among "people with an interest." You would have to be a particular sort of person not to be affected by the entangled nature of that setup. This was especially relevant for forensic anthropologists because we didn't just interact with the dead on a superficial level—we weren't exhuming bodies and then, say, counting them; we listened to them, studied them, knew them.

I told Barry's class that that entanglement did affect me at the time, but that the whole endeavor of the forensic missions has a legacy that continues to affect not only me but the families of the dead and the myriad living in those places. The medical anthropologist Linda Green once wrote that anthropologists "go to the field in an attempt to render intelligible the contradictions and complexities of people's lives. In doing so, we become at least temporarily both witnesses of and participants in those very lives." You mightn't think that forensic anthropologists participate in the lives of the living, but by interacting with the dead, we affect the living: we alter their memory and understanding of past events.

I reminded Barry's class that it's clear how our work influences the memories of families, as the dubious relief afforded by the contents of a body bag replaces fears and wonderings about missing relatives. At that moment, the event that has been remembered as responsible for the *disappearance* of a loved one is re-remembered as the event that caused that person's death. Memory is altered; for some the alteration may be subtle, for others, earth-shattering. As I talked, some people nodded; others closed their eyes, imagining it.

I thought it would be harder for the students to understand how forensic investigation alters the collective memory of postconflict communities. So I said, imagine that witnesses' stories about particular crimes are denied, derided, or deemed impossible by the witnesses' own government, military, or police—the very agencies believed responsible for those crimes. Then imagine that the stories are proven by physical evidence of facts most indisputable: human bodies in a grave that was said to "just" hold the carcasses of farm animals, for example. When we suspect a government of having committed crimes, the evidence isn't blatant; it's more likely to be hidden in obscure classified documents that are eventually dug up by investigative journalists. Usually, the deeds don't include mass murder, and the evidence doesn't take the form of bodies that, through forensic analysis, tell us that they were murdered or executed by government-issued bullets. The surfacing of the sort of evidence I've worked with serves to "challenge perceptions of respected institutions," as the historian Deborah Lipstadt put it in 1997.

Put those national institutions under the magnifying glass, I challenged the class. Take a closer look, not just because those institutions have denied illegal activities of which we now have clear evidence, but also because the bodies unearthed from supposedly different conflicts have told such similar stories. For example, Rwanda has been described as having experienced "spontaneous tribal violence" in 1994, while the former Yugoslavia was said to have experienced "war" between supposedly discrete "ethnic and religious" groups from 1991 to 1995. How could such different conflicts produce dead who tell a single story—a story in which internally displaced people gather or are directed to distinct locations before being murdered there? How could "spontaneous violence" or "war" leave physical evidence that reveals tell-tale signs of methodical preparation for mass murder of noncombatants? I'm thinking about countrywide roadblocks to check civilians' identity cards, supplies of wire and cloth sufficient to blindfold and tie up thousands of people, bodies buried in holes created by heavy earth-moving machinery during times when fuel alone is hard to come by.

Once I began to see hundreds of bodies on two continents telling a single story, I started to wonder what was really going on in those conflicts. What is the common denominator that produced a common story? One is being revealed in the Tribunal courtrooms: straightforward government-level decisions to gather and kill selected people and expel the rest, either actively or through the spreading of fear.

That leaves the question of why. Why did those governments decide to murder their own people? Why did soldiers and police and barbers and mechanics murder their own neighbors? I think the answer is self-interest. Particular people in a government of a single ideology with effectively no political opponents have supported national institutions that maintain power for themselves. What muddied the waters were the "reasons" the decision makers gave for their political agendas. Take Kosovo: were the killings and expulsions in the 1990s really meant to avenge the Battle of 1389, as Serbian president Slobodan Milošević was fond of stating? Or was it because mineral-rich parts of Kosovo can produce up to $5 billion in annual export income for Serbia? Or take Rwanda: did Hutus kill their neighbors *and* all their neighbors' children simply because they were Tutsi, as the government exhorted them to do? Or was it because the government promised Hutus their neighbors' farmland, land that otherwise could only have been inherited by those very children, and those children's children, ad infinitum?

In each of the places I've worked, the official "reasons" were in fact rhetoric-packaged justifications designed to dilute popular resistance to committing crimes against humanity. I do think those "reasons" played greater or lesser roles in influencing the way ordinary people behaved toward one another, but I don't believe government officials were materially concerned with ancient battles or religious or ethnic takeovers. Rather, they were focused on *real* issues of sustainability and power. Why was North Sector the only sector in "Code Black" (that is, experiencing active fighting or unrest) when I was in Kosovo in 2000? Because that sector, near Kosovo's border with Serbia, was the site of both the largest Kosovar Serb population *and* most of that region's mineral wealth and factories. Consequently, neither Kosovar Albanians nor Kosovar Serbs were willing to cede the territory, and because both Kosovar Serbs and Albanians lived there, fighting continued even in the presence of peacekeepers.

Why were Vukovar and its surrounds still under UN administration when I was there in 1996, while other areas of eastern Croatia were quiet though bullet-scarred? Because, along with its other attributes, Vukovar lies in one of the most oil-rich and fertile agricultural regions of the former Yugoslavia, and so both Croatia and Serbia continued to vie for ownership. So while various governments publicly rationalize their military and political decisions in terms of religion and ethnicity—and help them along with weapons and bribes, to exhort people to violence—the record strongly suggests they are really just employing elemental but well-thought-out grabs for power and wealth. The existence of such a reality would be neither complex nor peculiar to any group of people, any government or political party.

To Barry's class, I acknowledged that it might seem odd that I gained this insight after participating in *forensic* missions. But that insight is like a tool in a kit that helps me make sense of conflicts marked by the killings of civilians, wherever they are in the world. These same elements occur again and again, recognizable behind the headlines and the players' attempts to strip those events of their context.

It doesn't take long to see evidence of what's behind the headlines once you start looking. I was not surprised to learn that 40 percent of Israel's water comes from sustainable sources under Palestinian land that Israel occupies, fights over, and refuses to cede in any "land-for-peace" deal. It didn't surprise me to learn that the Israeli government has enabled groundwater to reach Israeli settlements in the desert by restricting Palestinians' access to their own water.

What *does* surprise me is that I rarely hear about competition over water resources when I see news of the fighting in the "Middle East." Instead, I see images of people throwing stones at tanks, and I hear voiceovers about "retaliatory attacks" and the numbers of Israeli and Palestinian children killed so far that month. The news sometimes obscures why this kind of violence has gone on for so long and how these places are inhabited by "regular people," not just by extremists. Similar confusion was produced by much of the mainstream news coverage of the 1994 Rwandan genocide and various conflicts in the former Yugoslavia in the 1990s. As a consumer of the news, I received a mixture of the participants' rhetoric, propaganda, selective mini–history lessons, and a lot of images I couldn't truly understand unless I tapped into alternative sources. After I came back from Rwanda in 1996, many people asked me, "Wasn't that about the Hutsis and the Tutus or something? All killing each other over some tribal thing? Thank heavens that couldn't happen here!"

Except for the power-mongers who conceived and incited the attacks in Rwanda, the people who lived there were just like you and me, responding to the same needs and desires for food, shelter, love, and life. Some of them were told to kill or be killed, while the names of others were on lists of those to be killed. This could happen anywhere in the world: west or east, "First" or "Third," developing or overdeveloped. I wouldn't be able to make that statement if what happened in Rwanda *had* been tribal violence, but it wasn't. Attempting to kill every "Tutsi" (because of their supposed innate evil) was about as arbitrary as attempting to kill everyone wearing a long-sleeved shirt on a given day. That is why it could happen anywhere, given the right ingredients: particular people in government, competing with others—or with each other—over natural and wealth-creating resources.

Another crucial condition seems to be a populace susceptible to bribes of both material and power, willing to accept looted big-screen televisions or plots of land in exchange for murdering their neighbors. Without that condition, it would have been difficult for the killing in Rwanda to claim almost a million lives in the short space of three months, or for the only houses shelled to their foundations in Vukovar to be those owned by Croats, not Croatian Serbs. The people who weren't on lists to be killed had to have believed, or simply gone along with, the propaganda asserting that those neighbors were different. *This* resonated with the people in

Barry's class. Everyone can imagine this, and see themselves in it, on one side or the other, or both.

When people feel they understand one another and the conditions under which they live in a way that cannot be swayed by government propaganda, a major basis for mass murder is nonexistent or at least severely challenged. A hint of this has already been seen in Rwanda: in 1997, gunmen burst into a school and told the students to stand up and divide themselves into groups of Hutu and Tutsi. The children refused, saying, "There is no Hutu or Tutsi: we are all Rwandan here." The gunmen shot most of the children. The incident is shocking; but buried in those children's stance is more hope than their parents' generation displayed. The confidence those children felt must have been based on the knowledge that they were closer to each other than any "group" of them were to the gunmen. And these were postgenocide kids, too, kids whose stance had overcome new propaganda about what "really" happened in 1994 as well as personal thoughts of fear or revenge. They had achieved improved communication in a postconflict situation, though they wouldn't have looked at it that way, and they had accomplished it in part because it was founded on truth about past events and people's roles in them. Forensic investigation contributes to this foundation because part of the truth comes from the dead, whose stories are unlocked by forensic anthropologists. Without forensics, mass graves of victims can easily be portrayed as mass graves of combatants.

Gathering all these disparate elements together for Barry's class, I thought back to a conversation I had had with Les Light, an old friend of the family, just after I returned from the first mission to Rwanda. "You know this is your mitzvah now," he told me. His serious tone made me feel I'd received a directive, but I wasn't exactly sure what "mitzvah" was. As I discovered, its original meaning of "commandment" now includes the idea of a meritorious deed, or duty. Les was telling me that, after what I had experienced in Rwanda, I now had a duty to share that knowledge. As a forensic anthropologist, I had always felt a duty to the dead, to help them speak, but I hadn't realized there would be a subsequent duty.

I once heard someone say, "Truth does not bring back the dead, but it allows their voices to be heard." Through working with Physicians for Human Rights and the UN tribunals, I've helped their voices be heard in the courtroom and the history books, and it has been an honor to do so. That was my primary duty, one that required detachment and discipline. But my mitzvah requires me to get personal, so I can really link other people to those events. I wouldn't be doing my duty if I simply flashed up a slide and said, "This is what we did" or "This is what I saw." Yes, I was in those places because I am a forensic anthropologist, but it was because of the *person* I am that after I "did" and "saw," I felt, thought, dreamed, cried, and connected.

Tribunal Appendix

Commenced and Completed Trials

—

KIBUYE CATHOLIC CHURCH

Clement Kayishema. Medical doctor and *préfet* (governor) of Kibuye. Convicted of four counts of genocide. Sentenced in 1999 to imprisonment for the remainder of his life.

Obed Ruzindana. Businessman in Kibuye. Convicted of one count of genocide. Sentenced in 1999 to twenty-five years' imprisonment.

KIGALI GARAGE

Georges Rutaganda. Businessman and second vice president of the National Committee of the Interahamwe, the youth militia of the MRND (Mouvement Républicain National pour le Développement et la Démocratie). Convicted of genocide and extermination as a crime against humanity. Further convicted, on appeal, of two counts of murder as a violation of common Article 3 of the Geneva Conventions; this was the first war crimes conviction at ICTR. Not convicted of one count of murder as a crime against humanity. Sentenced in 1999 to life imprisonment.

SREBRENICA

Dražen Erdemović. Officer in the 10th Sabotage Detachment of the Bosnian Serb army. Admitted to his participation in the murders of more than a thousand men at Pilica on July 16, 1996. Pleaded guilty in 1996 to one count of crimes against humanity. Sentenced in 1996 to ten years' imprisonment. In 1997, on appeal, the sentence was reduced to five years' imprisonment. He was released in 2000.

Radislav Krstić. Major general in the Bosnian Serb army and commander of the Drina Corps. Convicted of one count of genocide, one count of crimes against humanity, and one count of violations of the laws or customs of war (organized forced transfers, murder, suffering, persecution). Sentenced in 2001 to forty-six years' imprisonment; appeal filed.

Momir Nikolić. Assistant commander for security and intelligence of the 1st Bratunac Light Infantry of the Bosnian Serb army (the "Bratunac Brigade"). Pleaded guilty in 2003 to persecutions as crimes against humanity, but not guilty to genocide. Awaiting judgment.

Dragan Obrenović. Deputy Commander of the Zvornik Brigade of the Bosnian Serb army. Pleaded guilty in 2003 to persecutions as a crime against humanity. Awaiting judgment.

Vidoje Blagojević. Commander of the Bratunac Brigade of the Bosnian Serb army. Indicted for one count of complicity to commit genocide, four counts of crimes against humanity (extermination, murder, persecution, and inhumane acts), and one count of violations of the laws or customs of war (murder). Trial commenced 2003.

Dragan Jokić. Major and chief of engineering in the Zvornik Brigade of the Bosnian Serb army. Indicted for three counts of crimes against humanity (extermination, murder, persecution) and one count of violations of the laws or customs of war. Trial commenced 2003.

Slobodan Milošević. President of the Federal Republic of Yugoslavia. Indicted for crimes in Bosnia, consisting of two counts of genocide and complicity in genocide, ten counts of crimes against humanity (persecution, extermination, murder, imprisonment, torture, deportation, and inhumane acts), eight counts of grave breaches of the Geneva Conventions of 1949 (willful killing, unlawful confinement, torture, willfully causing great suffering, unlawful deportation or transfer, extensive destruction and appropriation of property), and nine counts of violations of the laws or customs of war (attacks on civilians, unlawful destruction, plunder of property, cruel treatment). Trial commenced 2002.

VUKOVAR HOSPITAL

Veselin Sljivancanin. Major and security officer of the 1st Guards Motorized Brigade of the Yugoslav People's Army (JNA). Indicted for two counts of grave breaches of the 1949 Geneva Conventions (willfully causing great suffering, willful killing), two counts of violations of the laws or customs of war (cruel treatment, murder), and two counts of crimes against humanity (inhumane acts, murder). Awaiting trial.

Mile Mrkšić. Colonel and commander of the 1st Guards Motorized Brigade in the JNA. Indicted as above for Sljivancanin. Also indicted for six counts of crimes against humanity (murder, imprisonment, inhumane acts) and three counts of violations of the laws or customs of war (murder, torture, cruel treatment). In 2002, he turned himself in. Awaiting trial.

Miroslav Radić. Captain in the JNA. Indicted as above for Sljivancanin. In 2003, he turned himself in. Awaiting trial.

Slavko Dokmanović. President of the Vukovar municipality and minister of agriculture of the "Serbian Autonomous District." Indicted as above for Sljivancanin. Trial began in 1998, but Dokmanović committed suicide while in the detention unit on June 29, 1998; his judgment had been scheduled for July 9, 1998.

Slobodan Milošević. President of the Federal Republic of Yugoslavia. Indicted for crimes in Croatia, consisting of ten counts of crimes against humanity (persecution, extermination, murder, imprisonment, torture, deportation, and inhumane acts), nine counts of grave breaches of the Geneva Conventions of 1949 (willful killing, unlawful confinement, torture, willfully causing great suffering, unlawful deportation or transfer, extensive destruction and appropriation of property), and thirteen counts of violations of the laws or customs of war (murder, torture, cruel treatment, wanton destruction of villages, destruction or willful damage done to historic monuments and institutions dedicated to education or religion, attacks on civilians and on civilian objects, plunder of property, cruel treatment). Trial commenced 2002.

BRČKO-LUKA CAMP

Goran Jelisić. Agricultural machinery mechanic and a commander at Luka camp who called himself the Serb Adolf. Pleaded guilty to sixteen counts of crimes against humanity and fifteen counts of violations of the laws or customs of war. Acquitted in 1999 of one count of genocide but sentenced to forty years' imprisonment for thirty-one counts of crimes against humanity and violations of the laws or customs of war, including murder, torture, and plunder of property.

Ranko Cesic. A commander at Luka camp. Pleaded guilty in 2003 to six counts of crimes against humanity (five of murder and one of rape) and six counts of violations of the laws or customs of war (murder, humiliating and degrading treatment). Awaiting sentencing.

SUB JUDICE SITES WITHIN KOSOVO

Slobodan Milošević. President of the Federal Republic of Yugoslavia and supreme commander of the Yugoslav army. Indicted for one count of violations of the laws or customs of war (murder) and four counts of crimes against humanity (deportation, murder, persecutions). Trial commenced 2002.

Milan Milutinović. President of Serbia. Indicted with Slobodan Milošević. Awaiting trial.

Dragoljub Ojdanić. Chief of General Staff of the Yugoslav army. Indicted with Slobodan Milošević. Awaiting trial.

Nikola Šainović. Deputy prime minister of the Federal Republic of Yugoslavia. Indicted with Slobodan Milošević. Awaiting trial.

ICTR OVERALL

Twelve completed trials, including that of the prime minister, Jean Kambanda; the minister for information, Eliezer Niyitegeka; and several mayors. Of these, four appeals are pending.

Twenty detainees on trial, including several military leaders, multiple governors, and the director of Radio Télévision Libre des Mille Collines (RTLM).

Thirty detainees awaiting trial, including six government ministers and three religious leaders.

One accused tried and acquitted.

ICTY OVERALL

Thirty-eight completed trials, including that of Biljana Plavsic, vice president of Republika Srpska. Of these, thirteen appeals are pending.

Ten detainees awaiting judgment or sentencing.

Four detainees on trial.

Thirty detainees awaiting trial, including Naser Oric, commander of the 2nd Corps, 28th Division of the Bosnian Government army in Srebrenica, and Vojislav Seselj, president of the Serbian Radical Party.

Five accused tried and acquitted.

THE BONE WOMAN

A Reader's Guide

C L E A   K O F F

To print out copies of this or other Random House Reader's Guides, visit us at

www.atrandom.com/rgg

1. Koff uses the term "double vision" to describe how she views the bodies she excavates—she looks at them as both objects of scientific evidence and loved ones of grieving families and friends left behind. How does this double vision help Koff complete her work? At what points in *The Bone Woman* does she find herself unable to maintain a balance between the two views?

2. When exhuming bodies, Koff often makes careful note of what they are wearing and the items they've retained, such as tax receipts, house keys, and identity cards. She states, "It wasn't until I had seen more of these artifacts that their significance dawned on me" (page 61). How do these artifacts help the anthropologists in their work? What conclusions can be drawn from them?

3. How did the book *Witnesses from the Grave* lead Koff from her university studies in archaeology to forensic anthropology? How did her parents and her upbringing contribute to her interests? What were her motivations for entering this line of work?

4. How do Koff and her teammates emotionally cope with working in mass graves? How do their strategies for dealing with this environment differ?

5. The shooting that Koff witnesses in Kibuye is a defining event in the memoir. Koff writes, "The episode and its aftermath underscored my concern that we weren't doing enough to help the living people associated with the bodies in the grave" (page 67). Discuss how this experience affects Koff.

6. Koff discusses "the importance of having team members who are team players, who look to each other for backup and can double-check each other's work without bristling" (page 97). What are other characteristics forensic anthropologists need to possess in order to succeed in their work?

7. Koff writes, "I knew that, despite the importance of the work we were doing, a toll would be exacted by this life. I didn't know what kind of toll, or when it would happen, or how long I would last" (page 150). What symptoms of trauma does Koff exhibit from her experiences? How do the team's emotional responses manifest themselves?

8. Reflecting on her experience in Kigali, Koff writes, "If I hadn't joined the second mission to Rwanda, I wouldn't have learned that my guilt was misplaced" (page 112). What does she mean by this? For Koff, how does the Kibuye mission differ from the Kigali mission?

9. What is Koff's explanation for the murders of noncombatants and civilians in such great numbers? How does she assess the reasoning behind these killings?

10. Throughout *The Bone Woman*, how does Koff change? Do you notice a significant transformation in her worldview, philosophies, and emotional thresholds at the end of her account?

CLEA KOFF was born in 1972, and is the daughter of a Tanzanian mother and an American father, both documentary filmmakers focused on human rights issues. Koff spent her childhood in England, Kenya, Tanzania, Somalia, and the United States. She earned her bachelor's degree in anthropology from Stanford University and went on to the master's program in forensic anthropology at the University of Arizona. At the age of twenty-three, she became a forensic expert for the UN International Criminal Tribunal for Rwanda, and was the youngest member of the first team to arrive in Kibuye in 1996. After two missions in Africa, Koff participated in five missions for the UN International Criminal Tribunal for the former Yugoslavia, including Kosovo in 2000. Koff earned her master's degree in anthropology from the University of Nebraska–Lincoln, and now divides her time between Los Angeles and Melbourne, Australia.

ABOUT THE TYPE

This book was set in Monotype Dante, a typeface designed by Giovanni Merdersteig (1892-1977) and conceived as a private type for the Officina Bodoni in Verona, Italy. The Monotype Corporation's version of Dante followed in 1957. Dante is a thoroughly modern interpretation of that venerable face.